V. S. Naipaul, Man and Writer

V. S. NAIPAUL,
MAN AND WRITER

Gillian Dooley

UNIVERSITY OF SOUTH CAROLINA PRESS

Published by the University of South Carolina Press
Columbia, South Carolina 29208

www.sc.edu/uscpress

Manufactured in the United States of America

15 14 13 12 11 10 09 08 07 06   10 9 8 7 6 5 4 3 2 1

Library of Congress Cataloging-in-Publication Data

Dooley, Gillian, 1955–
   V.S. Naipaul, man and writer / Gillian Dooley.
     p. cm.
   Includes bibliographical references (p.   ) and index.
   ISBN-13: 978-1-57003-587-6 (alk. paper)
   ISBN-10: 1-57003-587-3 (alk. paper)
  1. Naipaul, V. S. (Vidiadhar Surajprasad), 1932– I. Title.
   PR9272.9.N32Z665 2006
   823'.914—dc22
                             2005035538

This book was printed on Glatfelter Natures Natural, a recycled paper with
50 percent post-consumer waste content.

To the memory of my beloved parents,
Nanette Dooley (1922–2004) and Jim Dooley (1919–2004)

Until that illumination, I didn't know what kind of person I was, as man and writer—and both were really the same. Put it at its simplest: was I funny, or was I serious? So many tones of voice were possible or assumable, so many attitudes to the same material.

The Enigma of Arrival

CONTENTS

ACKNOWLEDGMENTS

I would like to acknowledge the advice, support, and encouragement of several past and present members of the English department at Flinders University of South Australia, including Joost Daalder, Michael Meehan, and John Harwood. I am grateful in particular for the feedback provided by Syd Harrex, who read this work in manuscript and who has played a large part in facilitating and promoting my academic publications. Satendra Nandan of the University of Canberra and Kavita Nandan of Australian National University also read and made useful remarks on the manuscript.

A special mention should be made of my friend and colleague Chandani Lokuge of Monash University, whose encouragement in her capacity as editor of scholarly journals and convenor of conferences has several times spurred me to pursue further research in the postcolonial arena.

My thanks also to the document delivery service at Flinders University Library for their prompt, expert, and friendly service over many years of study and research.

Thanks also to Barry Blose and the editorial and administrative staff of the University of South Carolina Press, who have made it easy and pleasant to deal with a publisher half a world away.

ABBREVIATIONS

All page references in the text are to the first American editions.

V. S. Naipaul, Man and Writer

Introduction

Understanding V. S. Naipaul as a writer entails understanding him as a man. Biographical knowledge provides insight into the work of any writer, but Naipaul more than most has been directly molded as an artist by his family and personal history. Theoretical notions such as the "death of the author" —the irrelevance of an author's biography in the interpretation of his works— make little sense when discussing Naipaul and his work. That said, one needs to be, as he has cautioned, aware "of the difference between the writer as writer and the writer as a social being. . . . All the details of the life and the quirks and the friendships can be laid out for us, but the mystery of the writing will remain."[1] However, without understanding something of the historical forces that placed Naipaul's forebears in the colonial backwater of Trinidad and the education and social forces that impelled him to leave for England, one runs the risk of seriously misunderstanding his work. Fortunately, he has provided his readers with all the information they need, if his works are read with attention and without prejudice.

Born in 1932, Vidiadhar Surajprasad Naipaul was the second child of a family of Hindu Indians living in rural Trinidad. His paternal grandfather had been an indentured laborer, lured or tricked into coming to Trinidad from India to work on the sugarcane plantations, like many of his compatriots. Naipaul's father, Seepersad, was a remarkable man. Unlike others in his family, he was lucky enough to receive some basic education. Seepersad Naipaul married Droapatie Capildeo, one of eleven children of an influential and comparatively wealthy rural Hindu family, and spent most of his subsequent life in an uneasy struggle to escape dependence on his in-laws. He eventually became a journalist in Port of Spain and nursed an ambition to become a "real" writer, an ambition that he transmitted to his son. Seepersad Naipaul wrote a few stories, some of which V. S. Naipaul edited for publication years after his death.[2] His life was the basis for Naipaul's fourth novel, A House for Mr Biswas (1961).

At the time of Naipaul's birth, Trinidad was still a British colony. The population was made up of a majority of Africans, descended from the slave population, with a large minority of Indians, descended from the indentured laborers who were imported to replace the slaves when slavery was officially abolished in the British Empire. It was an agricultural colony that produced mainly sugar. The Second World War brought a United States military base to the capital, Port of Spain, which had a significant impact on the society, as Naipaul records in books such as *Miguel Street* and *A Flag on the Island*.

Naipaul was academically capable and from an early age saw the possibility this provided of escaping from the limited society of Trinidad to the "real" world abroad. At Queen's Royal College, the leading secondary school in Port of Spain, he studied hard and gained a scholarship that enabled him to travel to Oxford University in 1950 and study English. While he was at Oxford, loneliness and homesickness caused a mental breakdown of a kind, from which he recovered gradually with the help of friends including fellow student Patricia Hale, later to become his wife.

In 1953 Seepersad Naipaul died in Trinidad at the early age of forty-six. Naipaul, shocked and grieved, stayed in England, a failure for which he would later reproach himself. He took his degree from Oxford and moved to London in 1954. During these anxious years, living in London with little money and the desperate ambition of becoming a writer, Naipaul started writing *Miguel Street,* the first of his books to be accepted for publication.

Once that book was written, the story of Naipaul's life is, in a way, reflected in his work. He himself said that before he could write *Miguel Street,* man and writer had to come together: he had to realize that his subject was within himself, not external "material" that he could observe with a detached and satirical eye (*EA,* 147). His travel books, beginning with *The Middle Passage* in 1962, are as much explorations of himself as of the places he visits. They trace his journeys to various, often neglected, parts of the world. He has traveled to and written about South America, Trinidad and other islands of the Caribbean, India, East Africa and Ivory Coast, Iran, Pakistan, Malaysia and Indonesia, and the southern states of the United States. Frequently a nonfiction account of his travels has given rise to a novel based on the same material. As his career has progressed, the distinction between his novels and his nonfiction has often been hard to draw.

Critically acclaimed from the first, he has won every major literary prize available to him but has only slowly built up a substantial readership. Although he has traveled extensively, he has lived in England since he left Trinidad in 1950. In 1990 he was knighted by the British government. In 1996 his wife, Pat, died. Shortly afterward he married again. His new wife is Nadira Khannum Alvi, a Kenyan from a Pakistani family.[3]

Although Naipaul's biography is that of a practically quintessential "post-colonial" writer, countless critics have shown, by attempting to fit him into this mold, how inadequate such a theoretical and political approach is to an appreciation of his work. Understanding Naipaul is a matter of empathizing, not theorizing, looking subjectively, as he does, rather than objectively, as many of his critics claim to do. As Lillian Feder writes, "At worst, such approaches dehumanize Naipaul: they strip him of his ambivalence, his spontaneity, his 'eye,' the immediacy of his experience, and his ever-changing reactions, and they recreate him as the offspring of their own formulas."[4]

Naipaul has a tendency to enrage some of his readers, especially people who feel he has let down their "side." Edward Said claims that Naipaul "has allowed himself quite consciously to be turned into a witness for the western prosecution."[5] Antiguan expatriate writer Jamaica Kincaid says, "He just annoys me *so* much, all my thoughts are intemperate and violent. . . . I think probably the only people who'll say good things about him are Western people, right-wing people."[6] However, novelist and critic Amit Chaudhuri contends that "it is a myth that Naipaul is cherished by the English literary establishment; that honour, till recently, belonged to Rushdie; Naipaul, in my experience, has long been an embarrassment to it."[7]

Kincaid implies that, if the response to him is political, Naipaul himself has a conservative political bias. This may be true to some extent, although Naipaul says that his forthright opinions have nothing to do with politics and arise instead from his interest in the truth: "Certain subjects are so holy that it becomes an act of virtue to lie . . . never say 'bush people,' never say 'backward country,' never say 'boring people,' never say 'uneducated.' But turn away from what is disagreeable and what happens in the end is that you encourage the chaps there to start lying about themselves too. So they lie because it's what is expected of them. Soon everyone begins to lie."[8]

There is no trace of the idealism that craves political change in his views. His conservative views, if they can be so described, are not dogmatic. They are skeptical and arise from an awareness of the danger of a desire for radical change. However, whether or not his views can be defined in political terms, there is certainly a personal bias, which he admits later in the same interview: "I do not have the tenderness more secure people can have towards bush people. . . . I feel threatened by them. My attitude and the attitude of people like me is quite different from people who live outside the bush or who just go camping in the bush on weekends."[9]

His editor, Diana Athill, says that "he was born with a skin or two too few."[10] He fears the enemies of civilization, and his fastidiousness can easily turn to disgust, but the other side of the coin is a fascination with the minute details of people's lives and the passion for accurate observation that make him such an exceptional writer. Asked by Adrian Rowe-Evans about the "conflict between the loving approach and what one might call the sur- gical approach to character," he replied, "Interesting question. One can't be entirely sympathetic; one must have views; one must do more than merely respond emotionally. I can get angry, impatient, like anyone else; I can be irritated, bored—but you can't turn any of that into writing. So you have to make a conscious effort to render your emotions into something which is more logical, which makes more sense, but which is more, and not less, true. . . . I long to find what is good and hopeful and really do hope that by the most brutal sort of analysis one is possibly opening up the situation to some sort of action; an action which is not based on self-deception."[11] To gloss tactfully over the truth is, as he sees it, neither helpful nor kind and would betray his ethical standards.

The story of how he became a writer has been related by Naipaul many times, in interviews and essays, in "Prologue to an Autobiography" (part 1 of *Finding the Center*), in *The Enigma of Arrival* and *A Way in the World,* and most recently in *Reading and Writing*. Again and again he describes his lack of talent and preparation ("My school essays weren't exceptional: they were only a crammer's work. In spite of my father's example I hadn't begun to think in any concrete way about what I might write" [*RW,* 20]); and the "roman- tic vision of the writer as a free, gifted, talented, creative, admired person" that he had developed "without pausing to consider what went before—and during—the writing of these fabulous things."[12]

Having committed himself to the vision, having left Trinidad for Oxford, there were years of waiting for the time when "his talent would somehow be revealed, and the books would start writing themselves" (*FC,* 32). In retro- spect, he sees his lack of talent as having worked to his advantage: "I think the body of work exists because there was no natural gift. I think if I had had a natural gift it would have been for mimicry. I would have been mimicking other people's forms. No, I really had to work. I had to learn it. Having to learn it, I became my own man."[13] What forced him to learn the art, to over- come the problems, is what he describes as "the element of panic,"[14] which is "a feeling you can't communicate, explain to other people; you can assuage it only by starting to write, even though your mind is as blank as the next man's. . . . And then, given the panic, the next thing you need is a certain fortitude, a tenacity, to carry on through all the ups and downs."[15]

The panic arises from his inability to envisage any other career: "I am nothing but my vocation," he told Linda Blandford in 1979;[16] and in 1983 he said, "I think if I hadn't succeeded in being a writer I probably would not have been around; I would have done away with myself in some way."[17] Even then, his ambition is not merely to write, or even to be published, it is to be the best writer possible: "This may shock you," he said to Charles Michener in 1981, "but I feel that I don't want to be a writer unless I am at the very top."[18] In *The Enigma of Arrival* he describes the "special anguish attached to the career: whatever the labour of any piece of writing, whatever its creative challenges and satisfactions, time had always taken me away from it. And, with time passing, I felt mocked by what I had already done; it seemed to belong to a time of vigor, now past for good" (*EA*, 101). He told Israel Shenker in 1971, "The thought of writing for the rest of one's life is a nightmare. . . . I'd be delighted to stop—now. Some years ago I remember thinking, if someone said to you, 'I'll give you a million pounds, you must stop writing, never write another word,' I would have said no, quite seriously, without any regrets. Today I would probably do it for much less."[19]

He has, however, continued; but Stephen Schiff wrote in 1994, "After every book, he complains of profound fatigue. 'I have no more than one hundred months left,' he told me one evening. 'One hundred months, I mean, of productive life. Yes. Yes. It's an immense relief to feel that you're near the end of things.' He stared gravely into the middle distance. I didn't have the heart to tell him that I recalled his announcing the very same thing—a hundred more months of productive life—to a British interviewer in 1979, when he was forty-seven years old."[20]

This fatigue and dissatisfaction are part of a creative cycle. The feelings of anguish described in *The Enigma of Arrival*, the sense of being mocked by past achievements, feed into the creation of the next book: "Emptiness, restlessness built up again; and it was necessary once more, out of my internal resources alone, to start on another book, to commit myself to that consuming process again" (*EA*, 101). The creative process is still something of a mystery to him, as he told Mel Gussow in 1994: "To this day, if you ask me how I became a writer, I cannot give you an answer. To this day, if you ask me how a book is written, I cannot answer. For long periods, if I didn't know that somehow in the past I had written a book, I would have given up. The idea of sitting down and 'invoking the muse' is so artificial. Writing a book is not like writing a poem. Prose narrative is quite different from the inspiration of a moment. One has to go on and on, and then, with luck, one day something happens, and you are transported into a state of exaltation."[21]

In *Finding the Center* he writes again about luck—that "for everything that seemed right I felt I had only been a vessel," although "for everything that was false or didn't work and had to be discarded, I felt that I alone was responsible." But he goes on to say, "This element of luck isn't so mysterious to me now. As diarists and letter-writers repeatedly prove, any attempt at narrative can give value to an experience which might otherwise evaporate away" (*FC*, 18). The element of surprise still exists, however, as he said in 1994: "I would say this is one of the beauties of imaginative writing; you have two or three things you want to do consciously, but if, in the writing, you arrive at a certain degree of intensity, all kinds of other things occur which you're not aware of."[22] This process involves refining the emotions that provide the initial urge to write. He gives *In a Free State* as an example in his 1971 interview with Rowe-Evans: "I began my recent book on Africa with a great hatred of everyone, of the entire continent; and that had to be refined away, giving place to comprehension. If one wasn't angry, wasn't upset, one wouldn't want to write. On the other hand it isn't possible to get anything down until you've made sense of it, made a whole of it."[23]

This refinement is necessary not only for the writer to "get anything down" but also for the work to communicate with its readers: "One can't write out of contempt. If you try to do that, the book won't survive and won't irritate. Contempt can be ignored."[24] The capacity of a book to irritate is clearly part of his intention as a writer. He feels that, for him, "a true communication with a society is non-existent and impossible," but he still aspires to "the communication of ideas . . . a simple desire to help—to serve";[25] and giving offense is an unavoidable aspect of this communication. Asked whether the reactions of Indians to his books about India, "their readiness to take offence, their deep feelings about foreign criticism," inhibited him, he replied, "No, it doesn't inhibit me, for several reasons. One is that I think unless one hears a little squeal of pain after one's done some writing one has not really done much. That is my gauge of whether I have hit something true. Also, in India, I find that people who respond violently usually haven't read the books. And I no longer forgive this."[26]

He has, however, become increasingly conscious of the need to help his readers interpret his work and the societies in which it is set. Bharati Mukherjee raised as an example a passage in one of the early novels that described a man beating his wife:

> Bharati Mukherjee: How did you, in the early novels, get across to
> the foreign audience the necessary sense of a wife-beating hero coming
> from a wife-beating culture? Your audience really couldn't know how
> to respond to a hero who is also a wife-beater. In a Cheever novel, if a
> character beats his wife, we know he is a bad guy. For you the situation
> had to be very different. . . . There's an easy assumption there about the
> couple's having fallen into their roles. Everything was comfortable, you
> suggest, the wife had been beaten, and each of them had fulfilled his
> assigned roles. I think that that kind of easy assumption . . . is no longer
> possible in your fiction.
>
> V. S. Naipaul: Not at all. Absolutely. You can no longer do that.
> Everybody, everything has to be explained very carefully. . . . These

things can be very funny, but you can't always be sure your reader will take them in as you'd like.[27]

On the whole, though, he tries not to concern himself with the reception of his work: "I never argue. . . . I loathe argument. I observe, and I think for a long time. My words are always well chosen. I'm not a debater. How can I be concerned about people who don't like my work? No, I can't cope with that. I can't cope with that. I don't *read* these things. I don't even read when people tell me nice reviews [*sic*]. I'm nervous of being made self-conscious. I've got to remain pure. You've got to move on to remain pure. . . . The books have to look after themselves, and they will be around as long as people find that they are illuminating."[28] He commented to Michiko Kakutani, "I can't be interested in people who don't like what I write because if you don't like what I write, you're disliking me."[29]

Nevertheless, he recognizes that reading can be idiosyncratic, and he is willing to allow his readers a wide range of interpretations as long as they read without prejudice. Of *A Way in the World* he says, "With this form everyone will read his own book, depending on his nature, depending on his need. Some people might pick up certain half-buried associations and not see others that are more prominent."[30] Some of the reactions to *In a Free State* he found more worrying: "I think . . . that what is wrong about the running down of this independent vision is that people seldom stay with the story. They feel that their principles are being violated by what the writer is saying. And then they stop listening."[31]

In all Naipaul's analysis of why and how he writes, the question of readers' interpretations and how they correspond with his intentions hardly seems to concern him. He never brings the matter up and only discusses it in response to interviewers' questions. One reason that this preoccupation, so marked in other writers, is lacking in Naipaul might be that he decided, early in his career, that he could not expect a large readership: "You write in London and you don't have an audience—you are just hanging in the air and being an artist in a vacuum, which is nonsensical. My reputation is dry, without dialogue, it stands by itself, without comprehension or feedback. But an artist needs to be nourished, needs an audience and a response. A writer must be supported by the knowledge that he comes from a society with which he is in dialogue. A writer like myself has no society, because one comes from a very small island which hardly provides an audience."[32]

Ten years later, in 1981, Mukherjee asked him if he still felt the same way, and he replied, "I think I've got a kind of audience now. At least I'm read by other writers," but still, "I am an exotic to people who read my work."[33] However, although "it's nice to think that there are readers who feel they can see their experience in what I've written, . . . finally the writer who thinks it's his business to get across the specificity of his material is making a great mistake."[34] He is ambivalent toward his audience. He "will always be dependent on outside opinion and encouragement"[35] but is afraid of compromising his "purity" by reading reviews, even if they are favorable. He has made few explicit comments on the qualities his ideal reader would possess. Only in a couple of later interviews has he considered the question in any detail. "A good critic," he told Aamer Hussein in 1994, "is someone who reads a text with a clear mind; most people are merely reading to find out what they already know."[36] He uses various techniques to break his readers' preconceptions and get their full attention: "In my writing there's no self-consciousness, there's no beauty. The writer is saying, 'Pay attention. Everything is here for a purpose. Please don't hurry through it.' If you race through it, of course you can't get it, because it was written so slowly. It requires another kind of reading. You must read it at the rate, perhaps, at which the writer himself likes to read books. Twenty, thirty pages a day, because you can't cope with more. You've got to rest after reading twenty good pages. You've got to stop and think."[37] He does not, however, expect or even wish to be universally esteemed and respected by his readers. Gussow reports his satisfaction with a comment by critic Christopher Hope that he passed on to him, to the effect that "his writing is always unexpected, and it's never entirely respectable."[38]

Unexpectedness is, according to Naipaul, a quality all good writing shares: "What is good is always what is new, in both form and content. What is good forgets whatever models it might have had, and is unexpected; we have to catch it on the wing" (RW, 62). He has not always been happy with the word "novel": he originally subtitled his 1994 book, A Way in the World, "A Sequence" but changed it to "A Novel" at the request of his publisher. He preferred not to use "novel," because "'if a novel is something that a person in public life does to show how much he or she knows about sex or shopping,' then the word is 'tainted.'"[39]

Earlier in his career he had regarded "the novel writing as engaging the truer part of me,"[40] but by 1995 he had come to feel that the novel was an outdated form: "There was a time when fiction provided . . . discoveries about the nature of society, about states, so those works of fiction had a validity over and above the narrative element. I feel that those most important works of fiction were done in the 19th century. . . . I feel that all that has followed since have been versions of those works."[41] As a form, it cannot, he believes, be applied to all societies: "If you take some literary form without fully understanding its origins and apply it to your own culture, it wouldn't necessarily work. You can't apply George Eliot country society to Burma, or India, for example, but people do try. It's one of the many falsities of the literary novel today. I can't help feeling that the form has done its work."[42]

Moreover, what he writes does not need to be classified: "This idea of categories is slightly bogus."[43] In 2001, however, he published his first conventional novel since *A Bend in the River* (1979). *Half a Life* is labeled "A Novel" and features third-person omniscient narration, fictional characters, and a reasonably straightforward plot. It was followed in 2004 by a sequel, *Magic Seeds*. At any rate, whatever he chooses to call them, there are certain qualities he feels are necessary to good books: "Literary art . . . *must have*" a moral sense;[44] it should be "fun . . . I'm willing to believe that the element of pleasure is almost invariably paramount";[45] and of course it must be original.

There should also be an element of instability: "I feel that the most interesting books have a certain instability about them which I don't find in current English fiction. . . . I much prefer writers who can carry in their writing some sense of what is, wasn't always, has been made, and is about to change again and become something else."[46] Too great a concern with plot, as opposed to narrative, is a danger: "Narrative is something large going on around you all the time. Plot is something so trivial—people want it for television plays. Plot assumes that the world has been explored and now this thing, plot, has to be added on. Whereas I am still exploring the world. And there is narrative there, in every exploration. The writers of plots know the world. I don't know the world yet."[47] Part of this professed ignorance of "the world" is perhaps manifest in his refusal to be enlisted on behalf of causes, social, political, or nationalistic. "A writer," as he told Rowe-Evans,

> should have a dialogue with his own society, and to have writers who
> have got one eye on an exterior world is to use writers as a tourist trade,
> as a cultural or political weapon. . . . To write honestly about one's own
> undeveloped society would offend it; ten years ago in Trinidad, if you
> called an African black, the man was mortally offended. In those days
> many people were offended by my writings. Now, I get letters from
> tourist boards asking if my work can be used, and so forth. What future
> can there be for a kind of writing which can be treated, or used, like
> that? . . . A man must write to report his whole response to the world;
> not because it would be nice to do something for the prestige of his
> country.[48]

In order to "report his whole response to the world" it is necessary to be receptive, whereas "people with causes inevitably turn themselves off intellectually."[49] Marxism is a prime example: "People love making simple distinctions —left, right, colonialist, anti-colonialist—and if they have trouble fitting you in, they do so just the same. People love clichés. It's a sign of being grown up to be able to use a cliché with authority. . . . Marxism is a very big and happy cliché to discover, manipulate and master."[50] The simple economic view is a dangerous reduction: "Unless you understand that everyone has cause for self-esteem, you make a terrible political error. The Marxists tend to reduce people to their distress, or to their economic position."[51]

In *The Enigma of Arrival* he admits that his distrust of causes is not merely an intellectual position; there is an emotional origin to these beliefs: "The fear of extinction which I had developed as a child had partly to do with this: this fear of being swallowed up or extinguished by the simplicity of one side or the other, my side or the side that wasn't mine" (*EA*, 152–53). But there is also the question of what could happen to one's political beliefs when the creative process takes hold, as he said to Derek Walcott in 1965:

> Writing, I think, is a very fraudulent thing. When you start writing about something it changes. It becomes distorted. It is extremely hard for a writer to know what is going to happen when he starts writing about a particular thing.
>
> A well-known English writer went to Kenya during the Mau-Mau emergency. His sympathies were with the Kikuyu; and it was for this reason that he couldn't write a novel about the emergency. He didn't know what would have come out. . . . In the process of writing one might discover deeper truths about oneself which might be slightly different from the day to day truth about one's reaction.[52]

The implication here is not so much that political beliefs distort one's creative response, but that the creative response cannot be constrained by preconceived political ideas, and writers who value their beliefs and want them to remain intact had better not subject them to the stress of writing fiction about them.

Naipaul's overriding aim in writing is "to achieve a writing which is perfectly *transparent*."[53] In order to do this, various temptations need to be fought. For one, there is the danger of "applying a type of dramatic pattern to what I am portraying, so that I falsify the situation as I really perceive it. Or I might be seduced by the rhythm of the words themselves to say something which isn't really what I see."[54] By 1981 he felt he had "sat out the Forster thing about relationships and a great many other temptations. You know how easy it would have been for me to subscribe to the pretentious stuff. How many people would have liked me to take as my slogan 'only connect,' that sort of thing."[55] He prefers to be thought of as an ironist rather than a satirist: "Satire comes out of a tremendous impulse of optimism. One simply does not indulge in satire when one is awaiting death. Satire is a type of anger. Irony and comedy, I think, come out of a sense of acceptance,"[56] he said in 1981.

Comedy has its place, however, to sugar the pill of the disturbing truths he presents to the reader as a result of his method of "direct looking": "When

I am writing, I always feel that to come to some comprehension or acceptance of what is true is itself a kind of liberation. Then I thought that perhaps that wasn't enough. Because when we read fiction we're like children to some extent. The strong instinct is for everyone to live happily ever afterwards. So then I thought, in addition to the truth, there was a way to combat the dissatisfaction the reader will feel at something that appears to end without solace for men. . . . Comedy. I thought, *that* is it. That all one could offer is comedy, real comedy."[57]

He is unwilling, however, to "beguile, to provide a respite from the constant anguish of reality" in the way of postmodern writers such as Gabriel García Márquez, whom he sees as "mystifiers": "There is too much that *needs* to be said," he insists.[58] Neither does he feel the need of experiment and innovation for its own sake: "What I am doing is sufficiently painful and novel to have no need of structural deformations."[59] He has no objection to shocking his readers. He believes the success of *Guerrillas* has come about partly because it is so shocking: "I know it's offended a lot of people. . . . But you see, the terror of that book is inevitable. It's a book about lies and self deception and people inhabiting different worlds or cultures."[60] Other less confrontational techniques he has used include repetition to create an "illusion of knowledge" in the reader that "makes it easier to approach unfamiliar material";[61] for example, in *A Way in the World* he repeated the story of Venezuelan revolutionary Francisco Miranda four times, in different ways, throughout the book. It was a moral consideration that led him to reject for many years the use of a fictional narrator: none of his books between *A Bend in the River* and *Half a Life* was in a voice not identifiably his own. He uses Graham Greene as another example of this problem: "He always has someone who is like Graham Greene in other parts of the world. And there's always someone . . . with doubts and a tormented soul in the Greene book . . . and it makes the work a little . . . false, really, because the world isn't like that. You don't always have a man and a tormented soul appearing in all these places. You have a writer who visits them there."[62]

As long as the narrator is himself, the other characters may be fictional, "because you can't use real people to hang philosophical ideas about flux and change":[63] this was at any rate his technique when writing about his life in England in *The Enigma of Arrival* in 1987. In 1971, however, he told Ian Hamilton that it was difficult to write about his experience as an immigrant in England: "I think the difficulty about that is that probably every time you try to devise a story to get some kind of symbol for your experience the whole apparatus of invention that you'd have to bring to bear would be so fraudulent. How do you ceaselessly introduce the foreign character into a setting? You just can't go on doing that. That *is* very tedious and boring."[64] Symbolism clearly interests him little: he wrote in 1961 that he could "enjoy *Moby Dick* without being too deeply concerned about the symbolism of the white whale";[65] and in 1971 the antagonism is greater: "I can no longer, at a time of crisis, in Bengal, take an interest in plays which don't have a proper setting, where people are in a way symbols, where incidents are always symbolic, where people are endlessly looking for their doubles, or acting out old myths, or where plays are set in madhouses."[66] Symbols, for him, need to arise more naturally: "The world abrades one, one comes to certain resolutions and then one devises by instinct and through dreams and all kinds of senses a story that is a symbol for all this. But one can't do it all the time."[67]

Justice for Naipaul is a dangerous mirage: "From the earliest stories and bits of stories my father had read to me . . . I had arrived at the conviction—the conviction that is at the root of so much human anguish and passion, and corrupts so many lives—that there was justice in the world. The wish to be a writer was a development of that. To be a writer as O. Henry was, to die in mid-sentence, was to triumph over darkness. And like a wild religious faith that hardens in adversity, this wish to be a writer, this refusal to be extinguished, this wish to seek at some future time for justice, strengthened as our conditions grew worse" (*FC*, 32).

As he matured, the concept of justice meant less and less: "As you get older and understand more, you no longer have the flat view of the world—flat and sometimes cruel. As you grow older you understand people a lot more; you have greater sympathy with people;"[68] but this does not mean not noticing their shortcomings: "I'm not interested in attributing *fault*. . . . I'm interested in civilizations. If Arabs piss on my doorstep in South Kensington, I can't *not* notice."[69]

Even the truth, his own ultimate aim, is not sacrosanct: "There probably are certain circumstances in which the only way you can be human and proclaim your humanity is by lying about yourself. I mean, having such regard for yourself that you can create a lie for yourself. It's very odd . . . because the truth is wonderful in certain societies. But, you know, in some places it probably isn't wonderful. I mean, why tell the truth in a work camp, in a gulag."[70]

Theoretical approaches to freedom do not preoccupy him, either. Clearly the concept is subjected to a certain amount of ironic treatment in *In a Free State*, but personally he regards his own career as having been benefited, even perhaps made possible, by his freedom: "I have never had to work for hire; I made a vow at an early age never to work, never to become involved with people in that way. That has given me a freedom from people, from entanglements, from rivalries, from competition. I have no enemies, no rivals, no masters; I fear no one."[71] In 1994 he told Gussow, "I'm very content. I've been a free man."[72]

The relationship between Naipaul and his narrative voice is one of which he is acutely conscious, and as a reader he prefers works where writers do not hide behind their prose: "I don't like things where the writer is not to be there. The writer has to take me, rather like Pepys."[73] He does not mind being thought of as elitist or snobbish; but prides himself on the honesty with which he records his admittedly subjective view of the world. Michener comments:

> There is "charity" in even his darkest books—the charity of seeing. He refuses not to see.
>
> His determination has not come easily. In Naipaul's books, as in his company, there is the sense of an opposing pull—into that withdrawal from the fray. Perhaps it is fear of giving in that brings such steel.[74]

The fear of giving in to the qualities he criticizes in others, the temptation to be corrupted by causes, to be bewitched by the beauty of language, to be lulled by its rhythms into saying what he knows to be untrue, to escape into the comfort of oblivion, to stop writing and become a "monkey": these are the tensions that give Naipaul the necessary impulses to get started on the next project, even while he comforts himself with visions of sudden death—in 1990 he told Andrew Robinson, "Nowadays I sleep with the idea of a bullet being put in the back of my head . . . it comforts me."[75] Although Naipaul claims to ignore his critics, their reactions are significant to him. He is clearly conscious of what he calls the "squeal of pain" that his works sometimes elicit: he perhaps deliberately provokes this reaction to some extent. Among the following chapters are three that discuss major works singly in depth: chapter 3, on *A House for Mr Biswas*, chapter 6, on *In a Free State*, and chapter 9, on *The Enigma of Arrival*. In these chapters more time is given to an examination of the critical reaction to these novels. The remaining seven chapters deal with works grouped by time period and form, insofar as this can be established. Chapters 4, 8, and 10 deal with nonfiction and travel, and the remaining chapters deal with the novels in chronological order.

"Apprentice Pieces" *Miguel Street, The Mystic Masseur,* and *The Suffrage of Elvira*

Naipaul said in 1964 that he "made a late start as a writer" and that his first three books were "an apprenticeship."[1] But these three books, all set in his childhood home of Trinidad, are funny, clever, and accomplished works in their own right, original in their vision and technique, and they are overshadowed only because they were directly followed by one of Naipaul's greatest works.

Miguel Street is so much a part of Naipaul's self-dramatization of his beginning as a writer—his discovery of his material and his voice—that it will be considered first, even though it was the third of his books to be published. It begins with a short character sketch—no more than six pages. The subject is Bogart, languid, enigmatic, and periodically absent from his small room in a backyard of Miguel Street, Port of Spain, Trinidad. There is nothing immature in the writing of this piece. Everything about the street and the life ebbing and flowing through its yards and verandahs is suggested in these few pages. Several characters are introduced, their pastimes and occupations sketched, their attitudes evoked, and the ethical framework of their world implied, all while the history of Bogart's arrivals and departures is related.

The narrative is poised and economical: "I don't know if you remember the year the film *Casablanca* was made. That was the year when Bogart's fame spread like fire through Port of Spain and hundreds of young men began adopting the hard-boiled Bogartian attitude" (*MS*, 9). This short passage reveals much about the world of the novel: the pervasive influence of American films (the source, of course, of Bogart's nickname); the setting—Port of Spain—mentioned in passing; the narrator's slightly knowing attitude, a little detached but still identified with this world.

Already Naipaul's trademark laconic wit is evident: Bogart plays solitaire "from morning to night. Yet he never liked cards. . . . He did everything with a captivating languor. Even when he licked his thumb to deal out the cards there was grace in it. He was the most bored man I ever knew" (*MS*, 9–10).

The narrator is an important element in the structure of the novel. He is a young boy, part of the street life yet new enough to it and young enough to be curious about it, clever and observant enough to make a pattern of what he sees. He learns and develops throughout the book to the extent that the innocent of the early stories outgrows this limited society, giving the narrative shape and meaning by walking away at the end to a new life.

Although this book is superficially a series of seventeen short stories, then, they form a continuous narrative. The story is built up much in the same way that the sentences quoted above combine to create a picture of this world. The impression is that the narrator is chatting casually to the reader about his memories of the people on the street, but, without any emphasis on a plot or a dramatic story, a vivid picture emerges of the events and personalities that shape this unique world. Each chapter concentrates on one of the inhabitants of Miguel Street. Their stories are told beginning to end, as far as the life of the street is concerned. This is in fact a natural way to relate this type of material, which is based on personalities and the way they interact rather than on a series of events. The first-person narrator is an integral part of both the form and the content, telling the story in a disarming but deceptively simple way, in precisely the way that someone would relate their childhood memories, building it around people rather than a chronological catalog of incidents.

Each story can stand alone, but as a whole they are carefully and cleverly fitted together. With every episode, more is revealed about the character of the narrator. The reader discovers that this boy is clever though not academically brilliant. His impulses are sound, and he is kind and perceptive. He has a winning way of ingratiating himself with adults by encouraging their obsessions. Without knowing the first thing about mechanics, for example, he endears himself to his uncle Bhakcu, the "Mechanical Genius," by pretending to hear the tappets knocking on his car, giving his uncle a welcome excuse to tinker with his engine. Although he is sometimes unwise, he is well intentioned and makes peace between his friends when he can, knowing when to keep quiet and when to put in a diplomatic word.

The stories tend to spiral inward as the book progresses. The book begins with Bogart, distant and enigmatic, while the last few stories concentrate more closely on the more central characters and the narrator himself. The fifteenth story, "Until the Soldiers Came," deals with Edward and his involvement with the Americans in Trinidad for the duration of the war, his ill-fated marriage, and his departure. The sixteenth, "Hat," concerns Edward's brother, Hat, who is ever present and influential in the life of the street, a role model to the boys and to many of the men and the principal member of the informal Miguel Street "Club." Hat, like his brother, suffers from the influence of a woman who plays him false, and a resulting period of imprisonment spells the end of the narrator's childhood:

> A long time. But it was just three years, three years in which I had grown up and looked critically at the people around me. . . . Everything had changed.
> When Hat went to jail, part of me had died. (*MS*, 213–14)

The last story, the seventeenth, deals with the narrator himself and his departure from Miguel Street. Now a late adolescent, he leaves on a scholarship to study in England, typically for this book not earned through academic merit, like the author's Oxford scholarship, but obtained with a bribe through his mother's influential connections.

Miguel Street was accepted for publication in 1955 but was not published until 1959, after two novels had appeared. In a letter to his sister Kamla in February 1956, he explains the reason for this delay. The publisher "said she liked the stories and everyone else did. But that they didn't know whether they should publish because no one likes to buy a volume of short stories, even connected short stories."[2] Consequently, they decided to publish his novel *The Mystic Masseur* (1957) first and keep *Miguel Street* for later. It is perhaps an indication of Naipaul's originality that the publishers, who could see the outstanding merit of these stories, lacked the imagination to view them—and make the decision to market them—as a single work with all the coherence of a novel. *Miguel Street* has gone on to become one of Naipaul's most popular works, and the fact that he continues to find this kind of form and technique useful is confirmed by his use of similar methods in later masterpieces such as *The Enigma of Arrival.*

In several works written decades later, Naipaul relates the beginnings of his writing career, starting always with the almost magical inspiration for *Miguel Street*. In *Finding the Center* (1984) he writes, "It is now nearly thirty years since, in a BBC room in London, on an old BBC typewriter, and on smooth, 'non-rustle' BBC script paper, I wrote the first sentence of my first publishable book. . . . Without having any idea where I was going, and not perhaps intending to type to the end of the page, I wrote: *Every morning when he got up Hat would sit on the banister of his back verandah and shout across, 'What happening there, Bogart?'*" (*FC*, 3–4)

There are, however, differences between Naipaul's later narrative of his youth, in works such as *Finding the Center* and *The Enigma of Arrival,* and what is evident in the letters he wrote to his father during the early 1950s, when he was at Oxford. In *The Enigma of Arrival,* for example, he describes "the separation of man from writer" that occurred when he left Trinidad for England in 1950:

> And then, but only very slowly, man and writer came together again. It was nearly five years . . . before I could shed the fantasies given me by my abstract education. Nearly five years before vision was granted me, quite suddenly one day, when I was desperate for such an illumination, of what my material as a writer might be.
>
> I wrote very simply and fast of the simplest things in my memory.
> (*EA*, 147)

Yet as early as April 1951 he was writing home, advising his father that "he should begin a novel. He should realize that the society of the West Indies is a very interesting one—one of phoney sophistication. . . . Describe the society just as it is—do not explain or excuse or laugh."[3]

In August 1953, it seems he is himself writing about Trinidad: "My, the stories that I seem to be writing. There is no lack of material. I feel sure a three-month stay in Trinidad would keep me writing for three years."[4] The suddenness of his revelation in 1954, "that afternoon in the Langham Hotel," of his "Port of Spain memories, disregarded until then" (*FC*, 10)—a "tract of experience I hadn't before contemplated as a writer" (*FC*, 18)—must therefore be exposed as a later adjustment of memory, a dramatic turning point that is, in essence, fictional.

Shaping the events of one's life into a narrative with a pattern is important to most people, and perhaps even more important to a writer. Naipaul feels, in addition, a strong impulse in this direction resulting from his colonial background—his inability to feel that he belongs in any particular place or to any particular group. By narrating the past, one is essentially creating form and order out of disorder in an attempt to defeat chaos. So it is understandable that, especially in Naipaul's case, the narrative he has created of his literary beginnings is simpler, more magical, and more easily told than the reality that has been revealed by the publication of his family correspondence.

Nevertheless, the influence of Naipaul's father, Seepersad, can scarcely be overemphasized. That part of the legend of his life seems to have a solid basis in fact. Although he said in his foreword to his father's stories, published finally in London in 1976, that in 1953 he "did not think the stories publishable outside Trinidad,"[5] he acknowledges their importance as an example of what was possible. The letters that passed between father and son in the early 1950s, before Seepersad's death in 1953, are largely concerned with writing. Advice and encouragement flowed in both directions. Naipaul Senior was confident enough in his son's abilities to trust him, flatteringly, to edit or even to rewrite his stories for broadcast or publication. And Naipaul Junior was constantly urging his father to persist with his writing against all discouragements: "You know that I can't write well. Not half as well as you. You manage a type of humour I cannot manage. Your view of life is surprisingly good-humoured. Well, don't write a novel then. Just let me have your short stories. And here: MAKE NO EFFORT TO THINK ABOUT DRAMATIC PLOTS. You can't manage them. Neither can I. Observe episodes."[6]

This young man, not yet twenty years old, is precociously clear-sighted about his own limits as a writer. Dramatic plots have never really interested him. His skill lies in the accretion of observation, building up a solid fictional world, vividly peopled. The example of his father's work, and his advice, helped Naipaul define his own strengths and weaknesses at this unusually early age, as well as providing him with a pattern and a model in subject matter and technique.

But Naipaul's vision has always been less romantic than his father's. He could see already the limits imposed by the difficulty his father had in acknowledging "some of the pain about his family he had once tried to hide," and understood that it was only toward the end of his short life that he was "able to blend romance and the later vision of dereliction into a purer kind of comedy."[7] After his father's death, he wrote to his mother that "in a way I had always looked upon my life as a continuation of his—a continuation which, I hoped, would also be a fulfilment."[8] In many ways, the son stood on his father's shoulders, having learned much about writing from their close, almost collegial, relationship. It was, despite Naipaul's claim to have come late to writing, an early and singularly effective apprenticeship, which was, perhaps ironically, made more telling by the shock of Seepersad's sudden death.

Miguel Street written in the year after his father's death, owed much to his influence, as did *The Mystic Masseur,* written soon afterward. Ganesh, the "mystic masseur" of the title, being something of a pretender to religious enlightenment, is reminiscent of Seepersad's Gurudeva in *The Adventures of Gurudeva,* an uneducated thug who comes to be regarded as a pundit. However, Ganesh is a much more fully developed character than Gurudeva, much more than a satirical figure. As Naipaul said in his foreword to *The Adventures of Gurudeva and Other Stories* (1976), eventually his father's "satire defeats itself" in this story,[9] and although the satire in *The Mystic Masseur* is sometimes overblown, on the whole it is well managed and controlled.

This novel, even more than *Miguel Street,* is obviously a young man's work. Its vitality and assurance are very occasionally flawed by the exuberance of the satirical urge. The novel is narrated by an admirer of Ganesh who plays no part in the story. This device gives the author an opportunity of adding an extra layer of irony with the young man's credulous acceptance of Ganesh at his own estimation, but this occasionally goes too far. Ganesh writes two books that "made his name a household word in Trinidad" (*MM*, 159). The first, *What God Told Me,* seems plausible in the satirical scheme, but *Profitable Evacuation,* a book "concerned more or less with constipation" (*MM*, 160), goes just a little further and breaks through the veneer of credibility despite the narrator's earnest assertion that this book, "printed on thick paper, with a cover of brightest yellow decorated with a lotus, established Ganesh finally, without question" (*MM*, 160).

But although *The Mystic Masseur* has satirical elements that contribute in a large measure to its comedy, it is more than mere satire. Ganesh and his wife, Leela, especially, are fully rounded characters despite the limited society that has produced them and that Naipaul clearly finds ridiculous. Leela's reaction to her increasing wealth and social status is comic, with the development of "a private accent which softened all harsh vowel sounds . . . and . . . a highly personal conjugation of the verb to be" (*MM*, 150). But her relationship with Ganesh is delicately drawn, while at the same time revealing something of their world. Sex, as in all early Naipaul, is never mentioned, but the reader might suspect that wife beating is used more or less as a sexual metaphor. Their "first beating" is described: "a formal affair done without anger on Ganesh's part or resentment on Leela's; and although it formed no part of the marriage ceremony itself, it meant much to both of them. It meant that they had grown up and become independent. Ganesh had become a man; Leela a wife as privileged as any other big woman. Now she too would have tales to tell of her husband's beatings; and when she went home she would be able to look sad and sullen as every woman should" (*MM*, 55).

Later, when it seemed that Leela was unable to bear children, Ganesh "lost interest in her as a wife and stopped beating her" (*MM*, 69). Difficult as it may be for many readers to accept, this is in no way intended as a criticism of Ganesh. Naipaul explained in an interview in 1981: "The treatment of the subject needn't be malicious. It's a serious thing. . . . These things can be very funny, but you can't always be sure your reader will take them in as you'd like."[10]

Some of Ganesh's pretensions are treated satirically, such as his justification of his claim to a B.A.: "Everybody start thinking is the little piece of paper that matter. It ain't that does make a man a B.A. Is how he does learn, how much he want to learn, and why he want to learn is these things that does make a man a B.A. I really can't see how I isn't a B.A." (*MM*, 96). But when it comes to his activities as a "spiritual healer," despite the obvious comic possibilities, Naipaul writes powerfully and seriously. Ganesh's first patient is a boy pursued by a black cloud that threatens to kill him, clearly a delusion brought on by the shock of his brother's death a year before. The boy is tormented by fear, "not the passing shock of momentary fear, but fear as a permanent state, fear so strong that it had ceased to thrill" (*MM*, 123). Ganesh, instructed by his aunt that "if you want to cure people, you must believe them, and they must know that you believe them" (*MM*, 114), with the help of a certain amount of mumbo jumbo which he admits to Leela is not really necessary, cures the boy by the power of persuasion. This incident is at the heart of the book. It shows that Ganesh is a genuinely benevolent person who uses his intelligence and skill to help people. It is true that he grows rich and influential through the exercise of this skill, but his exploitation is perhaps incidental, and anyway is relatively benign.

> Other thaumaturges who swarmed over Trinidad . . . knew an ineffectual charm or two but had neither the intelligence nor sympathy for anything else. . . . Ganesh elevated the profession by putting the charlatans out of business. . . . But more than his powers, learning, or tolerance, people liked his charity. He had no fixed fee and accepted whatever was given him. When someone complained that he was poor and at the same time persecuted by an evil spirit, Ganesh took care of the spirit and waived the fee. (*MM*, 133–34)

Ganesh, then, is not a charlatan. Although he profits by the fact that people believe in the "spirits" that he removes, he does not invent them—they are already real to those whom he helps. The narrative is suggestive but silent about what Ganesh himself believes. The implication is that, with all his intelligence, he tends to half-credit his own legend. Indeed, why should he not, since his success has been created by little more than his own clever manipulation of events, without malice or overt exploitation of the poor and unfortunate?

Much of the humor of *The Mystic Masseur* arises from Naipaul's already masterly use of language. He combines a grammatically correct, idiomatic English with reported speech suggesting the Trinidad dialect, to highly comic effect:

> My mother distrusted doctors and never took me to one. I am not blaming her for this because in those days people went by preference to the unqualified masseur or the quack dentist.
>
> "I know the sort of doctors it have in Trinidad," my mother used to say. "They think nothing of killing two three people before breakfast."
>
> This wasn't as bad as it sounds: in Trinidad the midday meal is called breakfast. (*MM*, 7)

The aplomb and timing of this passage is perfect. Combined with a genuine sympathy for all the characters, Naipaul's prose style gives this novel an enduring and graceful appeal. Sympathy does not destroy satire, but it elevates and enriches it. It is possible to see in Naipaul's later work a rather dismissive attitude toward women, if not a tendency toward misogyny, but the female characters in *The Mystic Masseur* are drawn with considerable understanding and tenderness, and there are references to injustices such as the poor education of women at the time.[11]

Ganesh's friend Beharry is undoubtedly a comic character. "When Beharry spoke he became rather like a mouse. He looked anxious and worked his small mouth nervously up and down as though he were nibbling" (*MM*, 65). The reader is constantly reminded of Beharry's "nibbling," always to humorous effect, but it characterizes rather than caricatures. And the comic description of the embarrassing dinner given by the governor of Trinidad to Ganesh and the other newly elected members of Trinidad's brand new legislative council in 1946, with the governor's wife taking a certain malicious delight in the discomfiture of her inexperienced guests, gains resonance when one reads a letter Naipaul wrote to his sister from Trinidad in 1949. He describes a similar dinner given by the Old Boys' Association, where he, like Ganesh, was "nauseated and annoyed" by the meat soup and committed "a gross breach of etiquette" by sending it away.[12] Food often becomes for Naipaul a deeply felt symbol of the difficulties faced by those brought up in ritualistic, superstitious societies in adjusting to the manners and customs of the wider world.

The Mystic Masseur is a kind of fictional biography, a form Naipaul has often used in preference to dramatic, event-driven fiction. His next novel, *The Suffrage of Elvira* (1958), was written, he said, "to prove to myself that I could invent, invent a story constructed carefully round a given incident."[13] It is a funny novel, full of wonderful scenes and vivid characters, but the plot, though carefully worked out, is a little too much like real life and never gains the impetus of a dramatic story. As he said in his letter to Seepersad, he could not—or would not—manage dramatic plots.

The Suffrage of Elvira tells the story of an election for Trinidad's legislative assembly—"the second general election under universal adult franchise" (*SE*, 181). The candidate whose fortunes we follow is Surujpat Harbans, a man who, as we soon come to see, has little interest in the electorate and regards the election as a financial investment from which he expects to make a good profit. The voters, in turn, see the candidate only as a source of handouts and favors, so much so that Harbans is worried that his investment will prove too expensive. Policies are never mentioned.

As always, the language is a delight. Naipaul's pure joy in words is evident in phrases such as "curious rural prudery" (*SE*, 183), used to describe the mode of dress of Elvira children, with the top half covered and the bottom bare. The dialogue is peppered with a universal kind of political jargon, which lumps people together in order to patronize them, like the "poorer people children" who are a constant target of petty bribery with sweet drinks and small change. The word "pussonal," the narrator writes, "had enormous vogue in Elvira in 1950" (SE, 186), as in the sentence, "Mr. Harbans, it have no reason why you should start getting suckastic and insultive in my pussonal" (SE, 300). Naipaul explained his technique for rendering dialogue in his foreword to his father's stories: "Phonetic dialogue—apart from its inevitable absurdities: *eggszactly* for 'exactly,' *w'at* for 'what'—falsifies the pace of speech, sets up false associations, is meaningless to people who don't know the idiom and unnecessary to those who do. The rhythm of broken language is sufficiently indicated by the construction of the sentence."[14]

The rhythm of Naipaul's dialogue is always effective. He spells an occasional word with a suggestion of its unconventional pronunciation—like "suckastic" for "sarcastic" and "pussonal" for "personal"—when it is justified, but does not overdo the phonetic dialogue enough to falsify the pace of normal speech.

The characters in *The Suffrage of Elvira* are a typical Naipaulian mixture of charlatans and fools. No one appreciates the meaning of democracy, and the implication is strong that the people have not been prepared and educated for self-government. They still see the government as something completely separate from themselves: they take bribes "easily, without acknowledgement, as though it was money from the government" (SE, 281). However, although political messages can be drawn from this novel, it is the social and personal interactions that really interest Naipaul. The comedy arises not so much from events and situations as from the way people behave with each other and the way they speak—language again—and the comic effects are achieved with economy and precision. The way the printer Harichand is described, for example, manages to convey information not just about Harichand but also about the village he lives in: "He was the only man in Elvira who possessed a raincoat; everybody else just waited until the rain stopped. . . . One of Harichand's idiosyncrasies was to wear a clean shirt every day" (SE, 269). In this way, wearing a raincoat and a clean shirt every day, nothing unusual to many of Naipaul's readers, becomes something which sets Harichand apart and illustrates his character. This is how the formidable Mrs Baksh, mother of seven children and wife of the "leader" of the Muslim community in Elvira, is introduced: "Mrs Baksh was combing out her thick black hair that went down to her hips. She nodded to Harbans, cleared her comb of loose hair, rolled the hair into a ball, spat on it and threw it into a corner. Then she began to comb again" (SE, 188). Without explicitly stating anything about her attitude toward Harbans, Naipaul has conveyed Mrs Baksh's characteristic combination of aggression and contempt in these two sentences. Mrs Baksh's children always refer to her in her absence as *"they,"* uniting respect and fear in their reluctance to speak of her in a more intimate way.

Two of Mrs Baksh's children, the eldest boy, Foam, and the ten-year-old Herbert, are the most sympathetic characters in the book and provide some hope for the future of this rather narrow, mean society. Foam, at seventeen, is not perfect. He is more interested in his own prospects than political ideals, and he becomes Harbans's campaign manager in order to outdo his rival, Lorkhoor, rather than to help Harbans. In this he is no different from everyone else in Elvira. He does, however, have the same sort of cleverness and generous impulses as the young boy in *Miguel Street*. He is aware of the consequences of his actions and never intentionally harms others, making amends when he accidentally does. His younger brother Herbert is a tender-hearted child in a difficult world. He adopts a stray mongrel puppy, Tiger, who virtually becomes a character in his own right. Tiger is seen by all the adults as an instrument of *obeah,* or magic, firstly as a sign of evil and later as a good omen. Only Herbert and Foam see him as a creature with his own independent existence, something approaching a pet, which is a foreign concept in Elvira. As Herbert says when confronted with the dead bodies of Tiger's mother and the rest of her litter, "Everybody only know how to say, 'Mash dog!' . . . Nobody know how to feed it" (*SE*, 276). Herbert endures beatings from his mother and, even worse, *jharay*—"spiritual fumigation"—from a pundit for Tiger's sake, and is rewarded by Tiger's survival as "the perfect street dog, noisy but discreet, game for anything, from chasing a chicken to nosing about a dustbin at night" (*SE*, 301).

Naipaul makes gestures in the direction of drama in this book. He frequently ends chapters or sections with a short, pregnant sentence, standing alone: "She was righter than she knew," of Mrs Baksh's prediction that "this election sweetness . . . going to turn sour sour" (*SE*, 244); and "This was to have disastrous consequences," of Ramlogan's decision to donate a case of whisky to the committee of the winning candidate (*SE*, 296). But the "disaster" and "sourness" do not really eventuate. There is a final scene of destruction and disorder, in which Harbans's new Jaguar is burnt, but there is no genuine catastrophe. The new member for Elvira, it is true, is committed only to his own profit, but nobody expects anything else. The novel ends with a short statement of losses and gains: "So, Harbans won the election and the insurance company lost a Jaguar. Chittaranjan lost a son-in-law and Dhaniram lost a daughter-in-law. Elvira lost Lorkhoor and Lorkhoor won a reputation. Elvira lost Mr Cuffy. And Preacher lost his deposit" (*SE*, 355). None of these wins and losses represents any great drama. The election has been a catalyst in the lives of several people, mostly for the good, although these consequences are all incidental to the democratic process.

Naipaul has had an abiding interest in elections and has written several essays covering election campaigns, but his interest is always in the social and personal behavior they inspire rather than the political process itself. Elections provide a wonderful setting for observation of human nature at its most manipulative and grasping, and the campaigns in Elvira provided Naipaul with the perfect fictional world for this small comic masterpiece.

Suman Gupta complains that Naipaul's Trinidad novels contain a "partial representation, which is made to appear comprehensive," of the "state of Trinidadian culture, politics, and society"[15] and that *The Mystic Masseur* and *The Suffrage of Elvira,* in particular, do not represent "with any clarity" the political history of Trinidad.[16] However, these novels are comedies about political behavior, not works of political science, and make no claims to achieve comprehensiveness. Fellow Caribbean writer George Lamming attacked Naipaul in 1962 for writing "castrated satire; and although satire may be a useful element in fiction, no important work . . . can rest safely on satire alone. . . . it is too small a refuge for a writer who wishes to be taken seriously."[17] Naipaul himself has claimed that he does not write satire, because "I fear no one. . . . I think it is . . . fear which underlies a good deal of what is called satire, or the attempt to be contemptuous of what you fear. That can't be done; rather you will be contemptuous of what you love, and exalt what you fear."[18] Although there are satirical elements in all these books, it is hard to see why Lamming should attack Naipaul in this way. There is indeed no contempt in Naipaul's writing. He writes clear-sightedly and humorously, but without malice and without patronizing his characters or his audience. His characters are what they are. They are clearly that way because of their upbringing, education, and situation in the world. These factors are not of their own making, but he will not turn that fact into a sentimental political point. He is a novelist, not a moralist.

CHAPTER THREE

Fiction versus Nonfiction *A House*
for Mr Biswas

In an interview in 1995 Naipaul said, in response to the question "Do you think you will ever go back to writing a pure novel or imaginative fiction again?,"

> I do write imaginative work, but I must say that I hate the word "novel." I can no longer understand why it is important to write or read invented stories. I myself don't need that stimulation. I don't need those extravaganzas. There is so much reading, so much understanding of the world that I still have to do. We are living at an extraordinary moment when so much knowledge is available to us that was not available 100 years ago. We can read books about Indian art, Indian history, Southeast Asian cultural history, Chinese art. . . . I don't see reading as an act of drugging oneself with a narrative. I don't need that. This other kind of reading is immensely exciting for me and there is so much of it to do.[1]

As novelist Ian McEwan commented in response to an edited version of this interview published in *The Observer* and provocatively titled "The Death of the Novel,"[2] "it's all very well" for the author of *A House for Mr Biswas* to spurn the novel: having accomplished a "comic masterpiece" before the age of thirty, he may have felt by his mid-sixties that the pleasures of fictional narrative had been exhausted for him. McEwan goes on, "I think he's giving an interview out of his current preoccupations and we writers tend to do that—we push out in manifesto mode and . . . say, well, because I'm not reading any fiction at the moment, the whole thing's dead."[3]

McEwan's analysis seems to be supported by Naipaul's publication of the novels *Half a Life* in 2001 and *Magic Seeds* in 2004. Naipaul's narrative style has never been the "drugging" variety anyway. Even in *A House for Mr Biswas*, one of his most formally conventional novels, he deliberately avoids suspense and relies instead on his sharp, perceptive insights into character and the dynamics of human relationships, and his fine eye for detail, to stimulate and sustain his readers' interest.

In any case, fiction provides a different type of information from nonfiction. A social history of the Hindu community in rural Trinidad might be factually informative, but it is likely to be dry reading matter beside *Mr Biswas*, a novel based on the life of a man like Naipaul's father, struggling to make a satisfactory life for himself and his family in colonial Trinidad. Even Naipaul's *The Loss of El Dorado,* a historical book about Trinidad written a few years after this novel, maintains, by its nature as an account of facts found in documents and archives, a far greater distance from its characters than any reader could sustain from Mohun Biswas and his children. Good fiction, with its subjective point of view and concern for the apparently trivial details of a life, a community, or a society, and its absence of an objectively testable corresponding reality, offers readers an opportunity to enter imaginatively into the setting and the lives of people they could otherwise understand only in a theoretical way.

Naipaul became a writer because of his father's expectations and, he claims, in spite of having demonstrated no talent. In *Finding the Center* he speaks of the fear of extinction that his father "so accurately transmitted" to him "without saying anything about it," which was linked with the writer's vocation and which "could be combated only by the exercise of the vocation" (*FC*, 72). For Seepersad Naipaul, and for his son after him, "to be a writer . . . was to triumph over darkness." (*FC*, 32).

Images of darkness and light are used often in *A House for Mr Biswas.* Mohun Biswas is born, his grandmother and the midwife assume, at "midnight, the inauspicious hour," and dire predictions are made for his future, but the next day in the morning's "bright light it seemed that all evil spirits had surely left the earth" (*HMB*, 16). The dark continues to hold terrors, however. The night his father dies, diving in a futile search for him in a dark pond, the boy finds himself "alone in the dark hut, and frightened" (*HMB*, 28). Later, his first sight of the private sections of Hanuman House, the home of the Tulsis, his future wife's family, is described in terms of darkness, blackness, dimness (*HMB*, 78–79). After his illness, which involves among other things a "billowing black cloud" which he feels "unless he was careful . . . would funnel into his head" (*HMB*, 239), he is recovering in Hanuman House and the darkness nearly overcomes him. In this case, however, it is not menacing so much as tempting: "The darkness, the silence, the absence of the world enveloped and comforted him: at some far-off time he had suffered great anguish. He had fought against it. Now he had surrendered, and this surrender had brought peace" (*HMB*, 269).

Mr Biswas's temptation by the peace and comfort of the dark and the void echoes Naipaul's temptation, as a young writer, to give up his vocation:

"Unless I had been driven by great necessity, something even like panic, I might never have written. The idea of laying aside the ambition was very restful and tempting—the way sleep was said to be tempting to Napoleon's soldiers on the retreat from Moscow."[4] This surrender, however comfortable, is dangerous. In a 1983 essay, Naipaul writes of his early twenties, the period before his writing career got under way: "Thirty years later, I can easily make present to myself again the anxiety of that time: to have found no talent, to have written no book, to be null and unprotected in the busy world. It is that anxiety—the fear of destitution in all its forms, the vision of the abyss—that lies below the comedy of the book."[5]

The temptation of the void is, however, outweighed by the terror it inspires, in both Naipaul and Mohun Biswas. For Naipaul, the failure to succeed as a writer would mean an unfulfilled life of displacement: in Trinidad "that society was such a simple one that I don't think there would have been room for me," while in England, although "I tried very hard . . . to get a job—to fit myself in," he found "there was nothing I could do."[6] For Biswas, the danger is in the capitulation of the individual to the suffocating system of conformity and repression that is the Tulsi clan. Although it is in the shelter of Hanuman House that he is able to recover from the panic and anxiety of his mental disturbance, he nevertheless knows that he must go "out into the world, to test it for its power to frighten" (*HMB*, 274).

Mr Biswas personifies the rebellion of the individual against the mass of nameless conformists. When he marries Shama and becomes aware of the way the household is organized, he finds that her sisters' husbands' "names were forgotten—they became Tulsis" (*HMB*, 88). Naipaul counteracts this by calling him "Mr Biswas" throughout the novel—even as a newborn baby. The effect of this is at once absurd and respectful. No one but the narrator calls him Mr Biswas. In dialogue he is usually addressed by his first name, if a name is mentioned at all. (The respect implied by addressing a low-status individual by formal title and surname is revisited in *The Enigma of Arrival,* where the narrator makes a point of addressing the gardener as Mr Pitton.) Other characters in the novel are commonly referred to by the names Mr Biswas uses: the carpenter who builds his house at Green Vale is Mr Maclean, his mother-in-law is Mrs Tulsi; but the brother-in-law whose library consists of the works of American western writer W. C. Tuttle becomes W. C. Tuttle, his wife Mrs Tuttle, and his children the little Tuttles. The narrative is seen so exclusively through Mr Biswas's eyes that no other names are given for these characters, even though no one but he and his family know them by these names.

One critic has argued that the Tulsi family is a symbol of imperialist organization, with the husbands as the colonized subjects: "There is something archetypal in the organization of Hanuman House. Mrs Tulsi is a powerful mother-figure, and rules through an understanding of the psychology of slavery. . . . Mrs Tulsi, good colonizer as she is, justifies her exploitation with the explanation that she is really doing her subjects good. Her argument is that which ex-colonial peoples most bitterly resent, and also the one which gives them pause."[7] This theory works well. It is supported by the way the Tulsis suppress Mr Biswas's identity, accuse him of ingratitude, and constantly harp on the fact that before he married he had nothing but what he could hang on a nail. But Naipaul, although he does not deny that his background formed him as a writer, denies any political purposes in his writing. In 1964 he wrote: "Mr [Chinua] Achebe says that his purpose is 'to help my society regain its belief in itself. . . .' Such a drive might produce good novels. But the attitude is political and one's sympathy with it can only be political. In the end it is the writer and the writing that matter. . . . We cannot share other people's obsession with their images. . . . A country is ennobled by its writers only if these writers are good. Propagandists help little in the end."[8]

Naipaul has consistently said that in his writing he is "not a spokesman for anything."[9] It is a personal vocation of his own "to explore the many sides of his past."[10] He has even described writing as "a sort of disease, a sickness . . . a form of incompleteness . . . a form of anguish, . . . despair."[11] This is not to say that he is apolitical, but that his purpose as a writer is not primarily political. His strength comes from his ability to control and channel his emotions in his writing. Interviewer Gordon Burn expressed surprise that his "distilled, simple prose" could be compatible "with what he regards as his genetically inherited tendency toward hysteria and panic," to which Naipaul replied, "Panic is there. Not in the writing. But panic is there in the writer."[12] Even when he was young, he says, he "was always amazed that out of such profound rage, one could end by writing quite calmly. One reacts rather strongly, but, as a writer, one distills that down. If those responses were not strong, probably one would not be a writer."[13]

The assurance of A House for Mr Biswas is sustained by a subdued, ironic tone. The distance he maintains between his narrator and the characters makes it possible to see this novel as principally a comic achievement, but in this he has taken his father's advice: "Be realistic, humorous when this comes in pat, but don't make it deliberately so. If you are at a loss for a theme, take me for it."[14] The early scenes of A House for Mr Biswas are, indeed, adapted from one of his father's short stories, "They Named Him Mohun," "the only piece of autobiography my father permitted himself, if autobiography can be used of a story which more or less ends with the birth of the writer."[15] The pathos in the father's story is, however, undercut in the son's novel by an ironic, skeptical narrator who points out that the birth of the baby at the "unseemly hour of midnight"[16] could only have been a superstitious guess on the part of the midwife and the child's grandmother. Also, the child's sixth finger, which in the story is regarded as a sign of "an incarnation of evil,"[17] falls off undramatically "before he was nine days old" (*HMB*, 18). The story is "a tale of pure romance, in which . . . old ritual, lovingly described, can only lead to reconciliation,"[18] while the novel continues after the reconciliation between Mohun's parents, telling the life story the father "could never take any further" although "he often spoke of doing an autobiographical novel."[19] Naipaul makes it clear, though, that *A House for Mr Biswas* is not a biography:

> For me to write the story of a man like my father was, in the beginning at any rate, to attempt pure fiction, if only because I was writing of things before my time. . . . I knew little about the Trinidad Indian village way of life. I was a town boy; I had grown up in Port-of-Spain. I had memories of my father's conversation; I also had his short stories. . . . So the present novel begins with events twice removed, in an antique, "pastoral" time, and almost in a land of the imagination. The real world gradually defines itself, but it is still for the writer an imagined world. The novel is well established, its tone set, when my own wide-awake memories take over.[20]

Even once his "wide-awake memories" took over, he still felt "that I didn't even really belong in the exotic world I was born into and felt I had to write about. That life I wrote about in *Biswas* couldn't be the true nature of *my* life because I hadn't grown up in it feeling that it was mine. And that world itself was in fact turning when I entered it. How could one avoid the feeling of floating around?"[21]

Along with these feelings of disorientation and displacement, the adult writer looks back upon his own childhood anger, which he embodies in Anand, Mr Biswas's son. Mr Biswas's anger is an uncertain lostness, never sure of its justification, and sometimes becomes mere petulance. In his teens he returns to his mother in her impoverished hovel, having been beaten by his uncle Bhandat, the rum-shop manager he was living with and working for. He tries to look for a job, but after a short time he announces his intention to kill himself. His mother's reply, "That would be the best thing for you. And for me," sends him into a "great rage" (*HMB*, 63). He is, however, soon mollified by the respect with which his sister's low-caste husband Ramchand treats him. Mr Biswas's moods are changeable. The despotic heads of the Tulsi household, Mrs Tulsi and her brother-in-law Seth, are the main antagonists in his life. They frequently claim that they are only trying to help him, and while he resents this argument, it also makes him feel guilty. When Anand is old enough to take a part in the action, however, his anger can be seen as well, explosive, but purer and more powerful because it lacks an adult's compulsion to register the enemy's point of view.

Humor is inherent in much of the novel's action, but it is rarely without a serious undercurrent. The description of Mr Biswas's father's funeral—the photographer trying to arrange the bereaved family around the propped-up coffin—is hilarious. But then the reader is reminded of their deprivation and poverty: the scene is immediately followed by a description of the photograph seen for the first time years later: "Mr Biswas was astonished by his own smallness. The scabs of sores and the marks of eczema showed clearly on his knobbly knees and along his very thin arms and legs. Everyone in the photograph had unnaturally large, staring eyes which seemed to have been outlined in black" (*HMB*, 38).

Sometimes Naipaul sets up deliberately comic scenes, only to shock the reader into awareness of the painful situation that lies beneath. When Shama discovers Mr Biswas's attempts at writing, for example, the scene begins as comedy, but the mood changes abruptly at the end:

> Forgetting that in his strictness, and as part of her training he had ordered Shama to file all his papers, he thought that these stories were as secret at home as his marriage and four children were at the office. And one Friday, when he found Shama puzzling over her accounts and had scoffed as usual, she said, "Leave me alone, Mr John Lubbard."
>
> That was one of the names of his thirty-three-year-old hero.
>
> "Go and take Sybil to the pictures."
>
> That was from another story. He had got the name from a novel by Warwick Deeping.
>
> "Leave Ratni alone."
>
> That was the Hindi name he had given to the mother of four in another story. Ratni walked heavily, "as though perpetually pregnant"; her arms filled the sleeves of her bodice and seemed about to burst them; she sucked in her breath through her teeth while she worked at her accounts, the only reading and writing she did.
>
> Mr Biswas recalled with horror and shame the descriptions of the small tender breasts of his barren heroines.
>
> Shama sucked her teeth loudly.
>
> If she had laughed, he would have hit her. (*HMB*, 312)

The comic tone allows him to explore the complex emotional lives of his main characters without lapsing into sentimentality. It makes the most painful situations bearable but stops short of ridicule.

Mr Biswas is both insignificant and profoundly important. Naipaul's narrative has endowed this unheroic figure with an unlikely heroism. His struggles and achievements echo the struggles and achievements of all individuals who refuse to conform, in whatever setting and circumstances. Critic Gordon Rohlehr notes that "the purity of motive and truth to instinct and necessity which marked Biswas's struggle against an apparently indestructible system make his rebellion an affirmation of universal values; transform it from being a sordid personal struggle to one undertaken on behalf of the group. Biswas doesn't know this, engaged as he is in the fight for a house; the Tulsis don't know it, engaged as they are in teaching their children to conform and mock at the rebel."[22] Naipaul apparently doesn't know it either: he rejects the suggestion that he intends to write universally. In 1965, reviewing a book of essays on Commonwealth writing, he wrote that one of the critics "sees my work, and that of others, demonstrating the 'essential kinship of various peoples.' I can see what is meant, but if I thought that this was to be the only effect of my work I might be tempted to be perverse the next time."[23] But Mr Biswas, with his vividly portrayed inner life and minutely described circumstances, has an impact on the reader that cannot be achieved in a nonfiction account. The following passage comes from *Finding the Center*. Seepersad Naipaul received an anonymous letter—possibly from members of his wife's family—threatening him with poisoning if he failed to perform a sacrifice to the goddess Kali in atonement for a critical article he wrote in the newspaper about "amazing superstitious practices" among the Hindu rural community:

> In the week that followed my father existed on three planes. He was the reporter who had becomes his own very big front page story: "Next Sunday I am doomed to die." He was the reformer who wasn't going to yield to "ju-jus:" "I won't sacrifice a goat." At the same time, a man of feud-ridden Chaguanas, he was terrified of what he saw as a murder threat, and he was preparing to submit. Each role made nonsense of the other. And my father must have known it. (*FC*, 68)

This describes vividly, but at some distance, the fear and humiliation of the time. It enters into the emotions to some extent, but the last sentence shows it for what it is—a nonfictional account: he cannot say "my father knew it," because that would be presuming beyond the boundaries of nonfiction and entering the realm of fiction. In contrast, the following passage from the novel makes bold, unqualified statements about Mr Biswas's state of mind when Anand and he are alone on a stormy night in their half-built house at Green Vale:

> "Say *Rama Rama Sita Rama,* and nothing will happen to you," Mr Biswas said.
> Anand repeated the words, faster and faster.

"You don't want to leave me?"

Anand didn't reply.

This had become one of Mr Biswas's fears. By concentrating on it—a power he had in his state—he managed to make it the most oppressive of all his fears: that Anand would leave him and he would be left alone. (*HMB*, 255)

Naipaul says his father's stories first gave him an appreciation of "the distorting, distilling power of the writer's art." English novels, he said, could not provide him with a tradition, but his father's Trinidad stories could help him: "Where I had seen a drab haphazardness, they found order; where I would have attempted to romanticise, to render my subject equal with what I had read, they accepted."[24] He insists that "all literatures are regional; perhaps it is only the placelessness of a Shakespeare or the blunt communication of 'gross' experience as in Dickens that makes them appear less so."[25] But Mr Biswas arouses sympathy in the reader, which inevitably expands into an awareness of "the essential kinship of various peoples."

Naipaul is no doubt right when he says that "every time you try to devise a story to get some kind of symbol for your experience, the whole apparatus of invention that you have to bring to bear would be fraudulent."[26] His method is more instinctive: even though he still claims that it is an artificial act to sit down to write, he finds, with imaginative writing, that "when it catches fire, it takes you to unexpected places."[27] In *Finding the Center*, he writes that "true, and saving, knowledge of my subject . . . always seemed to come during the writing" (*FC*, 17–18). So with the writer's gift for seeing the world through the eyes of others—"I could meet dreadful people and end up seeing the world through their eyes, seeing their frailties, their needs"[28]— and the power of narrative itself to distill experience into something of value, Naipaul in *A House for Mr Biswas* transforms "the life of someone like my father" into a modern-day Everyman's journey. In 1983 he recalled writing the novel: "Nothing had prepared me for the liberation and absorption of this extended literary labor, the joy of allowing fantasy to play on stored experience, the joy of the comedy that so naturally offered itself, the joy of language. The right words seemed to dance above my head; I plucked them down at will. I took chances with language. Before this, out of my beginner's caution, I had been strict with myself."[29] The joy in language he discovered at that time has obviously stayed with him, or at least revisited him when he wrote *The Enigma of Arrival*. The pleasure he clearly has in wrapping, or fixing, in words experiences "which might otherwise evaporate away" is never more happily displayed than in the later novel.

When he was writing *Mr Biswas*, Naipaul says, "I was writing about things I didn't know" (*FC*, 60). This belies the assurance and the profound understanding of the complexity of human relationships that characterize the novel. He remembers how, writing the novel, he regarded "with wonder what he had drawn out of himself, the unsuspected truths turned up by the imagination."[30] He claims that turning real life into narrative is a matter of simplification: whereas in real life, acts and events might be (or at least appear) random, in fiction they must have an internal logic, an explicable cause, in order that the reader's imagination may be engaged.[31] This might be true. Certainly, characteristic incidents and figures are selected or created to serve the needs of the story. However, there is little simplification of the feelings and relationships of the principal characters of this novel, which are so varied and convincingly inconsistent that they resist the reductions of political analysis or sentimentality, or even of rational cause and effect.

Mr Biswas's attitude toward his wife, Shama, for example, fluctuates wildly. By the time of his death, he has come "to accept her judgment and to respect her optimism" (*HMB*, 7). This comfortable reliance is hard-won, however. At the first sight of her, "though he disliked her voice, he was enchanted by her smile" (*HMB*, 74–75), and a rash love-letter catapults him into marriage and the clutches of the large, powerful machine that is the Tulsi family enterprise. Shama becomes alternately a focus for his resentment of her family and an ally. These contradictory roles mean that his attitude toward her is confused. Romance has no place at all in their marriage, but there are moments when happiness, or at least contentment, seems possible. On their first day at the derelict shop the family has assigned to them at the Chase village, "he was astonished at the change in Shama. Till the last she had protested at leaving Hanuman House, but now she behaved as though she moved into a derelict house every day. Her actions were assertive, wasteful and unnecessarily noisy. They filled shop and house; they banished silence and loneliness" (*HMB*, 131). And "feeling grateful to her, he felt tender towards her coffee-set." Mentioning the coffee-set tempers the hint of sentimentality with a note of absurdity. When she brings her first child, born at Hanuman House, back to the Chase, "he immediately began complaining of the very things that pleased him most. Savi cried, and he spoke as though she were one of Shama's indulgences. Meals were late, and he exhibited an annoyance which concealed the joy he felt that there was someone to cook meals with him in mind. To these outbursts Shama didn't reply, as she would have done before. She was morose herself, as though she preferred this bond to the bond of sentimentality" (*HMB*, 152).

Later, however, when she returns to Green Vale after one of their many separations, pregnant with their fourth child, he stays in bed for a week, "observing Shama closely, with suspicion, hatred and nausea. . . . One morning she came and placed her palm, then the back of her hand, on his forehead. The action offended him, flattered him, and made him uneasy" (*HMB*,

247). They begin an argument: "He was violently angry, never before had he been so disgusted by her. Yet he wished her to remain there" (*HMB*, 247). In his deranged state he decides that she wishes him dead, and in his panicky, irrational struggle to escape from her out the window, he kicks her, seeing, "too late, that he had kicked her on the belly" (*HMB*, 249). From this low point, their marriage gradually recovers and becomes the respectful partnership described in the prologue, but even when they have a house of their own and the threat of being engulfed by the Tulsis has diminished, arguments continue, because it has become their habit.

Relationships with his own family, and his children, are equally ambivalent. At his mother's funeral "he longed to feel grief. He was surprised only by jealousy" of those who had known her better (*HMB*, 433). He manages to make his grief genuine, however, through writing. Firstly, he writes a letter of complaint to the doctor who behaved rudely toward his brothers when certifying her death. Later, he writes a poem—"in prose"—to her memory.

Naipaul is in no doubt about what he owes his father: "His love was extremely important to me. It was a curious kind of love. I felt responsible for him, even as a child."[32] Fittingly, Anand's first major independent act in the novel is to decide to stay with his father, after the frightening scene at Green Vale. But he rejects a gift—a box of crayons—and Mr Biswas is puzzled:

> "Why did you stay then?"
> Anand looked exasperated.
> "Why?"
> "Because—" The word came out thin, explosive, charged with anger,
> at himself and his father. "Because they was going to leave you alone."
> For the rest of the day they hardly spoke. (*HMB*, 251)

The course of Anand's childhood proceeds very much as Naipaul's own did. The feelings ascribed to him are the anger, the satirical sense, the self-awareness, and the detachment that Naipaul admits were his own in childhood. The complexity of this father-son relationship is nowhere more evident than in the "ducking" incident. Shama's two brothers, Mr Biswas, and Anand go swimming at the harbor extension at Docksite. Clowning with his brothers-in-law, Mr Biswas fails to notice that Anand has disappeared into the water. Shekhar acts quickly enough to pull Anand from the water and resuscitates him:

> Anand spluttered. His expression was one of anger. He said, "I was
> walking to the boat."
> "I told you to stay where you were," Mr Biswas said, angry too.
> "And the bottom of the sea drop away."
> "The dredging," Shekhar said. He had not lost his look of alarm.

"The sea just drop away," Anand cried, lying on his back, covering his face with a crooked arm. He spoke as one insulted.

Owad said, "Anyway, you've got the record for ducking, Shompo."

"Shut up!" Anand screamed. He began to cry, rubbing his legs on the hard, cracked ground, then turning over on his belly.

Mr Biswas took up the shirt with the safetypin and handed it to Anand. Anand snatched the shirt and said, "Leave me."

"We shoulda leave you," Mr Biswas said, "when you was there, ducking." As soon as he spoke the last word he regretted it. (*HMB*, 320–21)

One might note that Shama's elder brother Shekhar, who has the least significant relationship with Anand, expresses the most concern about him.

On the next day, Anand writes an essay about this incident that gains him "twelve marks out of ten" at school. Mr Biswas is proud of his son and wishes "to be close to him. He would have done anything to make up for the solitude of the previous day" (*HMB*, 322), but Anand is impatient and already embarrassed by his composition, and a flogging ensues. Nevertheless, the incident also results in the recognition of Anand's academic aptitude, and he is started on a program of private lessons, milk, and prunes—the regimen that the Tulsis believe produces the best results in the scholarship stakes.

All these incidents exemplify the unpredictable nature of human responses to a variety of situations, which is one of Naipaul's consistent preoccupations. This is hardly a political position, but it does support his opposition to ideology that many have characterized as conservatism. For anyone to impose their beliefs about progress, human happiness, and correct behavior upon others is a dangerous presumption. Naipaul's dislike of causes no doubt arises from a personal fear of being subjected to such impositions. His consciousness of his own difference from the conventional, as well as what he observes of other people, feeds into the inconsistencies of his characters who show time and again the impossibility of the generalizations that are the essential basis for any radical ideology.

Naipaul was genuinely grief-stricken when his father died but realized that without his death, he would not have written *A House for Mr Biswas*: "If my father was alive, clearly, I wouldn't have been able to write it. I wouldn't have wanted to do it. I probably wouldn't have even seen the material, the way you don't see things in front of your face. . . . My talent wouldn't have been stretched at that early stage by this literary labor. You have the talent, but you have to *develop* it. I don't know whether his death wasn't a kind of creative liberation for me. No one was looking over my shoulder."[33] Without the perspective his father's death provided in his own life, the retrospective urge would not have arisen, and his writing career would have followed a different path.

In writing the life story of "someone like my father," Naipaul claims no political purpose. If he had intended simply to commemorate the father he felt he had disappointed in some ways, he would have succeeded: Mr Biswas, despite all his weakness and ineptitude, and his occasional bad behavior, commands the reader's respect and sympathy—James Wood names Mr Biswas as "one of the few enduring characters in postwar British fiction"[34]—and one can only be moved by the dispassionate way in which Anand's difficult relationship with his father is portrayed, when it is known that he is in essence an autobiographical figure.[35] But Naipaul has transcended the personal and has created a novel in which political, psychological, and social situations are shrewdly observed and analyzed in an imaginative and evocative way that would not have been possible in a nonfictional form.

The Journeys Begin *The Middle Passage, An Area of Darkness,* and *The Loss of El Dorado*

With four novels published in England to a favorable critical reception, Naipaul produced his first nonfiction book. *The Middle Passage* was written at the suggestion of the premier of Trinidad, Dr. Eric Williams, made when Naipaul was visiting in September 1960. He says in the foreword to the first edition, "I hesitated. The novelist works towards conclusions of which he is often unaware; and it is better that he should. To analyse and decide before writing would rob the writer of the excitement which supports him during his solitude, and would be the opposite of my method as a novelist. I also felt it as a danger that, having factually analysed the society as far as I was able, I would be unable afterwards to think of it in terms of fiction and that in anything I might write I would be concerned only to prove a point. However, I decided to take the risk" (*MP*, 5).

Five years later, after the appearance of his second travel book, *An Area of Darkness,* he told Derek Walcott, "I still find non-fiction extremely difficult; that is having to reduce disordered ideas into order."[1] As was seen at the beginning of the previous chapter, however, Naipaul came more and more to reject fiction in favor of nonfiction. It is ironic that he owes the fascination with travel and historical writing that has shaped his career to a colonial politician, a breed for which he has, on the whole, had little respect, targeting their shortcomings in such novels as *The Mimic Men.*

In *The Middle Passage,* Naipaul relates his travels in Trinidad and neighboring Caribbean states including British Guiana, Surinam, and Martinique. It is an uneven work in some ways, but in spite of his early reservations about venturing into nonfiction, he said later that it was "a very funny book" and that he "continue[d] to like it a great deal."[2] He stood by it despite the criticism it had aroused: "A writer's book has to stand even after the events have changed. My book was written in '61, published in '62. So 18 years later it has to stand up or not. You read it now and I think you see that it's fair—

it's fair. . . . If it remains true, if you cannot bring yourself to say, 'You were wrong here, and here, or here,' then there is no sense asking how I came to arrive at these things. I arrived at them because I refused to go in with preconceived notions."[3] He did have preconceived notions, however, and they marred part of this book. In British Guiana he traveled with Cheddi Jagan, the leader of the government, and his wife Janet, a government minister, on the campaign trail in the interior of the country. His preexisting sympathy with the Jagans, East Indian West Indians like himself, though not explicit, is obvious and makes for dull reading in parts.

Far more lively is the beginning of the book, describing the voyage from London to Trinidad. Boarding the train at Waterloo Station in London, he and his fellow travelers had already left England behind. With stabbing precision and a hint of malice, Naipaul vividly describes the other passengers, their clothes, and their conversations: "One man with a Nat King Cole hairstyle was dandling a fat bonneted baby that was gift-wrapped in ribbons and frills, and with a rubber nipple stuck like a gag and a final flourish in its drooping, dripping mouth" (MP, 11). Using his novelistic skills of characterization and dialogue, he deftly re-creates the train journey to Southampton and from thence the voyage on an immigrant ship bound for the West Indies to collect a new batch of seven hundred hopeful Caribbean islanders seeking a bright new life in England.

This boat trip, as he describes it here, seems to have provided Naipaul with ideas and characters for several later novels. There is a young man named Kripal Singh from a rich manufacturing family, who "smoked with nervous elegance" (MP, 20) and is very reminiscent of Ralph Singh (born Ranjit Kripalsingh) in The Mimic Men. West Indians on the boat anxiously discussing their children's English marriages foreshadow the terrifying story "Tell Me Who to Kill" in In a Free State, and that story might also owe something to the two West Indian "lunatics" who with their white "keepers" were traveling home on the boat.

Naipaul characteristically makes no apology for any offense he might cause by these often unflattering portraits. He explains his position in the section on Trinidad:

> Living in a borrowed culture, the West Indian, more than most, needs
> writers to tell him who he is and where he stands. Here the West Indian
> writers have failed. Most have so far only reflected and flattered the
> prejudices of their race or colour groups. . . .
>
> The insecure wish to be heroically portrayed. Irony and satire, which
> might help more, are not acceptable; and no writer wishes to let down
> his group. . . .
>
> It is not easy to write about the West Indian middle class. The most
> exquisite gifts of irony and perhaps malice would be required. . . . The

gifts required, of subtlety and brutality, can grow only out of mature
literature. (*MP*, 69)

Modestly, he does not explicitly lay claim to these gifts, but the connection
is certainly there to be made—malice, subtlety, and brutality are all present
to some degree in his work.

But Naipaul rarely lets the reader forget that this is his personal vision
and that he is far from a detached observer in this region, where he lived
for the first eighteen years of his life. He uses several different techniques
to convey his own engagement with his material. Early in the book, when
the first consignment of immigrants has been collected from St. Kitts, a
tourist who has never spoken to him before makes the remark that "the holi-
day is over. . . . The wild cows are coming on board." This comment sets off
a train of reflection beginning, "No attitude in the West Indies is new" (*MP*,
26–27). Going back as far as Christopher Columbus, he gives a brief history of the cynical exploitation of the region, asking, "How can the history
of this West Indian futility be written?" and replying, "The history of the
islands can never be satisfactorily told. Brutality is not the only difficulty.
History is built around achievement and creation; and nothing was created
in the West Indies" (*MP*, 28–29). Three pages of impassioned but apparently impersonal discussion come to an end with this controversial statement. There is a break, marked off with a row of asterisks; then comes the
revelation of personal engagement: "In the morning I was calmer" (*MP*, 29).
It is immediately clear, then, that this has been an emotional irruption, not
to be seen (as many critics have seen it) as a reasoned statement but as an
intemperate reaction to the opinion so casually expressed by the unwitting
"tourist"; a very specific reaction in a specific time and place, not a general
and considered political opinion. This technique of using juxtaposition to
establish context is extremely powerful, but dangerous. It relies on the attention and cooperation of readers and leaves the writer vulnerable to being
quoted out of context by hostile critics. It may, of course, be deliberately
provocative: Naipaul does not object to giving offense in order to make a
point.

Elsewhere in the book his subjectivity is more directly expressed. In
Georgetown, British Guiana, the daily frustrations typical of the traveling
life temporarily ruffle his customary cool detachment: "Georgetown, most
exquisite city in the British Caribbean, is for the visitor the most exasperat-
ing. Try getting a cup of coffee in the morning. The thing is impossible" (*MP*,
116). After three pages of petulance, recalling the bumptious, insecure boy
of ten years before as seen in his letters, the passage gradually broadens out
into a sociopolitical analysis of the legacy of slavery in this country. But the
personal irritation intrudes uncomfortably in a way that is rare in the later
books. In a similar passage in his next travel book, *An Area of Darkness*, he

subjects himself to more self-analysis, acknowledging the futility of his exasperation and the self-disgust aroused by indulging in anger and contempt in such circumstances. An earlier reaction in *The Middle Passage* to "the sight of exposed food in the midst of dust and mud" in an Amerindian hut, which gives rise to the feeling that "the reverence for food—rules for its handling, interdictions—was one of the essentials of civilization" (*MP*, 103–4), is more temperate and therefore also more effective.

There is a streak of contrariness in Naipaul—an unwillingness to be impressed by what is expected to impress him. In a later essay he complains, "'Characters' lie on my spirit like lead."[4] Leaving aside the question of whether he might find that such people interfere with the projection of his own unique persona, as a writer he finds it tiresome to meet "characters," people who present themselves as eccentric and who therefore, almost by definition, offer little scope for his novelistic skills. Similarly, in *The Middle Passage* he says: "I had tried hard to feel interest in the Amerindians as a whole, but had failed. I couldn't read their faces; I couldn't understand their language, and could never gauge at what level communication was possible. Among more complex people there are certain individuals who have the power to transmit to you their sense of defeat and purposelessness: emotional parasites who flourish by draining you of the vitality you preserve with difficulty. The Amerindians had this effect on me" (*MP*, 102). This is very clearly a personal opinion, directly related to his own inability to understand these people, and although it conveys a certain dislike, it does not show contempt or disapproval, only puzzlement and defeated intellectual effort. The people he can understand and therefore describe are much more rewarding for him—the black Trinidadians pursuing "the weary road to whiteness" (*MP*, 82), or the "cynical buffoons who form so large a part of the politically ambitious in every population" (*MP*, 133).

When he does make political points, Naipaul always takes the historical view—the long view. In a remarkable interview in 1971 with Adrian Rowe-Evans, he discusses the concept of length of vision:

> The people who are going to get things done are those of medium vision. The long-visioned ones, the people who had long vistas of eternity to play with, were so overwhelmed by all that that they weren't going to do much, whereas the short-visioned man, say the hunter in the South American bush who is going to kill an animal and eat it all at once, has no place in his thoughts for anything other than the immediate act. . . . I often wish I could have been a doer. But then I do have a great distrust of *causes,* simply because they *are* causes and they have to simplify, to ignore so much. As a man of action one would be continually weakened

by harking after the truth, by too-honestly reassessing the situation all the time.[5]

Naipaul's long vision is what gives him his power as a writer, but it also has the tendency to make him pessimistic and skeptical about political and social progress, an attitude that has excited much condemnation of his work from "postcolonial" critics who see him as contemptuous and insulting to societies that are struggling to make the best of their limited possibilities.[6]

In his foreword to a later edition of *The Middle Passage*, Naipaul lamented that he had been too "romantic about the healing power, in such a culture, of political or racial assertion."[7] "Romanticism" is far from obvious in this book, except perhaps in the approval implied for the Jagan regime in British Guiana, and this has nothing to do with approval of "racial assertion." But any residual romanticism was to be thoroughly eradicated in the next travel book, *An Area of Darkness*, which took Naipaul for the first time to his ancestral homeland of India. It was an uncomfortable awakening in a way that the trip to the Caribbean world he knew so well could never be.

An Area of Darkness begins with an anecdote of arrival, "A Little Paperwork," which, like the opening of *The Middle Passage*, is in many ways comic. But there is a difference, as has been noted, in the quality of the personal reaction. It is more thoughtful, more self-critical, and therefore more profound. He discusses with unsparing honesty the development of his response during the slow boat journey from Europe to India:

> From Athens to Bombay another idea of man had defined itself by degrees, a new type of authority and subservience. The physique of Europe had melted away first into that of Africa and then, through Semitic Arabia, into Aryan Asia. Men had been diminished and deformed; they begged and whined. Hysteria had been my reaction, and a brutality dictated by a new awareness of myself as a whole human being and a determination, touched with fear, to remain what I was. It mattered little through whose eyes I was seeing the East; there had as yet been no time for this type of self-assessment.
> Superficial impressions, intemperate reactions. (*AD*, 16)

Naipaul, as always, strives to move beyond superficial impressions. "India is the poorest country in the world. Therefore, to see its poverty is to make an observation of no value; a thousand newcomers to the country before you have seen and said as you" (*AD*, 47). So, in many ways, *An Area of Darkness* is a book about Naipaul himself rather than a book about India. "For the first time in my life I was one of the crowd. There was nothing in my appearance or dress to distinguish me from the crowd eternally hurrying into Churchgate

Station. In Trinidad to be an Indian was to be distinctive. To be anything there was distinctive; difference was each man's attribute. To be an Indian in England was distinctive; in Egypt it was more so. Now in Bombay I entered a shop or a restaurant and awaited a special quality of response. And there was nothing. It was like being denied part of my reality" (*AD*, 44–46). The remarkable thing about this passage is its frankness. To confess that one "awaits a special quality of response" is to put oneself in danger of accusations of conceit from those who lack the imagination to understand how ingrained this sense of identity-in-difference would be in someone like Naipaul, and who cannot see to what extent this consciousness has formed him as a person and a writer.

In his 1965 interview with Walcott, he spoke of the particular difficulties of writing *An Area of Darkness*: "After a few months in India, it seemed that I had nothing to write about. In fact, while I was there I abandoned the idea of writing a book."[8] It was, in the end, economic necessity that forced him to persevere, and he approached the work like a novel, "looking for a pattern in confused impressions. Writing a word like 'ruins' on a copybook page and looking at it for a day."[9]

Naipaul explains that the differences between his first two travel books relate to the differences in their subjects. *The Middle Passage* is about a "haphazard sort of society" and *An Area of Darkness* is about a "more profound" society that is "self-contained and unique." Therefore it is "possible to get at the truth, or to appear to get at it, more easily."[10] Looking for a pattern, reducing disordered ideas into order, is the quest of any writer, but it is especially urgent for Naipaul, with his commitment to the truth of his response, and the powerful anxiety that impels him in his writing. James Atlas asked for Naipaul's response to the claim of his critics that he "is an enemy of the Third World, that he condescends to it. 'The condescension is in those who don't notice,' he responds. 'You've got to be awfully liberal not to be moved by distress. When you see human degradation on that scale, you can never be the same again.'"[11] But determined as always to look beyond the superficial, he is not content to notice only the poverty and deprivation, but seeks the humanity that is also present:

> The smiles on the faces of the begging children, that domestic group
> among the pavement sleepers waking in the cool Bombay morning,
> father, mother and baby in a trinity of love, so self-contained that they
> are as private as if walls had separated them from you: it is your gaze
> that violates them, your sense of outrage that outrages them. You might
> have seen the boy sweeping his area of pavement, spreading his mat,
> lying down; exhaustion and undernourishment are in his tiny body and
> shrunken face, but lying flat on his back, oblivious of you and the

thousands who walk past in the lane between the sleepers' mats and house walls bright with advertisements and election slogans, oblivious of the warm, over-breathed air, he plays with fatigued concentration with a tiny pistol in blue plastic. (*AD*, 47–48)

Naipaul looks to literature for help in interpreting this society. While he acknowledges that his reading of Indian novels has not been comprehensive, he doubts their capacity to do anything but produce "documents of the Indian confusion" (*AD*, 228). Apart from R. K. Narayan, who is "inimitable" and therefore not a viable role model for younger writers, Naipaul sees only a "mimicry of the West" in Indian novels. "The sweetness and sadness which can be found in Indian writing and Indian films are a turning away from a too overwhelming reality; they reduce the horror to a warm, virtuous emotion. Indian sentimentality is the opposite of concern" (*AD*, 226–27). However, later in the book he had still not settled the question of how to respond to this country: "From the railway train and from the dusty roads India appeared to require only pity. It was an easy emotion, and perhaps the Indians were right: it was compassion like mine, so strenuously maintained, that denied humanity to many. It separated; it permitted the surprise and emotion I felt . . . at these simple exhibitions of humanity. Anger, compassion and contempt were aspects of the same emotion; they were without value because they could not endure. Achievement could begin only with acceptance" (*AD*, 263). This book is at its most moving in passages like these, where Naipaul, groping for order and meaning, expresses in his clearest prose the uncertainty and confusion that everyone shares when confronting immense and intractable facts such as India's poverty.

An Area of Darkness is divided into three parts. The middle section is set in Srinigar, Kashmir, where Naipaul stayed for four months in the Hotel Liward, built on a island in the lake. (Although he does not say so, it was here that he wrote the novel *Mr Stone and the Knights Companion*, set in London. It seems almost a universal rule that he never writes about a place while he is living there: he needs the perspective provided by distance.) Readers are introduced to the hotel's proprietor, Mr Butt, and his assistant Aziz, who is one of Naipaul's most memorable characters in fiction or nonfiction: "a very small man, bare-footed, with a dingy grey pullover tight above flapping white cotton trousers gathered in at the waist by a string. A touch of quaintness, something of the Shakespearean mechanic, was given him by his sagging woollen nightcap. So misleading can first impressions be: this was Aziz" (*AD*, 108).

Almost a mininovel, this part of the book becomes a story about the complex developing relationship between Naipaul and Aziz. Aziz accompanied him on several excursions. On a trip to Gulmarg to visit some friends, Naipaul found it "especially interesting to watch him at work on our friends, to see applied to others that process of assessment through service to which, in the early days, we ourselves had been subjected. They had servants of their own: nothing bound Aziz to them. Yet he was already taking possession of them; and already he was binding them to himself. He had nothing to gain; he was only obeying an instinct. He could not read or write. People were his material, his profession and no doubt his diversion; his world was made up of these encounters and managed relationships. His responses were acute" (*AD*, 161).

Naipaul, tacitly recognizing a kindred spirit of a sort—surely people are also *his* material, profession, and diversion—is clearly intrigued by this man, and there is respect and admiration, untainted by pity, in this portrait: "To us illiteracy is like a missing sense. But to the intelligent illiterate in a simpler world mightn't literacy be an irrelevance, a dissipation of sensibility, the mercenary skill of the scribe?" (*AD*, 161). As Naipaul leaves Srinigar, Aziz sees him off at the bus. "Tears were running down his cheeks. Even at that moment I could not be sure that he had ever been mine" (*AD*, 192). The exquisite comedy and pathos of this moment encapsulates much: the unfamiliar dynamics of master and servant in a strange but familiar country; Naipaul's frank admission of his uncertainty about reading other people accurately; his own emotional rawness, never far below the surface of the book.

Nearer the end of the book there is a more disturbing encounter. Naipaul visits the village from which his grandfather had traveled to Trinidad as an indentured laborer sixty years earlier. At first the homecoming seems to go well. Welcomed warmly by his relatives, he is surprised by the "exaltation" he feels, but his subsequent meetings with the head of the family end "in futility and impatience, a gratuitous act of cruelty, self-reproach and flight" when Naipaul refuses the insistent entreaties of his kinsman to finance a lawsuit he wants to initiate (*AD*, 277). Once again, he is almost self-punishingly frank about his own failure to cope with India's demands on him. The darkness of the title is in Naipaul's knowledge of India, not in India itself.

Naipaul's next major nonfiction project, *The Loss of El Dorado*, was an immense undertaking. Commissioned to write a book about Trinidad, he spent two years immersed in the archives, having found, to his surprise, that there was little or nothing already written on the subject to draw upon. He describes his work on this book in *The Enigma of Arrival*.

> A great packed education those two years had been. And I had such
> faith in what I was writing, such faith in the grandeur of my story, that
> I thought it would find the readers that my books of the previous twelve
> years had not found. And I behaved foolishly. Without waiting for that

response, I dismantled the little life I had created for myself in England and prepared to leave, to be a free man. . . . ·

The calamity occurred four months later. The book in which I had placed such faith, the book which had exhausted me so much, could not please the publisher who had commissioned it. We had misunderstood one another. . . . He had wanted only a book for tourists, something much simpler than the book I had written; something at once more romantic and less romantic; at once more human and less human.

(*EA*, 101–2)

Once again, in *The Loss of El Dorado* it is the characters who live in the reader's imagination: "For the two years that I lived among the documents I sought to reconstruct the human story as best I could" (*EA*, 101). The search for the illusory City of Gold in South America in the sixteenth century by the Spanish conquistador Antonio de Berrio and his English rival Sir Walter Raleigh, from a historical perspective insanely foolish and misguided, is the subject of the first part of the book. It is not the events that interest Naipaul so much as the characters. Even the fact that the Spanish empire was too big and had overreached itself is put in the human context of the vulnerable people left stranded at its outer reaches, waiting for help that never comes. And the image of Raleigh returning to England for the last time, having failed again, as he surely knew he would, to find El Dorado and knowing he will pay for his failure with his life; old, sick, and grieving for his dead son, is a haunting one.

But the substance of the book comes with part 3, "The Torture of Luisa Calderon," describing the British regime in Trinidad after the defeat of the Spanish in 1797. It is a story of infighting, intrigue, and hypocrisy among the British governing elite, and rival factions among the French planters, Spanish peons, new English settlers, and free Negroes. A British colony administering Spanish law to a disunited population, with no lawyers or reliable legal authorities and with the sickening brutality of a slave society forming the incessant background, provides a compelling if horrifying scenario. Into this society is introduced the Venezuelan revolutionary Francisco Miranda, attempting to enlist British help to defeat the Spanish on the Caribbean mainland. Miranda clearly fascinates Naipaul, and he later wrote about him even more comprehensively in *A Way in the World*. Miranda's dream of a revolution is shown to be as illusory as Raleigh's dream of El Dorado: Naipaul's choice of title for this book implies the comparison. Meanwhile, the first British governor, Thomas Picton, was being tried in London for ordering the torture of a free mulatto woman, Luisa Calderon. The crux of the case was whether torture was allowed under Spanish law but justice was not really the issue. The case was brought by Picton's successor, Colonel William Fullarton, purely out of a desire to discredit him.

Naipaul investigates the shortcomings of these men, their weakness and vanity, their incompetence and moral failings; but at the heart of the problem of this slave colony was the slave system itself: "Principle and generous anger had become impossible" (*LED*, 228). The slaves themselves are "as anonymous as the Indians of Las Casas three centuries before. It is the silence of all serfdom" (*LED*, 250). Naipaul does not spare his readers the details of the savagery of punishments visited on the slaves; he reconstructs what he can of their misery and their compensating fantasy world. But individuals are difficult to excavate when people become possessions and merchandise. "In the records the slave is faceless, with an identification rather than a name. He has no story" (*LED*, 319). With one exception: Naipaul tells the story of Jacquet, an old slave who had been driven, by the desperate logic of the slave mentality, to poison fellow slaves. He had poisoned a baby of his master's family without realizing "that the grief would be so great, that he himself would grieve so much" (*LED*, 320). Soon afterward he himself died of poisoning, perhaps self-administered. This story was told to the governor by the slave's owner in 1806; the events had taken place in 1803. It is a poignant story, full of small, unexpected sidelights: the compassion of the master, the grief of the poisoner after his victim's death, and the silence of the other slaves, suspicious of Jacquet but preferring to risk death rather than expose him to their owner. This kind of insight is often missing from histories of slave societies, and Naipaul has worked hard to bring it to his readers.

Miranda, the revolutionary, "dealt in romance. In Trinidad . . . he preferred not to see the Negroes. They formed no part of his revolutionary romance, no part of his vision of a world made classically pure and beautiful. The Indians did, noble and not savage, descended, in his fantasy, from the legendary Incas; and Miranda lamented their degradation in Trinidad."[12] The end of his romance of revolution, his "appalling discovery . . . that the society was wrong, the cause was wrong, that the good words didn't fit," is, however, not regarded by Naipaul as an unwelcome revelation. "It must also have been like reconciliation, because Miranda had lived out this truth in his own life" (*LED*, 297).

Something of Naipaul's own temptation by the comforts of inactivity and failure discussed in chapter 3 is evident in his elegiac description of Miranda's last years in prison: "Prison was perhaps the setting that Miranda, like Raleigh, subconsciously required. It dramatized inaction, failure and the condition of exile" (*LED*, 309). Miranda's exile, like Naipaul's exile, is not a simple matter of banishment from a homeland held dear; it involves "the deeper colonial deprivation, the sense of the missing real world, that Miranda had spent a lifetime making good" (*LED*, 266). The word "colonial," in this book, conveys straightforward criticism:

> "Trinidad itself, visibly corrupt, where the English immigrants had already gone as colonial as the French and had reduced the complex drives of their culture to the simplicities of money and race, no longer referring their actions to any ideal" (*LED*, 269).

To be colonial, for both Miranda and Naipaul, is a condition of exile from the "real world," from the "complex drives" of a metropolitan culture that they instinctively prefer to the "simplicities of money and race," the typical values of the colonial society. The deficiencies of the colonial mentality resonate through much of Naipaul's fiction: it is a continuing preoccupation for him. In *The Middle Passage*, too, he describes "how imprisoning for the West Indian his colonial culture is. Europe, the Surinam Nationalist says, is to be rejected as the sole source of enlightenment; Africa and Asia are to be brought in as well. But Europe is in the Nationalist's bones and he feels that Africa and Asia are contemptible and ridiculous" (*MP*, 165).

Trinidad's particular colonial history, however, has "combined to give it its special character, its ebullience and irresponsibility. And more: a tolerance which is more than tolerance: an indifference to virtue as well as vice" (*MP*, 54). This might have its drawbacks, but the picture Naipaul paints is not an unattractive one:

> The Trinidadian is a cosmopolitan. He is adaptable; he is cynical; having no rigid social conventions of his own, he is amused by the conventions of others. He is a natural anarchist, who has never been able to take the eminent at their own valuation. He is a natural eccentric, if by eccentricity is meant the expression of one's own personality, unhampered by fear of ridicule or the discipline of a class. If the Trinidadian has no standards of morality he is without the greater corruption of sanctimoniousness, and can never make pleas for intolerance in the name of piety. . . . Everything that makes the Trinidadian an unreliable, exploitable citizen makes him a quick, civilized person whose values are always human ones, whose standards are only those of wit and style. (*MP*, 77)

Again, after his year in India, Naipaul says he "had learned my separateness from India, and was content to be a colonial, without a past, without ancestors" (*AD*, 266). It can be seen in the earlier two books that the colonial condition is not so wholly rejected: it has its compensations.

In *The Middle Passage*, in a moment of distress and despair, Naipaul had asked, "How can the history of this West Indian futility be written?" (*MP*,

28). In *The Loss of El Dorado* he found a way. Although he said in *The Middle Passage* that "history is built around achievement and creation; and nothing was created in the West Indies" (*MP,* 29), in *The Loss of El Dorado* he aimed not to "abstract principals from human events" (*EA,* 101) in the manner of a historian, but to give the human story behind the events. This provides a much more comprehensible picture of these events: without Naipaul's novelistic insight into the complex motives of these historical figures, their actions would indeed seem absurd and extraordinary. Perhaps nothing was created or achieved in the West Indies, but from the evidence of *The Middle Passage* these societies that have been formed, however accidentally, from the fallout of imperial exploitation have an enduring vitality that has more to offer than Naipaul is sometimes prepared to admit.

Branching Out *Mr Stone and the Knights Companion, The Mimic Men, and A Flag on the Island*

The two novels that followed *A House for Mr Biswas* are different from each other in many ways. Their differences in style and subject account for a large disparity in their treatment by critics. A search in the Modern Languages Association Bibliography for critical articles on *The Mimic Men* (1967) produces thirty-one results, whereas a corresponding search for articles about *Mr Stone and the Knights Companion* (1963) produces only four.[1]

Mr Stone and the Knights Companion is a short, spare novel with a rich vein of comedy. Unlike *The Mimic Men*, it contains little philosophical rumination by the narrator for a critic to dissect. Another reason for its lack of critical attention is that the subjects it deals with, superficially at least, are unlike those Naipaul has treated either before or since. In addition, the point of view in this novel is detached and none of the characters can easily be identified with the author. Many critical approaches depend upon the interpretation of the author's political and moral views as they appear in his work, and Naipaul seems to attract this type of criticism more than most. *Mr Stone* provides little scope for this kind of criticism.

Paul Theroux has claimed that Naipaul "may be the only writer today in whom there are no echoes or influences."[2] This is an extraordinary statement to make about any author, even Naipaul who has had to invent his own traditions to a large degree. Influences from the mainstream of English literature are present in *Mr Stone*. It is clear, for example, that Oscar Wilde was in his mind while writing this novel. Early on, Mr Stone's niece Gwen performs a scene from *The Importance of Being Earnest*. Further, the humor often echoes Wilde's famous ironical bons mots. The head of Mr Stone's firm Excal is known as Old Harry "to those who did not know him, but Sir Harry to those whom he admitted to converse which they hoped to suggest was intimate," and "the impression of grandeur and inaccessibility was completed by his reported left-wing leanings" (*MSKC*, 76–77). And Mr Stone's friend Grace's "radiant" widowhood (*MSKC*, 129) recalls the widow in *The Importance of Being Earnest* who "looks quite twenty years younger" and whose "hair has turned quite gold from grief."[3]

The wit of this novel, as well as its brevity, also recalls the satirical novels of Evelyn Waugh, with their themes of death and decadence. Waugh was still an eminent figure on the English literary scene when Naipaul's writing career began, and it is only in this context that Naipaul occasionally mentions him.[4] However, Waugh's style of jaundiced, uncompromising social criticism conveyed by means of devastatingly comic satire, although on the whole crueler and less humane than Naipaul has ever been, must certainly have influenced the younger writer, particularly in his early days. *Mr Stone*, especially, with its London setting and its emphasis on the inexorable passage of time and the approach of old age and death, contains many echoes of this supreme stylist. Waugh's satire on death and funeral rites in California, *The Loved One*, was published only a few years before *Mr Stone*, and it is likely that Naipaul would have read and enjoyed it as well as his earlier novels and travel books. It is unlikely that he found Waugh's worldview entirely congenial, but Waugh had much to teach a young writer interested in the fastidious and exact use of English. Here is Waugh, describing his heroine:

> Aimée walked swiftly down the gravelled drive to the mortuary entrance. In the reception room the night staff were drinking coffee. They glanced at her incuriously as she passed silently through them, for urgent work was done at all hours. She took the lift to the top story where everything was silent and empty save for the sheeted dead. . . . She indited no letter of farewell or apology. She was far removed from social custom and human obligations.[5]

And here is Naipaul, describing Mr Stone:

> As he walked up the street to his home with long, hard strides, he felt himself grow taller. He walked as the destroyer, as the man who carried the possibility of the earth's destruction within him. Taller and taller he grew, firmer and firmer he walked, past the petty gardens of petty houses where people sought to accommodate themselves to life. (*MSKC*, 159)

In both these passages, the language, although direct and concrete, conveys much about the mood of the character. It is detached and cool, with a hint of amused irony at the delusions it describes. The subjects, respectively a young American woman about to commit suicide and an elderly English office worker walking home after a disappointing day at the office, may not have a great deal in common, but they share a feeling of distance from the rest of the human race, an illusion of dedication to a higher power, which is in both cases profoundly comic as well as quite disturbing.

The title character of *Mr Stone and the Knights Companion* is an employee of a large firm, Excal. Approaching retirement, he rather suddenly marries a widow of about his own age. Subsequently he achieves some local celebrity by designing a welfare scheme for retired employees of the company—The Knights Companion. It is a remarkable portrayal for a writer of only thirty. Naipaul has said that he was "still very shaky" when he wrote *Mr Stone*.[6] But, as with his earlier books, there is assurance and, despite the evidence of influences mentioned above, a confident, original voice in this novel. Confidence shows in the muted humor, easy to miss on a superficial reading, in his characterizations. Mr Stone's jokes and funny stories are feeble, and those of his new wife, Margaret, despite her noted wit, are not much better. Even so, they are not made objects of ridicule: their shared jokes and pet names are pathetic and endearing.

Naipaul charts the course of their courtship and marriage delicately. Their wedding itself he dismisses in one sentence, but he devotes more time to their first meeting and Mr Stone's changing impressions of Margaret; from his initial speechless admiration of her brilliance and glamour, through the difficulties of accommodating a new and unfamiliar presence in his bachelor home, to the "affection he had begun to feel for her clothes . . . once the arresting attributes of a new person, now the familiar, carefully looked-after parts of a limited wardrobe" (*MSKC*, 87). The new marriage is neither a disaster nor a romantic triumph for this couple in late middle age, as it could easily have been. As usual, Naipaul resists the drama of extremes in favor of a perceptive realism. The humor is subtle: "In the bathroom, which before had held his own smell, to him always a source of satisfaction, there was now a warm, scented dampness. Then he saw her teeth. It had never occurred to him that they might be false. He felt cheated and annoyed. Regret came to him, and a prick of the sharpest fear. Then he took out his own teeth and sadly climbed the stairs to their bedroom" (*MSKC*, 35). The irony of his shock at finding that his new wife, quite normally for a woman of her age and time, has false teeth is brought home to the reader gently with the passing mention of his own. But this incident shows more than Mr Stone's illogical attitude: it conveys vividly the unexpected emotions gripping a man in his early sixties embarking on his first marriage.

Naipaul had said in 1958 that he couldn't write about England. "I feel I know so little about England. I have met many people but I know them only in official attitudes—the drink, the interview, the meal. I have a few friends. But this gives me only a superficial knowledge of the country, and in order to write fiction it is necessary to know so much."[7] The London he creates in this novel is, however, recognizable as the same city written about by English writers of the same period. The observations he had made of English society since arriving in 1950 had allowed him to re-create this narrow, middle-class

London world where there is scarcely an immigrant to be found. Years later, in 1994, he was still worried by the errors he felt he had made in *Mr Stone:* "In the past few months, it's been tormenting me more and more. I like the excellent material, still, but I felt it was thrown away by my suppression of the narrator, the observer who was an essential part of the story. To write a book as though you were this third-person omniscient narrator who didn't identify himself was in a way to be fraudulent to the material, which was obtained by me, a colonial, living precariously in London in a blank and anxious time, observing these elderly Edwardian people trying to postpone death."[8]

It is revealing that the error of which he accuses himself is fraudulence, the failure to be true to his material, and that this is expressed as the absence of himself either as the narrator or a character. His fastidious sense of ethics, very much his own notion of the rights and wrongs of writing, is, remarkably, still exercised by this work from more than thirty years earlier. He even said that he "might do something about it, rework it in some way."[9]

However, despite the third-person omniscient narrator and thorough Englishness of the characters in *Mr Stone,* beneath the surface there are intimations of common Naipaulian themes such as the ambivalence of close human relationships, so much a feature of *A House for Mr Biswas.* Mixed with the resentment Mr Stone feels toward his wife after their first two weeks of marriage is "the feeling that his thoughts about women and his marriage . . . were a betrayal of her who sat beside him, not at all fat, not at all parasitic, full only of loving, humiliating, killing concern" (*MSKC,* 71). Although he said in his essay "London" that "we are not all brothers under the skin,"[10] he has found enough common ground to draw a faithful picture of the joys and pains of the married state, expressed in an idiom quite different from the more exuberant and outspoken way of his Trinidad characters.

There are glimpses, too, of Naipaul's own London. On his first visit to Margaret's flat in Earl's Court, Mr Stone considered it "a disreputable, overcrowded area. . . ; and the streets were full of young people in art-student dress and foreigners of every colour." However, "the address Mrs Springer gave turned out to be a private hotel. . . . A small typewritten 'Europeans Only' card below the bell proclaimed it a refuge of respectability and calm" (*MSKC,* 32). Naipaul lived in Earl's Court when he first arrived in England and would have experienced for himself the other side of Mr Stone's instinctive disapproval of "foreigners" and his reassurance at the "Europeans Only" sign. Margaret seems to have spent time in India, a fact that is suggested by a "framed sepia photograph of a dead tiger on whose chest lay the highly polished boot of an English cavalry officer, moustached, sitting bolt upright in a heavy wooden armchair . . . with three sorrowful, top-heavily turbanned Indians, beaters or bearers or whatever they were, behind him" (*MSKC,* 42).

Once again, Mr Stone's point of view is in the foreground, but in the "sorrowful" Indians there is a fleeting glance of another perspective. It might be noted that Naipaul wrote this novel when he was in Srinagar, India.

But the chief reflection of Naipaul's recurrent preoccupations in *Mr Stone* is the one he mentions in his interview with Aamer Hussein: the specter of these people "trying to postpone death." The struggle Mr Stone has in common with Naipaul's other characters is his search for meaning and purpose, which for a person of any intelligence in Naipaul's world is doomed to failure. In Mr Stone, the mixture of English reserve and a kind of fatalism that could be seen almost as a Hindu cultural trait makes for an intriguing character. Naipaul's own feelings about writing can be traced in Mr Stone's reflections on his own creation: "In that project of the Knights Companion . . . the only pure moments, the only true moments were those he had spent in the study, writing out of a feeling whose depth he realized only as he wrote. What he had written was a faint and artificial rendering of that emotion. . . . All that he had done, and even the anguish he was feeling now, was a betrayal of that good emotion. All action, all creation was a betrayal of feeling and truth" (*MSKC*, 149). Mr Stone is a disappointed creator, looking back, like Naipaul in *The Enigma of Arrival,* on his creation and feeling "mocked by what I had already done; it seemed to belong to a time of vigor, now past for good" (*EA*, 101).

Mr Stone, then, has more in common with his author and with Ralph Singh, the main character in *The Mimic Men,* than might at first seem likely. Ralph is also a creator. He is the first-person narrator and explicitly the writer of *The Mimic Men*: the labor of writing forms part of the story. It is tempting to see in its many reflective passages a revelation of Naipaul's feelings and beliefs as a writer, and to go on from there and interpret Ralph as a mere mouthpiece for his author. After all, writers must draw their material at least partly from their own experience. Theroux describes his reaction to reading the typescript of *A Bend in the River*: "The difficulty I always had with Vidia's scenes of sex or violence became almost overwhelming. Was it because I did not want to read such scenes for what they disclosed about my friend? A writer is never more unconsciously confessional than when he writes of sex."[11] This may be true, but it is a part of an unknowable creative process, and it is a mistake to assume, for example, that because Ralph feels that "wife" is "a terrible word" (*MMen*, 90) the same feeling is shared by Naipaul. Ralph has an affair with his cousin that he says is a "relationship based on perfect knowledge, in which body of one flesh joined to body of the same flesh, and all external threat was diminished" (*MMen*, 155). If one takes the first opinion about the word "wife" as revealing an attitude shared by Naipaul, what is to prevent one from believing also that he believes incest is the most perfect form of sexual relationship? This interpretive caution must be applied not only to matters of sex and marriage but also to all the opinions expounded by a character in a novel. In a 1981 interview Naipaul was asked "To what degree can the narrator in that novel [*The Mimic Men*] be said to speak for you?" His response was clear: "No, no, no. That isn't *me*."[12]

However, the narrator in *The Mimic Men* is unlike many narrators in modern fiction. Many first-person narrators are obviously unreliable, and the author has ways of conveying to the reader that this is the case. This certainly happens in *Miguel Street* and *The Mystic Masseur*, Naipaul's previous first-person novels. In *The Mimic Men* there is no evident dichotomy of this kind between author and narrator, no sense that the author is communicating with the reader behind the narrator's back. The fact that Ralph is so explicitly engaged in writing this book could make it even more difficult to distinguish him from the author in some ways, although the explicitness might also help. The concrete details of the narrator's life—his hotel room, his desk, his solitary life in London—could encourage the reader to make the distinction between the character and Naipaul. In any event, even a writer who uses his own life in his work to the extent that Naipaul does must be assumed to transform his experience and combine it with invented material in an imaginative way that precludes the simple assumption of direct correspondence between life and art.

There is a more general fusion of fact and fiction in *The Mimic Men*. The travel writer of the nineteenth century James Anthony Froud, a real historical figure, is mentioned as having visited Isabella, the fictional Caribbean island where *The Mimic Men* is set (*MMen*, 77–78), and having written about it in his book *The Bow of Ulysses*.[13] Again, there is a reference to Stendhal's *Le rouge et le noir* (*MMen*, 173–75): an anecdote about a friendship between Stendhal and an ancestor of one of Ralph's friends that is said to be mentioned in Stendhal's novel. This blurring of the boundaries between fact and fiction can have the effect of heightening the realism, but in a way, because the reader knows that Isabella is a fictional place, not to be found on any map, these touches of realism might sometimes have the opposite effect and broaden the area of doubt to take in the fact as well as the fiction. Isabella is taken by many as a straightforward portrait of Trinidad, but a passing reference to Trinidad as a different place with different problems (*MMen*, 146) contradicts that potential identification.

Nevertheless, an author such as Naipaul has a purpose in writing that is implied in his concern about the fraudulence of *Mr Stone*. He told Hussein that he writes fiction "to deliver the truth, really, to deliver a form of reality. Because if you were dealing with real people, when you start writing about them, it becomes too particular: and one wants to make a larger point, so you fabricate."[14] Thus Ralph, although he is a highly individualized character, is not based on any real colonial politician and can stand as an example of all those who "pretended to be real, to be learning, to be preparing ourselves for life, we mimic men of the New World, one unknown corner of it" (*MMen*, 146). In the same way, Naipaul creates Isabella instead of writing about Trinidad directly in *The Mimic Men*: he wants to make a point about all similar former colonies and their difficulties coping with self-government after gaining their independence.

Ralph Singh, born Ranjit Kripalsingh on Isabella to a rich mother and a poor father, goes to college in London. He meets and marries Sandra, a London girl, and returns to Isabella to take up a life of relative privilege there, making a fortune from land development. After a few years his marriage fails and he goes into politics. Although he is still quite young at the time of writing, his political career, always a precarious matter of bluff and chance, is finished, and he has retired in disgrace to London, where he is writing this book in a seedy hotel.

The Mimic Men was Naipaul's least comic novel to date. Humor had played an important part in all his previous novels, and also satire, although this had become less and less prevalent. Pure satire refuses to understand and only attacks. Ralph writes, "The colonial politician is an easy object of satire. I wish to avoid satire; I will leave out the stories of illiteracy and social innocence. Not that I wish to present him as grander or less flawed than he is. It is that his situation satirizes itself, turns satire inside out, takes satire to a point where it touches pathos if not tragedy" (*MMen*, 208–9). In this passage, the narrator is talking of every one of his fellow colonial politicians, but he intends to include himself despite the fact that he is writing in the third person. When he does write satirically, Naipaul, unlike many satirists, leaves much to the reader. As he says, some situations—and no doubt people —"satirize themselves" and there is no need for the author to do anything but describe events with minimal comment. Ralph, although he writes about his younger self with the advantage of hindsight after his career has finished, criticizes but does not satirize himself.

He is more critical of himself than of his wife, Sandra. Sandra is one of Naipaul's most successful female characters. She has strength and a clearly defined personality, and Ralph blames himself rather than her for the failure of their marriage: "I had willed the gift away" (*MMen*, 76). He expects a great deal from Sandra. When they arrive in Isabella, his mother stages a scene of frenzied rejection, proclaiming to all the world that her son has killed her by bringing home an English wife. He readily sees that this is "pure self-indulgence" on his mother's part but fails to understand that "Sandra could not have been expected to make my swift assessment . . . I relied on her forthrightness and what I thought was her vision; but to her this reliance must have seemed like abandonment at a moment when she was most insecure. I don't think she ever forgave me or the island" (*MMen*, 53–54). There is a touch of comedy in Sandra's quick adaptation to the luxurious life the island had to offer her. "Even before the fortnight was out Sandra could be heard disdaining demisec and expressing a preference for Mercier above all others. The splendid girl! Sprung so sincerely from her commonness!" (*MMen*, 56).

The sexual element in their marriage is not strong, and Ralph feels free to pursue other women. However, it is when he finally discovers—or intuits—that Sandra has also been sexually unfaithful that he realizes the marriage is over. She in this case is the freer agent: "Other relationships awaited her, other countries. I had nowhere to go; I wished to experience no new landscapes; I had cut myself off from that avidity which I still attributed to her. It was not for me to decide to leave; that decision was hers alone" (*MMen*, 76).

It is now that he takes up politics, the career of a colonial politician that, as he says at the beginning of the book, is typically "short and ends brutally" (*MMen*, 8). Even at the beginning the seeds of disenchantment are present: he talks of "that moment of success which, after long endeavour, is so shatteringly brief: a moment that can almost be fixed by the clock, and recedes and recedes, leaving emptiness, exhaustion, even distaste: dissatisfaction that nags and nags and at last defines itself as apprehension and unease" (*MMen*, 199). Once again, this is reminiscent of the feelings Naipaul describes in *The Enigma of Arrival*. The absorbing nature of the effort of creation, whether it be a book or a political victory, is never rewarded by a sustained feeling of contentment or pride in achievement. Further effort is always called for, and unease is always lurking near the surface.

The malaise Ralph associates with public life makes failure almost welcome, and this gives a clue to the ruminative, almost elegiac nature of the novel. Ralph seems to have achieved equilibrium at the time of writing, away from the excitement and difficulty of striving for success. He is content to live a narrow life on a narrow income, reflecting on his past and re-creating scenes from his marriage. There is a striking passage of two or three pages, written in the present tense; a scene at a Sunday morning gathering of the social set. It is precisely detailed—the "recurring inconvenience" of having no pockets in the tropical clothes, the weekly game of scanning the society pages of the local newspaper that hold a private joke for the initiated. But already Ralph is noticing "the attention of studied inattention. The talk is a bit too loud, too hearty, too aggressive or too defensive; these people are overacting, overdoing domesticity and the small details, over-stressing the fullness of their own lives" (*MMen*, 63). Signs of rivalry and envy in the group are beginning to appear, and, despite the nostalgic tone, there is a feeling of relief combined with the regret for the passing of these good times. Ralph describes "the period between my preparation for life and my withdrawal from it . . . when I was most active and might have given the observer the impression of a man fulfilling his destiny" as a "period in parenthesis" (*MMen*, 32). Real life is the time of preparation before, and reflection after, the active life of achievement. The act of narration, although it can revive the unease it describes, also imposes order on events that now become "historical and manageable" (*MMen*, 243). Ralph finds, to his surprise, "that the writing of this book [became] an end in itself, that the recording of a life [became] an extension of that life" (*MMen*, 244). At the end of the task, the "fear of action" remains with him (*MMen*, 251). A quiet, constricted, but ordered future awaits him.

In 1965, while he was writing *The Mimic Men,* Naipaul also wrote a novella of about ninety pages called "A Flag on the Island," and this was published along with ten short stories in a book of the same name in the same year as *The Mimic Men.* The stories span fifteen years, from Naipaul's first arrival in England, and display a wide range of styles and subjects, from the Trinidad teacher—"They don't pay primary school teachers a lot in Trinidad, but they allow them to beat their pupils as much as they want" (*FI*, 25)—in the story "The Raffle," to the London landladies of "Greenie and Yellow" and "The Perfect Tenants." One very early story, "The Mourners," written in 1950, gives an idea of Naipaul's youthful skills, clearly influenced by his father, at setting a scene and sustaining an atmosphere.

In the novella "A Flag on the Island" these skills are used to full effect. In a note at the beginning of the book, Naipaul explains that this story, subtitled "A Fantasy for a Small Screen," "was specially written for a film company. The story they required was to be 'musical' and comic and set in the Caribbean; it was to have a leading American character and many subsidiary characters; it was to have much sex and much dialogue; it was to be explicit" (*FI*, 7). The story failed to please the director who commissioned it, and the film was never made.[15]

The purpose for which it was written explains to some extent the nature of this story, which is, in contrast to *The Mimic Men,* wild, almost frenzied. The narrator is Frankie, an American former serviceman who had been stationed on this unnamed Caribbean island during the Second World War and who unexpectedly and unwillingly revisits the island, about twenty years later, when the ship on which he is traveling seeks refuge there from a hurricane.

This narrator is decidedly unreliable. He seems to be a lover of extremes. On the ship, "abstemiousness, even self-mortification, had settled on me almost as soon as I had gone aboard; and had given me a deep content" (*FI*,

150). Nevertheless, almost immediately after making the decision not to go ashore and make unsettling and unwelcome reconnections with people and places there, he goes ashore and lets his mood of "confusion and threat . . . take possession" of him (*FI*, 152). Confusion and threat are everywhere in the story, which has a nightmarish, surreal atmosphere. The narrator quickly becomes drunk and unable to tell the difference between a bar and a literary meeting. A dreamlike shifting of identities pervades the narrative. One character is both a preacher, an insurance salesman, and a television personality; another is a black writer, unpublishable in previous times when writing English aristocratic romances under the name H. J. Blackwhite but now a best-seller as H. J. B. White, author of interracial love stories and anti-white tracts such as *I Hate You: One Man's Search for Identity*. There is a cleverly choreographed scene in a restaurant where representatives of international philanthropic foundations with large sums of money to give away absurdly compete for the privilege of patronizing Mr Blackwhite and other local artists.

Counterpointing this chaotic narrative is a flashback to the war years when Frankie lived on the island with a local beauty, Selma, and became part of the life of a street not unlike Miguel Street in Naipaul's first novel. As a serviceman with access to the goods of the army base, Frankie was able to help the local people, distributing the United States armed forces' unwitting largesse generously among his new friends. But prosperity brings with it discontent, ambition, and even, for some characters, an early death. The wise publican, Henry—a man very like Hat in *Miguel Street*—points out to Frankie, "You know, I don't think people want to do what they say they want to do. I think we always make a lot of trouble for people by helping them to get what they say they want to get. Some people look at black people and only see black. You look at poor people and you only see poor. You think the only thing they want is money. All-you wrong, you know" (*FI*, 194). A recurring theme in Naipaul's work is his resistance to simple solutions to the complex problems of people's lives, and Frankie's disastrous inability to help his friends despite his good intentions is a vivid dramatization of this point.

This whirlwind of a story, full of irony and biting satire, is less subtle than many of Naipaul's other works. Its origin as a story for a film is clear in its strong use of visual images and exact descriptions of people and places, and the unusually large proportion, for Naipaul, of dialogue in comparison with narration and reflection. The expected hurricane and the devastation that were welcomed with "cries of joy" (*FI*, 232) fail to arrive: "Benediction never came. Our dancing grew listless. Fatigue consumed anguish" (*FI*, 233), and "each exhausted person had once more to accommodate himself to his fate" (*FI*, 235). Life goes on relentlessly, despite one's efforts to improve the lot of oneself or others and even despite one's wish for the drama and finality of destruction and apocalypse.

Naipaul sees that the apocalyptic vision is as false as the related dream of a golden age in the past that can be recreated in some Utopian future, which is the staple of radical political theories. His next novel, *In a Free State,* is an uncompromising statement about the impossibility of reducing modern life to the platitudes of political ideologies such as Marxism and postcolonialism.

CHAPTER SIX

Finding the Correct Form *In a Free State*

You have to be very clear about the material that possesses you, and you've got to find the correct form for it. . . . One narrative goes with a particular kind of life, a particular moment in history; another narrative comes at another time, and you have to find the correct one. The one that feels true to you.[1]

Naipaul's 1971 Booker Prize–winning novel *In a Free State* is, like his first book, *Miguel Street,* a series of stories. Unlike the earlier novel, however, there is little continuity in the usual aspects of character, setting, and plot; and critics have developed a variety of interpretive glosses to explain its thematic continuity. There are five sections in the novel: a prologue and an epilogue, two short stories, and one long story. Only the prologue and epilogue have a character in common, a first-person narrator who appears to be Naipaul himself.

Critical explanations for the unity of themes in this novel include the image of the journey, the many facets of the idea of freedom, and the accommodating of a variety of subject positions.[2] John Rothfork infers that Naipaul sees the state of exile to be universal: "In the twentieth century man has entered 'a free state,' a state without values or direction. Man is in exile, lost in the desert."[3] But in a world where everyone is in a state of exile, the concept would lose much of its meaning. Naipaul's world in *In a Free State* is peopled by displaced persons and perpetual travelers to whom the security of home is hopelessly out of reach for one reason or another. Either they have thoughtlessly chosen to abandon their homes, like Santosh, or they have never valued them, like Bobby, or home is itself a place of desolation, as is the case with Dayo's brother. However, these characters all experience their "freedom" as exclusion from a society they believe exists, even though it might not; and their attitudes toward it are complex and various. In a television interview with Melvyn Bragg, Naipaul described *In a Free State* as being about "loss, fear and independence—personal themes."[4] What was it about these themes that gave rise to the peculiar form of this novel?

Naipaul talks dismissively about other writers, who prefer to write novels about "ordered societies"[5] or "enclosed societies," and goes on to claim that "to write about a world which is much more shattered, and exploding, and varied, write about it in fiction, is very difficult."[6] *In a Free State,* in form as well as content, is shattered and varied, and its explosiveness—its violence— varies in intensity through the course of the book. What is shattered, however, has first been whole and does not preclude wholeness elsewhere and at another time. To know what has been lost is not granted to all Naipaul's characters, and those who lack this knowledge are finally the more deprived: their freedom is of even less use to them.

Santosh, the narrator and main character of the story "One out of Many," is well aware of the happiness and security he has lost. A domestic servant, he has chosen to move with his employer to Washington from Bombay, only to find the American lifestyle perplexing and difficult. In his regret for the life he left behind in Bombay and his alienation in his new, free life in Washington, he is able to be calm, and his narrative voice communicates his calmness. His narrative style is rather like the dialogue Naipaul uses in his Trinidad novels when his characters are speaking in Hindi; a clear, pedantic, and formal use of English, with its own undramatic, regular rhythm that refuses to panic. He attempts to account for his new circumstances—"the particular moment in my life, the particular action, that had brought me to that room. . . . I could find no one moment; every moment seemed important. An endless chain of action had brought me to that room. It was frightening; it was burdensome" (*IFS,* 59). He is not happy, but he understands what has happened, takes responsibility for himself, and does not try to deflect the blame onto other people, institutions, or abstractions.

He admits that he is himself implicated in the "endless chain of action," although it would have been open to him to blame his employer, or the government that sent his employer to Washington, or the accident of his birth in a poor country, or the imperial system. Naipaul believes the colonial state of mind is one that does not accept responsibility: "One of the terrible things about being a Colonial . . . is that you must accept so many things as coming from a great wonderful source outside yourself and outside the people you know, outside the society you've grown up in. That can only be repaired by a sense of responsibility, which is what the colonial doesn't have."[7] Santosh, with his secure and stable, though not prosperous, background, has the most profound understanding of his lot and of his own part in bringing it about, of the three protagonists in the central stories of this novel. Santosh is not a "colonial." He is materially richer in Washington than he was in Bombay, but he has lost the feeling of belonging to a society. Having made his decision, even though it was made in ignorance, he knows he must accept his new life, its emptiness and its unpalatable mysteries: "It is as though I have had several lives. I do not wish to add to these" (*IFS*, 61).

The formal aspects of "One out of Many" make it the least "explosive" of the three stories. Its resigned first-person narration—in what Peter Hughes calls his "lapidary prose and stoical tones" that "transform his life into fate"[8]—together with Santosh's acknowledgment of responsibility and his consciousness of cause and effect, lulls the reader into a calm melancholy that is shattered in the next story.

The nameless narrator-protagonist of "Tell Me Who to Kill" is a more bereft and shattered individual than Santosh. He goes to England from his home in the Caribbean to help his younger brother Dayo, whose "studies" he is financing; but although he is able to earn well in London, when he buys his own shop his life goes seriously wrong. Once again, material security is beside the point. He has paid for his colonial status with insanity, the fate Naipaul himself feels he narrowly missed by becoming a writer: "One must make a pattern of one's observations, one's daily distress; one's daily knowledge of homelessness, placelessness; one's lack of representation in the world; one's lack of status. . . . If daily one lives with this, then daily one has to incorporate the experience into something bigger. Because one doesn't have a side, doesn't have a country, doesn't have a community; one is entirely an individual. A person in this position risks going mad."[9]

Dayo's brother has not been able to "make a pattern"; he does not know whom to blame for the wreck of his life—and being a "colonial," he does not take responsibility for himself; therefore he has gone mad. His madness makes him a chaotic narrator; the fractured form of his story reflects the state of his mind. Freedom here is terrifying, and all the more so because the narrator fails to make clear the events that have led him to this situation.

Santosh tells his story in the past tense, as one might when one can look back on one's troubles and "make a pattern." "Tell Me Who to Kill" is narrated in a modified form of Trinidad English and in the present tense, whether past or present events are being described. Uncertainty is built into the story, which is a stream-of-consciousness narrative where the lines between past and present, between fact and dream or fantasy, are blurred. The present tense increases the feeling of panic and desolation, the incapacity to stand back and detach oneself from one's experience, "to incorporate the experience into something bigger." The narrator is confused and the reader remains confused with him. Several times he refers to an incident: "It is like a dream. I see myself in this old English house. . . . No weather. I am there with my brother, and we are strangers in the house. My brother is at college or school in England, pursuing his studies, and he is visiting this college friend and he is staying with the boy's family. And then in a corridor, just outside a door, something happen. A quarrel, a friendly argument, a scuffle. They are only playing, but the knife go in the boy easy, and he drop without making a noise. I just see his face surprised. I don't see any blood, and I don't want to stoop to look. I see my brother opening his mouth to scream, but no scream coming" (*IFS*, 68).

The incident, it seems, is imaginary. It is a projection of the narrator's fear: "I know at that moment that the love and the danger I carry all my life burst. My life finish. It spoil, it spoil" (*IFS*, 68).

This vision is an image of a panic that causes trouble of itself: "it is as though because you are frightened of something it is bound to come" (*IFS*, 68). From what the reader is able to piece together, however, a real act of violence has taken place in the narrator's roti shop in London. Provoked beyond endurance by the "white boys who come in the shop," he locks himself in with his tormentors. He says, "'I am taking one of you today. Two of us going today.' I hear nothing else" (*IFS*, 102). His mind is taken over by the nightmare of the imaginary accident with his brother; "it is like a dream, when you can't move, and you want to wake up quick. Then noise come back, and I know that something bad happen to my right eye. But I can't even move my hand to feel it" (*IFS*, 102).

The reader is not given enough information to reconstruct the train of events reliably, so the imagination is prompted to fill in the gaps. At the time of the narrative it is three years since the narrator last saw his brother Dayo, so presumably three years after the "trouble" caused by the incident in the roti shop, but the reader can infer that he is, or perhaps has been, in an institution and that his "friend" Frank, who travels with him to his brother's wedding, is some kind of professional "carer." Landeg White, with no justification, refers to their relationship as "apparently homosexual."[10] Andrew Gurr calls the narrator an "asylum inmate" and sees Frank as "his keeper, the male nurse, the warder of his prison,"[11] which is nearer to what the story suggests. The West Indian "lunatics" with their keepers who appeared in *The Middle Passage* seem to foreshadow the narrator's relationship with Frank. It is characterized by the inevitable resentment of a dependent, demonstrating the irrelevance of stock politico-social analyses: "Frank will never understand. . . . He is only querying and probing me about foremen who insult me at the factory, about people who fight with me at the restaurant. He is forever worrying me with his discrimination inquiries. He is my friend, the only friend I have. I alone know how much he help me, from how far he bring me back. But he is digging me all the time because he prefer to see me weak.

He like opening up manholes for me to fall in; he is anxious to push me down in the darkness" (*IFS*, 91).

The major theme of this story is the madness of the narrator, his torment, and its connection with his inability to find someone or something to blame. He is unable to say glibly with critic Rothfork that "the colonial system is undeniably responsible for the tragedy of the narrator's life."[12] His situation is an illustration of the impossibility of laying blame on anyone. The long chain of cause and effect is too complicated.

The symptom that Dayo's brother personifies is the reverse side of the success stories of other postcolonial lives, such as that of Naipaul himself. Dayo, indeed, has himself made a life in England. He has found a job and is marrying an English woman; he "make his own way" (*IFS*, 103), and although he is in England principally owing to the efforts of his brother, he has grown distant and does not show any gratitude or reciprocal responsibility. "He do better without me; he don't need me," the narrator says, bitter but resigned (*IFS*, 103); and, although during the story he tries out several scapegoats, in the end he cannot identify anyone as the cause of his misfortunes. The reason he is more lost than Santosh is that he is unable to accept not blame, but any responsibility at all, for the mess of his life. He feels that forces far beyond his understanding and control have conspired against him, and he can only thrash about blindly and dangerously, looking for someone on whom to wreak revenge—someone "to kill." The narrative ends with the recurring nightmare of his brother's childhood illness in their Caribbean village, and the soundless scream, "like in *Rope*" (*IFS*, 108).

Following the taut horror of this ending, the title story begins with a fable-like simplicity: "In this country in Africa there was a president and there was also a king. They belonged to different tribes" (*IFS*, 111). The change of pace, tense, and point of view relaxes the tension, and the reader is now led by a disengaged third-person narrator through the ironies of this mordant story.

The point of view stays almost entirely with Bobby, an English expatriate government worker traveling with fellow settler Linda through an unnamed African country in the throes of civil war. The only deviation is a short description of the life of a young Zulu whom Bobby tries to pick up in a bar, and who, after leading him on, spits in his face (*IFS*, 115). Apart from this short passage—less than half a page—early in the story, the reader has no knowledge of events or other people's thoughts that is not, or at least could not be, available to Bobby, with his taste for uncomplicated sexual adventures with Africans. However, the narrator's voice is not Bobby's and is able to present with ample irony the inconsistencies between his words and his behavior. To some extent Bobby is an innocent victim of circumstances that have led to the difficult position in which he has found himself, but of the three protagonists in the three stories he is the least sympathetic. The stark contrast between his use of power in sexual transactions, his exploitation of "the other Africans, boys built like men. . . . Sweet infantilism, almost without language" (IFS, 117), and his liberal aversion to Linda's settler attitudes and her "expatriate gossip" (IFS, 120) is far more damning than Santosh's Hindu-based racism or Dayo's brother's pathological confusion.

The choice of the third-person narrator for this story and the first person for the others is vital in making these distinctions. Bobby is also more ridiculous than either of the others—more truly laughable than Santosh, who makes comical mistakes but is not hypocritical. The tiny defensive moves he makes minute by minute are mercilessly charted: "Bobby set his face. He decided to be sombre, to give nothing away" (IFS, 120). "He had spoken too much; in the morning he would be full of regret; Linda would be another of those people from whom he would have to hide. He set his face, the silent man" (IFS, 170). He says, "I am here to serve. . . . People who don't want to serve have no business here. That sounds brutal, but that's how I see it" (IFS, 126). But his true priorities lie with self-protection and saving face, meanwhile enjoying Africa and Africans, in the most superficial sense, as much as he can. He prides himself on his liberal relationship with his houseboy, Luke, but in the end he sees him as a threat and decides to sack him. He will stay in Africa, in the compound that "was safe; the soldiers guarded the gate" (IFS, 245). He has nowhere else to go. He is not wanted back in England and asserts, "My life is here" (IFS, 134). Any sympathy the reader does feel is on account of the restrictions that life in the new regime is beginning to involve, which, it seems, will increase significantly and for which Bobby is not personally responsible. But, as Bruce King says, "In a Free State explores the nature and illusions of commitment. Naipaul appears critical of the Sartrean strategy of transcending the self in a larger community, in some ideal."[13]

Some critics have attacked Naipaul's decision to represent white settlers in Africa as an example of racial bias,[14] but it is clear that his sympathies in the novel as a whole, as far as he displays them, are principally with the two less self-conscious and hypocritical narrator-protagonists, who are not white. He chooses to write about these white settlers in order to expose their shortcomings.

In this book, the narrators can never simply be identified with Naipaul, however similar their language and attitudes seem on the surface. Only a very shallow reading would interpret the narrators of the two first-person stories as simply representing Naipaul's opinions, but in this story, with its seemingly detached narrator, more care must be taken to make the distinction. For example, the following passage, read carefully, is full of irony: "And Bobby understood that the barboy was trying to start a conversation. It was what some young Africans did. They tried to start conversations with people they thought were visitors and kindly; they hoped not only to practise their English but also to acquire manners and knowledge. It moved Bobby to be singled out in this way; it moved him that, after all that had happened, the boy should show such trust; and it distressed him that he had allowed himself to be influenced by the colonel and had so far not looked at the boy, had seen only an African in uniform, one of the colonel's employees, part of the hateful hotel" (IFS, 198). The reader does not need to be told that Bobby's response to this boy is not disinterested. Bobby realizes that he has a chance to take advantage of yet another young African's desire for education and money, by paying for sexual favors; so his distress at not having "looked at the boy, seen only an African in uniform" is not an objective statement on the state of Bobby's mind but another hint at his capacity, by now clear to the perceptive reader, for self-deception.

Words and phrases used by the narrator also reflect Bobby's changeable attitude, for example, to Linda. When she holds up her shirt to display an insect bite, he sees "the thin yellow folds of the moist skin, the fragile ribs, the brassiere, put on for the day's adventure, enclosing those poor little breasts" (IFS, 160), and he kisses the insect bite out of pity. But later, at dinner, irritated by her "casual feminine demand" that he investigate a mysterious presence in his own hotel room, he goes into her room and finds a "vaginal deodorant with an appalling name" (IFS, 184), which he uses the next day to insult her when the tension between them breaks into open conflict. The "poor little breasts" and the "appalling name" represent the extremes, of pity and fellow-feeling on one hand and revulsion on the other, of his feelings toward Linda during their eventful journey, and the evaluative words, although not attributed to Bobby, are his words, not the narrator's.

The relationship between Naipaul and the narrator of the prologue and epilogue is even more difficult to disentangle. Both pieces are subtitled "from a journal," but even Naipaul's journals would hardly be so polished and well-constructed in their original form. It is not important whether these narratives are based on fact. Their significance lies in the adoption of this particular Naipaul-like narrator—a "reliable" voice—and the behavior of those who witness these episodes of persecution. Both incidents are staged for the benefit of an audience, and once the audience loses interest, the persecution ceases.

The title of the epilogue, "The Circus at Luxor," seems initially to refer to the Chinese circus, the members of which the narrator sees at Milan and then at Luxor; but a kind of circus entertainment is provided at Luxor for the visitors by an Egyptian with a whip. The Chinese circus people, in contrast, are a model of civilized behavior: "so self-contained, so handsome and healthy, so silently content with one another: it was hard to think of them as sightseers" (*IFS*, 255). Sightseers, "travelling only for the sights" (*IFS*, 10), it is implied, are apt to behave badly and will demean others merely to engineer the "sights" they wish to see, like the Italians at Luxor, and the Lebanese, Egyptian, and Austrian travelers on the steamer to Alexandria in the prologue, "The Tramp at Piraeus."

The incidents in both stories are described as games with rules. The game on the steamer, in the prologue, "was to be like a tiger-hunt, where the bait is laid out and the hunter and the spectators watch from the security of a platform. . . . Hans smiled and explained the rules of the game as often as he was asked" (*IFS*, 17). An English tramp to whom his fellow passengers have taken a dislike is attacked, according to the rules of the game (of which he has not been informed), but he revenges himself by locking himself in the cabin he shares with his persecutors, denying them entry so they have to sleep in the dining room. But the game loses its interest, except as a tired, private joke; and when the tramp reappears to disembark at Alexandria, "he was of less interest than he thought" (*IFS*, 22). The other passengers have the last word by ignoring him.

The narrator's part in this episode is that of an observer, a first-hand witness, taking an almost anthropological interest in the proceedings. The narrator's character is only lightly sketched; he is disconcerted by the crowding on the steamer, and later, seeking solitude, he comes upon the tramp, but "I didn't disturb him. I feared to be involved with him" (*IFS*, 14). Apart from these suggestions of a fastidious nature, the narrator is seen only as a neutral observer of the other passengers and their diversions.

The narrator in the epilogue is identifiably the "I" of the prologue but is different in one respect: he does act, once. The game this time involves an Egyptian waiter at a tourist rest house using his camel-whip on the desert children: "this was an Egyptian game with Egyptian rules" (*IFS*, 252), played for the benefit of the Italian tourists who collaborate by continuing to bait the children with food scraps, and then by photographing the results. Other tourists in the rest house take no notice, but the narrator is provoked into action:

> I saw that my hand was trembling. I put down the sandwich I was eating on the metal table; it was my last decision. Lucidity, and anxiety, came to me only when I was almost on the man with the camel-whip. I was shouting. I took the whip away, threw it on the sand. He was astonished, relieved. I said, "I will report this to Cairo." He was frightened; he began to plead in Arabic. The children were puzzled; they ran off a little way and stood up to watch. The two Italians, fingering cameras, looked quite

calm behind their sunglasses. The women in the party leaned back in their chairs to consider me.

I felt exposed, futile, and wanted only to be back at my table. (*IFS*, 253–54)

Having acted, he expects "some gesture, some sign of approval" from his Egyptian driver, but "I couldn't tell what he thought. He was as correct as before, he looked as bored" (*IFS*, 254).

Critical reactions to the narrator's intervention have ranged from Fawzia Mustafa's interpretation of it as a "parable of despair" at the "almost immediate erasure of the narrator's intervention,"[15] to Robert K. Morris's rather grandiose assertion that "seldom can we find a novelist so openly linking arms with his protagonists nor converting poetic justice into a current truth about the human condition."[16] Is it despair or solidarity, or perhaps both, that Naipaul is dramatizing here? His final remarks put the whole book into context. The penultimate paragraph refers to an ancient Egyptian tomb painting depicting "the pleasures of that life" (*IFS*, 251), speculating on the purity of that ancient time; but "it was hard to believe that there had ever been such innocence" (*IFS*, 255).

Critic Rob Nixon writes, "Naipaul does not admit any remedial, purer realm outside the west in space or time and is unable to harbor dreams of an idealized organic society."[17] He intends this as a criticism, but it is an unwitting testament to one of Naipaul's greatest strengths. P. S. Chauhan writes that Naipaul's vision might seem heartless, but "its heartlessness is but the measure of Naipaul's honesty and of his artistic integrity. He deliberately refuses to hold out any sentimental salves."[18] Naipaul himself has said, "In Africa you can get a profound refusal to acknowledge the realities of the situation; people just push aside the real problems as if they had all been settled. As though the whole history of human deficiencies was entirely explained by an interlude of oppression and prejudice, which have now been removed; any remaining criticism being merely recurrence of prejudice and therefore to be dismissed."[19]

Naipaul sees colonialism as an example of a fundamental aspect of the human condition, rather than something that has occurred within the past few centuries, which is now in its final stages, and after which the world will return to some "purer realm." Rothfork criticizes him for refusing "to accept the Marxist position that the corrupt colonial system must be destroyed. . . . Naipaul refuses to accept political solutions, even though he himself has described the political causes of injustice and tragedy in colonialism."[20] This is exactly Naipaul's point. Colonialism is unjust and has tragic consequences, but it does not follow that he should accept "the Marxist position" that destroying it will immediately and automatically lead to utopia. Even Suman

Gupta, after a sustained attack on Naipaul's "black-and-white colonial psyche," has to concede "that there is an objective basis to Naipaul's sentiments" about Africa.[21] Naipaul is "not interested in attributing *fault*."[22] He sees the "true forces of history" as "dreams, lies, lusts, and rages,"[23] and these are decidedly not specific to any one civilization. He explains his predilection for "Western civilization"—really a universal civilization based on the rights and responsibilities of the individual—to an interviewer: "We all in a way—even when we violate the rules—know that there are certain good ideas of public behavior. We can't torture people; people have human rights; people must have access to the rule of law. This is comparatively new to have these principles honored across the globe."[24]

And as to being prejudiced, he does not deny it. He says, "For works to last, they must have a certain clear-sightedness. And to achieve that, one perhaps needs a few prejudices."[25] He will not, in a bogus attempt at objectivity, suppress his own point of view, and it became more and more important to him, in the years following *In a Free State*, that his narrators were scrupulously himself.

The form of this work allows Naipaul to give a number of examples of "casualties of freedom" (*IFS*, 10) (as he describes Egyptian Greek refugees on the steamer), and they are not always the examples the reader might expect. He shows that the English are not immune to suffering from the new freedoms of the postcolonial world along with the Indians, Egyptians, West Indians, and Africans of the nations they formerly subjected. The subjection, also, is only part of the story. He said, talking to Ian Hamilton in 1971, "One of the things that struck me, and has struck me for many years, is that even at the height of imperial power, even when people make the most fantastic assumptions about their place in the world, they still have these enormous personal problems, problems that can make their power seem meaningless to them, make it merely the background to their own anguish."[26]

Reading these stories in sequence, one is reminded constantly of the variety of resonances in the word "free"—and one realizes that freedom is always relative, and freedom from one subjection will, almost inevitably, lead to another. Santosh, in Washington, is "a free man":

> I could do anything I wanted. I could, if it were possible for me to turn back, go to the apartment and beg my old employer for forgiveness. I could if it were possible for me to become again what I once was, go to the police and say, "I am an illegal immigrant here. Please deport me to Bombay." I could run away, hang myself, surrender, confess, hide. It didn't matter what I did, because I was alone. And I didn't know what I wanted to do. It was like the time when I felt my senses revive and I wanted to go out and enjoy and I found there was nothing to enjoy. (*IFS*, 58)

"Freedom" for Dayo's brother comes when he discovers Dayo is not studying but hanging aimlessly around London:

> I have nowhere to go and I walk now, like Dayo, where the tourists walk. The roti-shop: that noose I put my neck in. I think how nice it would be if I could just leave it, leave it just like that. Let the curry from yesterday go stale and rotten and turn red like poison, let the dust fall from the ceiling and settle. Take Dayo home before he get foolish. . . .
>
> The life is over. I am like a man who is giving up. I come with nothing. I have nothing. I will leave with nothing.
>
> All afternoon as I walk I feel like a free man. I scorn everything I see, and when I tire myself out with walking, and the afternoon gone, I still scorn. I scorn the bus, the conductor, the street. (*IFS*, 101)

This freedom—the feeling of release from all responsibilities—gives him the courage and desperation to turn on his tormentors in the roti shop and leads to the greater bondage to which he is now subject. And the "free state" in the title story is full of captives—imprisoned by their "liberal" beliefs, like Bobby, or their knee-jerk "settler" attitudes, like Linda and the Colonel; or by the exigencies of civil conflict, like the Africans in their newly independent, "liberated" states. Freedom as a political concept is virtually meaningless, as is its related term "liberalism." Naipaul's "free state" is more dangerous, implying lostness, irresponsibility, and despair.

CHAPTER SEVEN

Sex and Violence   *Guerrillas* and *A Bend in the River*

> I cannot write Sex. I haven't the skill, or the wide experience which is
> necessary if one's work is to have variety. And then I would be embar-
> rassed even at the moment of writing. My friends would laugh. My
> mother would be shocked, and with reason.[1]

So wrote Naipaul in his essay "London" in 1958. As observed in the discussion of *The Mystic Masseur*, wife-beating often seems to stand in for sex in
Naipaul's early work. It was many years before he could bring himself to be
as frank about sexuality as he was in *The Mimic Men*, and even then the
hero's sexual drive was "low and unreliable" and Naipaul was not compelled
to be very explicit.

However, in *Guerrillas*, written in 1973 and 1974 and published in 1975,
the material that "possessed" him required a more direct approach. "I dislike
writing about sex, but I had to in that book," he told Mel Gussow.[2] Indeed,
the relationship between sex and violence, relatively benign in the early novels, takes on in this novel a far more sinister aspect.

Guerrillas is Naipaul's most dramatic novel, a shocking book about unpleasant, inadequate characters. The action takes place in a period of only a
few weeks, involving a small group of people. It is written in the third person,
moving between the points of view of these three or four people. This not
only helps the reader to understand these characters and their actions, it also
shows how dangerous they are, and how vulnerable.

The setting is a city very like Port of Spain, Trinidad, but it is explicitly not
Trinidad—a historical figure "left Trinidad and came over here," one character tells another (*G*, 67). The novel is, however, based on real events. It was
written after the publication of Naipaul's article "Michael X and the Black
Power Killings in Trinidad"[3] in the *Sunday Times*. He told Melvyn Bragg that
although "the fact of the murder gives one confidence to write about murder,

fiction must have its own internal logic. Fiction must have a simplicity in order to draw the reader in imaginatively. A factual account will be full of absurdities, things which can't be explained, will contain some mysteries, but fiction must contain an act of provocation, while in real life a murder might be a random act."[4] This is not to say that the events themselves have no explanation, but that the reasons and motives are hidden to journalists and other observers. Even an exhaustive court case will often not penetrate the mystery of a violent crime. The novelist, in contrast, can imaginatively reconstruct the sequence of events leading to these shocking actions.

In *Guerrillas*, Jane, a white Englishwoman, arrives at this unnamed Caribbean island to live with Roche, whom she has met in London. He is a hero of the South African freedom struggle who has written a successful and respected memoir. Roche has come out with vague ambitions of trying to help this newly independent country; Jane has followed him on little more than a whim, a short-lived infatuation. They become involved with the "Black Power" leader Jimmy Ahmed, a half-Chinese, half-Black man who has gained some celebrity during a visit to England and has come home to start an agricultural commune for urban delinquents. Roche tries to help them, gradually realizing the impossibility of the task, while Jane is drawn into a foolish and eventually fatal sexual relationship with Jimmy.

Jane is an unlikable character. She is shallow, stupid, and self-deceiving. Naipaul himself said of *Guerrillas*, "The fact that it shocks you is part of its success. But it's the wrong kind of success if you just think, God she was such an unpleasant girl. If she was really all that unpleasant, if you hadn't been made to understand her, you wouldn't have found her death to be so appalling."[5]

The book's success hinges directly on the character of Jane, and Naipaul does not manage to excite much sympathy for her. She appears irredeemably selfish and vain, incapable of tender feelings even for her lover Roche, whom she begins to reject as she gets to know him well: "She had invested little in this relationship. She had from the start, as it now seemed, held herself back, for this moment of withdrawal. The gesture, of leaving London and coming out to live with him, so soon after meeting him, had appeared to him grand, part of her passionate nature; yet it was contained within this sense of inviolability, her belief that everything could be undone. And he saw that he had moved from the role of comforter to that of violator. He was another of her failures, someone else who wasn't what she had thought he was" (*G*, 96).

Naipaul's comment that the book is "moralistic . . . it has very hard things to say about people who play at serious things, who think they can always escape, run back to their safe world"[6] is illustrated most clearly with this character. On her first visit to the commune, she looks "provocative . . .

foreign, wrong . . . white enough to be unreadable" (*G*, 8), but although this makes Roche feel protective toward her, the feeling is not likely to be shared by the reader. It is clear that she is vulnerable, but she is willfully blind to the consequences of her actions. For example, she has no conception of the importance of Bryant, Jimmy's young protégé and lover, whose jealousy is to be appeased with her murder. The closest Naipaul brings the reader to sympathy for Jane is when, driving home after her first sexual encounter with Jimmy,

> Words began to go through her head, words addressed to no one in particular, yet words which she fancied herself speaking with tears, like a child: "I've looked *everywhere*. I've looked and looked". . . .
>
> A whole sentence ran through her head, at first meaningless, and then, as she examined it, alarming. She thought: I've been playing with fire. (*G*, 78)

But in her vanity, she ignores her instincts, believing that she is free to act as she pleases with impunity. She has the selfishness of a spoiled child, along with the same feelings of invulnerability and irresponsibility for the consequences of her behavior. There is no room in her imagination for the needs or feelings of other people. She tells Roche she is going to leave him but, ignoring the hurt she has caused, sleeps with him whenever she wishes in spite of his appeal that it would be "better if I get used to sleeping alone" (*G*, 79). She delays her departure for no good reason and is unable to resist a last adventure with Jimmy. Even the deluded Jimmy, while fascinated with her in his self-fantasizing way, can see that she is "weak, spoilt, with the cruelty of the weak and the spoilt" (*G*, 65). She is "playing at serious things," and although her murder is shocking, it is not as confronting as it might have been had she shown some trace of feeling for another person, some slight leaven to her unremitting self-centeredness, her "casual, instinctive cruelty towards people with whom she was not concerned, this cruelty part of her laziness, her refusal to be bothered" (*G*, 131). Naipaul has made the morality of the book more clear-cut than he intended. Jane appears to invite her horrible fate. Even Roche, who has become obsessed with her and longs for her approval—even he comes to value her so lightly that he covers up her murder.

Roche is himself lost, but he at least looks outward and understands other people. Jane's jaundiced view of him is tainted for the reader by the knowledge that she looks to other people only to fulfill her own needs, and when she senses vulnerability she rejects rather than attempts to give comfort. Roche is a complex man:

> He knew that to many people around him he appeared as a man given
> over to a cause. It was understandable, but it was strange; because he

had no political dogma and no longer had a vision of a world made good, and perhaps had never had such a vision. If he had had a system, a set of political beliefs, it might have been easier for him to have set it aside, to have admitted error, as some of his associates had done, to have blamed the system or to have blamed the world for not living up to the system, and without any sense of reneging to have made a fresh start. But he had had no system; he distrusted systems; he had a feeling of responsibility for what he had done. (G, 87–88)

In his distrust for causes and systems of belief, he echoes Naipaul's sentiments, but although he is the most sympathetically drawn and admirable character in the book and provides most of the moral focus, he is in the end a weak and passive man. He allows himself to be mistreated by Jane, even while he is quite aware of her failings. He is in a way a victim of his reputation: people who "knew his South African history . . . wished to test him further," and "in spite of real respect for his past, Roche became a kind of buffoon figure to many. He was a doer of good works, with results that never showed" (G, 47). In the radio interview that forms a kind of intellectual climax to the novel, he is reproached for not "hold[ing] out hope for the rest of us," and he responds, "But I don't know why you should want me to hold out hope" (G, 206). He has unwillingly become a symbol. He says, "I wish the world were arranged differently, so that afterwards I didn't feel I had been landed with a side. I wish I hadn't walked into that particular trap . . . thinking I had somehow committed myself to one kind of action and one kind of cause. There is so much more to the world" (G, 204). His failure at the end of the book to report Jane's disappearance, telling his friend that she has left and taken her passport, the passport he is holding in his hand as he talks on the telephone, is weakness and indecision rather than a bold attempt to defend Jimmy, who he knows has killed her. The book ends unresolved: Roche apparently intends to leave the island, but neither he nor the reader can predict whether, in the unstable, violent atmosphere of the city, he will be able to get away.

Jimmy is a fraud who believes his own lies, and his fantasy of power is sustained by his writing. He usually writes "out of disturbance, out of wonder at himself, out of some sudden clear vision of an aspect of his past, or out of panic" (G, 32). He writes a fantasy of Jane's fascination with him, in her own voice: "I wonder how a man of those attainments can waste his life in a place like that with all those good for nothing natives for whom to speak in all candour I cannot have too high an opinion" (G, 32). Naipaul creates long passages of Jimmy's text, revealing Jimmy's warped perspective on the world, on Jane, on England, and especially on himself. The writing is not quite ungrammatical, but the style is inept and the sentences are too long. Naipaul is careful not to make Jimmy too ridiculous. The menace he represents is always real, even though he is clearly not the great leader, the "High Command, James Ahmed (Haji)," that he claims to be (G, 6).

The novel, as Naipaul says, "hangs between two sexual scenes. The first explains the second."[7] After the first, Jimmy feels humiliated by Jane's remoteness: "So cool she looked now; so triumphant. He was full of hate for her" (G, 76). The second, then, is Jimmy's revenge upon her. Her humiliation of him, probably unwitting and certainly careless, leads inevitably to his need to humiliate her; the humiliation as necessary a sacrifice to his wounded pride as the murder is a sacrifice to Bryant's jealousy.

Naipaul said, "I was careful enough to remove from the sex scenes any association of the standard erotic writing, but I was appalled."[8] Shocking as these sexual scenes are—and the removal of the "standard eroticism" increases rather than diminishes their power—there are other scenes in the novel that are just as dramatic. One is when Jimmy is quietly writing, creating his twisted fantasy of sex and violence, and Bryant interrupts: "'The rat!' Bryant screamed, throwing down the paper on the carpet. 'Jimmy, I see the white rat today!'" (G, 85). The reader is as startled as Jimmy and feels the emotional logic of Jimmy's promise to Bryant: "I'll give her to you" (G, 85).

Another strangely shocking and memorable scene describes a trivial incident:

> Jane was standing on the other side of the bed, next to the window.
> She was naked below her cotton blouse; her blue trousers, with the
> pants inside them, were thrown on the bed. . . . She glanced at Roche
> as he came in; then, turning her back to him, and facing the window,
> she seemed about to sit on the bed. She came down hard on the very
> edge of the bed . . . but she didn't sit; she threw herself backwards in
> an apparently abandoned attitude, opened her legs, raising her feet up
> against the wall, and inserted what Roche now realized was the tampon
> she held in her hand; and then almost immediately she was sitting, had
> seized the blue plastic tampon-case from the bed and sent it spinning
> with a low, level flick of the wrist to the corner of the room. (G, 122–23)

The reader shares Roche's shock at this abrupt and somehow contemptuous action. It is not that he is offended that she should do such a thing in his presence—they have been living together for several months. It is rather that he is stunned by the suddenness of it and the fact that she sees him but ignores him. His shock is perhaps intensified by the knowledge that she is about to leave him and is merely biding her time. The scene is carefully described exactly as Roche perceives it: she "seemed about to sit"; he "now realized" what she had in her hand. This scene, although far more powerful, recalls Mrs Baksh's hair-combing reception of Harbans in *The Suffrage of Elvira,* the action of a woman demonstrating her contempt for a member of the opposite sex.

Guerrillas is not really a novel about politics. Jimmy is not politically astute. He knows how to work on the guilt and fear of people with money so that they support him up to a point, but he has no future, and his brief moment of glorious insurrection—his procession round the town with the body of his murdered associate—merely underlines the fleeting nature of his influence. If anything, *Guerrillas* is about the impossibility of politics in a world like this, full of "lies and self deception and people inhabiting different worlds or cultures."[9]

A Bend in the River (1979), Naipaul's next novel, is a little closer to what is usually thought of as a political novel. It is about the effect of politics on lives, the violence that arises from political actions, and the victims of political power, whether they be racial minorities, discarded advisers, or even anxious, overstressed government officials.

A Bend in the River is a less dramatic novel than *Guerrillas.* The violence, although always threatening, is usually not dramatized but reported at one remove, or rumored. At the beginning of the book, the narrator, Salim, leaves his family home on the east coast of Africa. Although his family, originally from India, has lived in the town for many generations, he can see that he will have no future there. He buys a shop in central Africa in a provincial town that has recently endured postindependence wars. Salim does not stay long enough in his hometown to experience the violence he foresees but hears of it when Metty, a member of his family's long-standing slave community, comes to join him. The violence is described in terms of Metty's melodramatic reaction to what he has seen: "He went on about those cut-off arms and legs that belonged to people we had known since we were children. It was terrible, what he had seen. But I was also beginning to feel that he was trying to excite himself to cry a little bit more after he had stopped wanting to cry. I felt that it worried him to find out that from time to time he was forgetting, and thinking of other things" (*BR*, 32).

Again, when the violence and troubles come to Salim's new town, the disturbances keep their distance from the center where Salim spends his time. "The very size and unregulated sprawl of the town muffled all but the most extraordinary events. . . . In the centre of the town life went on as before" (*BR*, 214). Even when Salim is carried off to jail for a few days, although he witnesses other prisoners, Africans, "being maltreated in ways I don't want to describe" (*BR*, 269), he is himself left alone. He escapes at the end of the novel to an uncertain future. The only act of violence that is reported directly is his own abuse of his mistress.

Yvette is the wife of a historian, Raymond, who comes to the city's new university. He is "the Big Man's white man," the president's adviser before and during his rise to power, and his influence is now waning. Salim finds happiness for a time with Yvette, much younger than her husband. However, ultimately, enraged by something in her manner—her assumption of his own pliability, her lingering loyalty to Raymond, or perhaps something even more indefinable: his ideas about what might happen on "those blank days when she was away from me, those days about which I didn't inquire, [which] would have been full of possibilities for her" (BR, 216)—he one night beats and humiliates her shamefully. "An idea like that is like a vivid dream, fixing a fear we don't want to acknowledge," Salim says of his jealous imaginings (BR, 216). Sex and violence here take on a new aspect again. Their sexual life has been described as "a physical fulfilment which could not be more complete" (BR, 197), but now it seems that the violence of their ending is virtually inevitable. As always seeking the nuance beneath the expected, Naipaul describes Yvette's phone call to Salim that night after she arrives home, bruised and sore.

> "You must try to sleep. Make some hot milk and try to sleep. It helps to have a hot drink. Let Metty make some hot milk for you."
> Never closer, never more like a wife, than at this moment. (BR, 221)

The violence is not condoned, but neither is Salim condemned. As the point of view is his, it is his pain that is seen at first hand, while the suffering of Yvette, not fully understood by Salim but nevertheless still deeply connected with his own emotional state, is also shown. In scenes like this Naipaul is at his most powerful: never offering obscene or unnecessary words but dramatizing with great economy events that become etched on the reader's mind. It is telling that the three-year affair with Yvette is contained within only about fifty pages of the three hundred or so in this book, so sparingly is it delineated: it assumes in retrospect a significance and richness of detail out of proportion to the space it occupies in the text.

Wayne C. Booth, in his influential book *The Rhetoric of Fiction,* sets out the complexities and variations authors use in their choice of narrators.[10] There is much more involved in this choice than merely who is telling the story—whether it is one of the characters or an impersonal observer, or whether the narrator is omniscient or has only partial or subjective knowledge of what is being related. A common type of narrator in twentieth-century fiction is the first-person unreliable narrator, whose opinions and knowledge of events are easy to distinguish from those of the author. The reader understands, for example, that Alex in Anthony Burgess's *A Clockwork Orange,* or Holden in J. D. Salinger's *Catcher in the Rye,* are not in any sense mouthpieces for their authors' beliefs.

Naipaul has not often used the device of the obviously unreliable narrator. Striking examples, of course, are the narrators of the stories "One out of Many" and "Tell Me Who to Kill" from *In a Free State,* and "A Flag on the Island"; and another, where the device is less integral to the narrative, is *The Mystic Masseur,* where the narrator is brought in occasionally to make a satirical point, the author rather obviously winking at the reader over the innocent boy's shoulder. However, usually Naipaul's narrators are less obviously "unreliable," and they need to be carefully distinguished from the author, as discussed in relation to *The Mimic Men.* In some cases, it is possible to decide that they are virtually the same, as will be shown in chapter 9.

In *A Bend in the River* Salim is certainly not Naipaul in any biographical sense. His world is very different from Naipaul's. He comes from a family of some standing and privilege in their community, although these advantages are being rapidly undermined. His education, however, finished when he was sixteen: "Not because I wasn't bright or didn't have the inclination, but because no one in our family had stayed at school after sixteen" (*BR*, 18). Salim also has a type of innocence that Naipaul lacks. Perhaps where the distance between them is clearest is in chapter 9, which is almost wholly narrated by Salim's friend Indar.

Indar is a childhood friend from the east coast. His family was richer than Salim's: "He was handsome, careful of his appearance, and slightly effeminate, with something buttoned-up in his expression. I put that expression down to his regard for his own wealth and also to his sexual anxieties" (*BR*, 18). Indar arrives unexpectedly in the town at the bend in the river, to teach at the new polytechnic, and it is he who introduces Salim to Raymond and Yvette. Indar's self-assurance and apparent contempt for Salim's drab, limited life in the town are initially disconcerting, but they resume their friendship, and Indar tells the story of his studies in England and his subsequent career.

Here a striking parallel can be seen to Naipaul's own experiences when he first arrived in England to study:

> The word "university" dazzled me, and I was innocent enough to believe that after my time in the university some wonderful life would be waiting for me. . . . But I hadn't understood to what extent our civilization had also been our prison. I hadn't understood either to what extent we had been made by the place where we had grown up, made by Africa and the simple life of the coast, and how incapable we had become of understanding the outside world. . . .
>
> When we land at a place like London Airport we are concerned only not to appear foolish. . . . That is the nature of our stupidity and incompetence. And that was how I spent my time at the university in England,

not being overawed, always being slightly disappointed, understanding nothing, accepting everything, getting nothing. (*BR*, 142–43)

This is remarkably similar to Naipaul's description of his early years in England in later books like *The Enigma of Arrival,* as well as what can be gleaned from his letters home in the 1950s. Again, after university, Indar says,

Everything which I thought had made me powerless in the world had also made me of value, and . . . I was of interest precisely because I was what I was, a man without a side. . . .

I'm a lucky man. I carry the world within me. . . . In this world beggars are the only people who can be choosers. Everyone else has his side chosen for him. I can choose. (*BR*, 153–55)

This echoes Naipaul's many statements about the advantages of being "without a side." After reading this chapter, one might begin to believe that Indar is more of an autobiographical figure than Salim: more sophisticated, better educated, more widely traveled. But Indar comes to grief. His self-created job, of arranging intellectual exchanges between educational institutions in African countries, acting as a kind of broker of philosophy and ideas, peters out, and he refuses to take up any further options: "He knows he is equipped for better things, but he doesn't want to do them. . . . He enjoys being told he can do better. . . . He doesn't want to risk anything again. The idea of sacrifice is safer, and he likes the act" (*BR*, 244). So here is another cautionary tale, another Ralph Singh retreating from the world, and here the resemblance to Naipaul, fleetingly glimpsed, falls away. Indar is exposed as another failed exile and alien, wishing only to go home. As Salim explains, "The idea of going home, of leaving, the idea of the other place—I had lived with it in various forms for many years. . . . It was a deception. I saw now that it comforted only to weaken and destroy" (*BR*, 244).

Almost all the other characters in whom Salim sees strength and wholeness are similarly undermined. Ferdinand, an African village boy who rises through government sponsorship, becomes one of the Big Man's officials. Salim thinks that for him the world is "ready-made and easy" (*BR*, 271). But when he meets him in his office near the end of the novel, "he was, after all, like other high officials. . . . These men, who depended on the President's favour for everything, were bundles of nerves. The great power they exercised went with a constant fear of being destroyed" (*BR*, 271). Political power, then, is a two-edged sword. And at the other extreme of the social hierarchy, Salim's servant Metty, at one time a friend of Ferdinand, seems to Salim carefree, until he is discovered to have a woman and child. Salim feels shocked and betrayed, and Metty changes in his eyes: "He lost the brightness and gaiety of the servant who knows that he will be looked after, that others will decide for him; and he lost what went with that brightness—the indifference to what had just happened, the ability to forget, the readiness for every new day" (*BR*, 108).

Raymond, Yvette's husband, at first impresses Salim deeply. This is part of Salim's innocence, his exaggerated respect for Raymond's "intelligence and intellectual labours" (*BR*, 129) and his initial willingness to fall into line as a disciple. But soon after his first sexual encounter with Yvette, he reads an article by Raymond and discovers that his historical work is worthless: "His subject was an event in Africa, but he might have been writing about Europe or a place he had never been. . . . He didn't seem to have gone to any of the places he wrote about; he hadn't tried to talk to anybody" (*BR*, 181). His better understanding of Raymond begins subtly to color his attitude to Yvette: "To have understood more about Raymond . . . might have made me see her more clearly—her ambition, her bad judgement, her failure" (*BR*, 183). When it seems that Raymond's position with the government is under threat, Salim realizes that "my life with Yvette depended on the health and optimism of all three of us. . . . I couldn't bear the idea of the lost coming together for comfort" (*BR*, 215). With his customary perception, refraining from moral judgment, Naipaul shows yet another aspect of human life: the corrosive effect pity can have on a passionate relationship.

The absence of moral judgment is significant. It is explicitly part of the rootlessness of Salim's life:

> It was the opposite of the life of our family and community on the coast. That life was full of rules. . . . Here I had stripped myself of all the rules. . . . With Yvette—and with Yvette and Raymond together—I had acquired a kind of domestic life: the passion in the flat, the quiet family evening in the house in the Domain. . . . It was only when the life was disturbed that amazement came to me at the coolness with which I had accepted a way of living which, if it had been reported to me about someone else when I was younger, would have seemed awful. Adultery was horrible to me. I continued to think of it in the setting of family and community on the coast, and saw it as sly and dishonourable and weak-willed. (*BR*, 101)

So, along with the reality of a home and family, Salim loses his moral code and even finds it hard to know "what to think or feel. Fear or shame—there seemed to be nothing in between" (*BR*, 76). Africa is the only home Salim has ever known until he travels overseas when he is perhaps thirty years old, after his affair with Yvette. And yet he is not at home in Africa: he is used only to the feeling of being racially different from most of the population, a feeling Naipaul shares, and of living in the country belonging to "people who didn't know their own mind. They had suffered so much; they had brought so much suffering on themselves. . . . They looked so much like people needing the food and the peace that the town offered. But it was people like them, going back to their villages, who wished to lay the town low again. Such rage!" (BR, 67).

Salim is frightened of both sides in this war and realizes his disadvantage: "We could all cope with the good times. It was for the bad that we had to be equipped. And here in Africa none of us were as well equipped as the Africans. . . . Even the raggedest of them had their villages and tribes, things that were absolutely theirs" (BR, 71).

A Bend in the River is a bleak vision of Africa and of the difficulties of any alien communities and expatriates who find themselves adrift there. Once again, Naipaul refuses to offer any remedies or identify any scapegoats. The opening sentence of the book, "The World is what it is; men who are nothing, who allow themselves to be nothing, have no place in it" (BR, 3), takes on an even grimmer aspect when considered in the light of the novel's close. It is impossible to believe that Salim, escaping with virtually nothing on the river steamer, has made something of himself and that he has a place in the world. It is open to the reader to hope that he will yet find that place, fleeing as he is to the protection of Nazruddin, the one figure in the novel who has always managed to succeed, to get out in time when necessary and make the best of a life elsewhere. Nazruddin now lives in London, and Salim will marry his daughter, but it is difficult to be confident in a secure future for them, given the uncertainty of the last few pages of the novel.

Naipaul said, perhaps mischievously, that Guerrillas "is full of jokes" and that A Bend in the River "is a little funnier than" Guerrillas. [11] Little comedy is, however, apparent in either book. It is difficult for the reader to relax enough to laugh at anything in Guerrillas. A Bend in the River is calmer than Guerrillas, which was written "in about five months of controlled frenzy."[12] It has passages describing great joy and passion, in Salim's affair with Yvette, and a couple of mildly satirical scenes, mocking the pretensions of characters such as Indar and Raymond, but there is little one could truly describe as humorous or comic. Any momentary amusement is soon swept away by the sense of menace, insecurity, and desolation that pervades both these novels.

After A Bend in the River, Naipaul forsook the conventional novel for twenty years and embarked on more travels. He did not abandon fiction entirely during this period but used autobiography and history in a number of idiosyncratic ways in the fiction and nonfiction of the 1980s and 1990s. Violence, or the possibility of violence, is always present in his work, but until Half a Life (2001) he left aside, no doubt with a sense of relief, the question of sex.

CHAPTER EIGHT

Investigations Abroad Middle-Period Nonfiction

After the publication of *In a Free State,* no full-length work of nonfiction or fiction appeared from Naipaul for four years. The gap was bridged by two books of collected nonfiction, *The Overcrowded Barracoon* and *The Return of Eva Perón.*

The Overcrowded Barracoon draws together essays dating from 1958 to 1972. The first section, "An Unlikely Colonial," contains four short magazine articles on the theme of Naipaul's adjustment to life in England. They are witty and idiosyncratic, if sometimes petulant. He considers the problems and possibilities of being both a writer and a colonial, an ethnic oddity, in English society. In "London" he complains of "the barrenness of my life in London," but goes on "and yet I like London. . . . It is the best place to write in" (*OB,* 16). "Cricket" discusses the West Indian politician and writer on history and cricket, C. L. R. James, and the place in West Indian culture of the game of cricket: "For West Indians, as one cricket writer says, the game is a carnival. But what a game to choose for a carnival! It is leisurely, intricate, difficult to appreciate, its drama often concealed or curtailed; and the players stop for tea" (*OB,* 18).

In "Jasmine" Naipaul considers the oddity of English language, literature, and culture in faraway Trinidad: the difficulty of comprehending the literature of a complex society when "the only social division I accepted was that between rich and poor, and any society more elaborately ordered seemed insubstantial and alien" (*OB,* 24). "East Indian" is the funniest of these pieces, recounting an air trip from London to Paris, a special "Epicurean" service, where Naipaul sits beside an Indian and has his usual trouble explaining his background as an "East Indian West Indian" (*OB,* 34). The description of his conversation with his companion is amusing and only faintly malicious, and his complaint that "to be an Indian from Trinidad is . . . to be the embodiment of an old verbal ambiguity" is witty but leads on to a more serious discussion of the difficulties of what has now come to be known as the Indian Diaspora.

Part 2 contains a collection of pieces on India—travel writing and book reviews. The first piece, "In the Middle of the Journey," once again mentions the amusing difficulties Naipaul has when asked "the Indian question": "Where do you come from?"

> My answer that I am a Trinidadian is only puzzling.
> "But you look Indian."
> Three or four times a day the dialogue occurs, and now I often abandon explanation. "I am a Mexican, really." (OB, 43)

In "Jamshed into Jimmy" he makes a study of a particular species of English-educated Indian working for British firms in India, whose first name is often changed to Jimmy or Bunty. With his customary incisiveness—and scatological fascination—he notes that "it is impossible to write of Bunty without making him appear ridiculous," but he is nevertheless "admirable in the Indian context. . . . Not least of his virtues is that he keeps a spotless lavatory. East and West blend easily in him" (OB, 53). "A Second Visit" and "The Election in Ajmer" are longer pieces analyzing various aspects of Indian society in a similar vein to An Area of Darkness and his later books on India. Themes that recur are the "special Indian psychology of dependence" (OB, 97), and the drama, personalities, and moral issues involved in election campaigns. Naipaul follows the activities and fortunes of rival candidates, as he has in places as diverse as New York, British Guiana, and Mauritius. In this case he observes with a mixture of fascination and disturbance the behavior of everyone involved in the campaign, supporters and principals alike, in an electorate in Rajasthan.

The next part of The Overcrowded Barracoon, titled "Looking Westward," is the least cohesive and might have been more accurately labeled "Miscellaneous." Its four essays concern four very different figures: the novelist John Steinbeck and the efforts of the business community in Monterey, California, to exploit the tourism potential of his novel Cannery Row; Norman Mailer, campaigning for mayor in New York in 1969; Jacques Soustelle, exiled French politician, ethnologist, and scholar; and, most bizarre of all, Morihiro Matsuda, a Korean immigrant to Japan, a businessman who had a scheme for "bringing about peace in Vietnam in a day or, at the outside, three days" and other similarly ambitious schemes to help and protect America, for which purpose he needed to make a million dollars: "This is how he will do it. He will go to Chicago, to deal with the newspapers that have invited him. Then he will give lectures to the university about happiness and the seven degrees of beauty. He might also make a model of his indestructible motor car—no more deaths in road accidents—and sell the development rights. From Chicago he will go to New York . . . " (OB, 144). And so his plan goes on. Naipaul describes Mr Matsuda's projects, hopes, and philosophies, allowing their patent absurdity to reveal itself without unnecessary interpretive comment. The final sentence of the essay, "Mr Matsuda will die" (OB, 154), conveys not only confidence in the restoration of sanity but also some pathos.

The last section of the book, "Columbus and Crusoe," contains essays seemingly united by the theme of colonization. The essay from which the title of the section comes, although it appears nominally to be a review of a book on Christopher Columbus, is a short discussion comparing Columbus with Daniel Defoe's *Robinson Crusoe,* seeing in both "the dream of being the first man in the world: . . . the dream of being suddenly, just as one is, in unquestionable control of the physical world" (OB, 206). A selection of Naipaul's characteristic travel writings follows, describing the societies of British Honduras, St. Kitts, and Anguilla in 1969, and a discussion of black power in Trinidad, Jamaica, and other Caribbean nations. The last piece in the book, "The Overcrowded Barracoon," describes with Naipaul's customary deadpan wit and pessimism the island nation of Mauritius in the Indian Ocean, where he discerns overpopulation and disaffection fueling a desire for escape to a prosperous life overseas, in this place where "the dodo forgot how to fly, because it had no enemies" (OB, 256).

The Overcrowded Barracoon is a useful collection of characteristic essays. Covering as it does nearly fifteen years of nonfiction writing, it shows the development of Naipaul's style and the broadening of his concerns from a necessary early preoccupation with his own life and situation, to a vision that encompasses a range of societies, old and new, and the plight of individuals and groups trying to make their way in these societies.

The Return of Eva Perón contains a group of more intense pieces written between 1972 and 1975, although not published in book form until 1980. In his author's note, Naipaul explains this intensity, their "obsessional nature," by the fact that "they bridged a creative gap: from the end of 1970 to the end of 1973 no novel offered itself to me." The creative energy that was not being consumed by full-length works of fiction or nonfiction during this time must have built up into anxiety bordering on panic, the panic that Naipaul has always felt in connection with his work and that he feels he inherited from his father.

The first of the four essays, "Michael X and the Black Power Killings in Trinidad," covers some ninety pages and contains the material from which *Guerrillas* was developed. As carefully structured as any of Naipaul's novels, it begins with a chilling, concrete image: "A corner file is a three-sided file, triangular in section, and it is used in Trinidad for sharpening cutlasses" (REP, 3). In this one sentence, both the setting and the murder weapon are established. Two of the murderers are introduced in the following few sentences:

Steve Yeates, "Supreme Captain of the Fruit of Islam, as well as Lieutenant Colonel (and perhaps the only member)" of the "Black Liberation Army" of Michael de Freitas, also known as Michael X and Michael Abdul Malik (*REP*, 3). The details he gives of the place of purchase and the price paid for the file—"a Trinidad dollar, 20p"—contrast absurdly but ominously with the self-assumed titles and deluded visions of these men. The corner file reappears later, used by the hired killer to sharpen his cutlass before the murder.

The sense of menace is as strong throughout this piece as it is in *Guerrillas*. Malik, like Jimmy in *Guerrillas*, fancied himself a writer. For both Malik and his associate Hakim Jamal, the lover of the murder victim Gale Benson, "uneducated but clever, hustlers with the black cause always to hand, operating always among the converted or half-converted, writing had for too long been a public relations exercise, a form of applauded lie, fantasy" (*REP*, 73). Malik was writing a fictional narrative from the point of view of two white, upper-middle-class English characters who, in his story, are obsessed with "Mike," obviously an idealized version himself with barely an attempted veneer of fiction. But, as Naipaul says, "an autobiography can distort; facts can be realigned. But fiction never lies: it reveals the writer totally" (*REP*, 63). The events of Malik's "novel" are prophetic; in the end he is, like his hero, on the run.

However, Naipaul reserves his harshest judgment for those who, in their security and complacency, encouraged Malik's delusions: "England made many things easy for Malik. But England in the end undid him. . . . Malik exaggerated the importance of the fringe groups which seemed to have made room for him. . . . He failed to understand that section of the middle class that knows only that it is secure, has no views, only reflexes and scattered irritations, and sometimes indulges in play: the people who keep up with 'revolution' as with the theatre: the revolutionaries who visit centers of revolution, but with return air tickets, the people for whom Malik's kind of Black Power was an exotic but safe brothel" (*REP*, 29).

Exposing himself to accusations of blaming the victim, Naipaul criticizes people like Gale Benson and carries the criticism over even more trenchantly to Jane in *Guerrillas*. But such simple formulas are never reliable: sometimes, perhaps, the victim is at least partly to blame.

The title story in this collection discusses at some length the political situation in Argentina from 1972 to 1974. Rampant inflation, an inaccurate and glorified sense of the country's history, and the wish for a strong leader have led to the re-emergence of Juan Perón, former dictator and widower of the legendary Eva Perón. As usual, Naipaul is not content with a superficial political analysis. He approaches Argentina in several ways. One is a series of discussions with and meditations upon its most famous writer, Jorge Luis

Borges: "Borges is a great writer, a sweet and melancholy poet. . . . But his Anglo-American reputation as a blind and elderly Argentine, the writer of a few very short and very mysterious stories, is so inflated and bogus that it obscures his greatness" (*REP,* 118). Even Borges is not immune to the myth-making tendencies of his compatriots, although he is not fooled by the legend of Perón, refusing even to use his name, referring to him only as "the horrible man" (*REP,* 127). But the damage Perón did to Argentina came about because "he intuited the needs of his followers" (*REP,* 147), despite expressing "in himself, and in his movement . . . so many of his country's weaknesses" (*REP,* 147–48).

Naipaul's political analysis of the country seems acute, but what makes this piece uniquely his is the detailed and nuanced observations he makes of people's behavior, such as the trade union leaders making "free trips to Europe on Aerolineas Argentinas . . . flashy provincial machos . . . each man, after supper, settling down with his pile of comic books and photo-novels, light reading for the long night flight, the tips of ringed fingers wetted on the tongue before the pages were turned" (*REP,* 159). Even more revealing is the Trotskyist who, asked by Naipaul about his plans for the abolition of torture under a socialist regime, "noticing my concern, . . . promised, speaking very quickly, as to a child to whom anything could be promised, that torture would disappear 'with the downfall of the bourgeoisie'" (*REP,* 162). He recognizes, with ironic de-emphasis, that the poor Spanish and Italian Argentinians "know how to protect themselves against the ghosts and poltergeists with which they have peopled the alien land" where they have settled (*REP,* 104): that their need for a system of belief creates both their terrors and the means of conquering them. And Perón is the straw these hapless people have been induced to clutch at, an aging, macho dictator without a program. "Like all Argentines, he was a victim, someone with enemies, someone with that pain about others" (*REP,* 167): envy and resentment standing in for positive, practical political ideas.

"To write realistically about this society has peculiar difficulties; to render it accurately in fiction might be impossible," Naipaul writes of Argentina (*REP,* 153). No novel arose directly from "The Return of Eva Perón," but the next essay in this collection, "A New King for the Congo: Mobutu and the Nihilism of Africa," a shorter piece than the first two, is clearly revisited in *A Bend in the River.* There is no character in *A Bend in the River* who is directly drawn from life in the way in which Jimmy Ahmed in *Guerrillas* is a fictional portrayal of Michael Abdul Malik. Instead, Naipaul's description of Kinshasa, the capital city of Zaire, and the regime of Joseph Mobutu is the basis for the setting for Salim's fictional world in his unnamed town on the bend in the unnamed river.

Naipaul's manifold concerns recur. He describes "the new men of the new state who, in the name of Africanization and the dignity of Africa, were so often doing jobs for which they were not qualified and often were drawing salaries for jobs they were not doing at all. This . . . was their fear: to be returned from the sweet corruptions of Kinshasa to the older corruption of the bush, to be returned to Africa" (*REP,* 179). And he concludes that although "Mobutu's peace and his kingship are great achievements . . . the kingship is sterile. . . . African dependence" and "nihilistic assertion" are all it has to offer (*REP,* 203).

Much of the essay describes Naipaul's trip on the river steamer, which plays an important part in the novel, and there are many other minor details in the novel that appeared first in this piece. But there is a great leap of the imagination between "A New King for the Congo" and *A Bend in the River,* even greater than that between "Michael X" and *Guerrillas.* A rounded character and his environment, however insecure and fragile, have been created from a much smaller amount of information in the later novel, in a setting where Naipaul has much less personal experience. That such a convincing fictional world can be conjured from so little shows not only Naipaul's novelistic skills but also his strong affinity with people from postcolonial societies, whether they are in Africa, India, or the Caribbean.

The final piece in this book, "Conrad's Darkness," is an extraordinary work of literary criticism that quite explicitly says as much about Naipaul as it does about the novelist Joseph Conrad. Naipaul describes his early reading of Conrad and his youthful judgment that "in his fictions Conrad had refined away, as commonplace, those qualities of the imagination and fantasy and invention that I went to novels for." But, he goes on, "we read at different times for different things" (*REP,* 213), and he later found, when discovering his own true subject as a writer, that Conrad "had been everywhere before me. Not as a man with a cause, but a man offering . . . a vision of the world's half-made societies" (*REP,* 216). This short essay offers not only an assessment of one major writer by another, but also an analysis of what Naipaul sees as the failure of the modern novel to "awaken the sense of true wonder . . . a fair definition of the novelist's purpose, in all ages" (*REP,* 227).

After writing *Guerrillas,* Naipaul revisited India during the Emergency of 1975, and the book that resulted was *India: A Wounded Civilization.* A trenchant and often gloomy view of the country, it is preceded by Naipaul's explicit disclaimer of objectivity:

> India is for me a difficult country. It isn't my home and cannot be my home; and yet I cannot reject it or be indifferent to it; I cannot travel only for the sights. I am at once too close and too far. . . .

> An inquiry about India—even an inquiry about the Emergency—has quickly to go beyond the political. It has to be an inquiry about Indian attitudes; it has to be an inquiry about the civilization itself, as it is. And though in India I am a stranger, the starting point of this inquiry—more than might appear in these pages—has been myself. (*IWC*, ix–x)

With his customary combination of minute observation and broad generalizations, Naipaul investigates many aspects of Indian society, starting, as he often does, by looking at one of the country's major writers. He finds much to admire in R. K. Narayan, who at least did not "regard the novel, and all writing, as an opportunity for autobiography and boasting" (*IWC*, 10). Nevertheless, he finds Narayan a misleading guide to Indian society, which seemed, in his novels, "oddly like the Trinidad of my childhood" (*IWC*, 12): "In the books his India had seemed accessible; in India it remained hidden. To get down to Narayan's world, to perceive the order and continuity he saw in the dereliction and smallness of India, to enter into his ironic acceptance and relish his comedy, was to ignore too much of what could be seen, to shed too much of myself: my sense of history, and even the simplest ideas of human possibility. I did not lose my admiration for Narayan; but I felt that his comedy and irony were not quite what they had appeared to be, were part of a Hindu response to the world, a response I could no longer share" (*IWC*, 13).

A comparable Indian/Hindu response to India is represented by a young woman who insists that "the poor people in Bombay . . . are beautiful." Naipaul comments, "The poor of Bombay are not beautiful, even with their picturesque costumes. . . . The idea that the poor are beautiful was, with this girl, a borrowed idea. She had converted it into a political attitude, which she was prepared to defend. But it had not sharpened her perception" (*IWC*, 125).

He vividly demonstrates the reality of Indian poverty with a couple of scenes. In a shanty town he comes upon "a hellish vision": two scrawny cows being dragged away by two scrawny women, to be hidden from the authorities, a "scene of isolated, feeble frenzy . . . the frightened cows and the frantic starveling women" (*IWC*, 68). And a little later he observes a woman using "a tiny strip of rag held between her thumb and middle finger" to brush the causeway of a huge dam: "veiled, squatting, almost motionless, but present, earning her half-rupee, her five cents, she does with her finger dabs in a day what a child can do with a single push of a long-handled broom" (*IWC*, 75).

Indian politicians do little to change these conditions. Naipaul draws a damning portrait of Vinoba Bhave, Gandhi's influential successor, who, "even if he understood Gandhi's stress on the need for social reform, was incapable of undermining Hindu India; he was too much part of it. The perfect disciple, obeying without always knowing why, he invariably distorted his master's message" (IWC, 181). Asked in an interview about what he would like to see happening in India, Naipaul said, "A more cogent, a more lucid play of mind. I would like to see people getting away from an unexpressed faith in magic . . . opening oneself to inquiry of all sorts, asking about history . . . getting some sense of human contract."[1] He realizes, however, that this would be a painful awakening: "The poverty of the land is reflected in the poverty of the mind; it would be calamitous if it were otherwise" (IWC, 189). He perceives something of this kind of creative calamity in his later book India: A Million Mutinies Now.

Naipaul's description of the work of the National Institute of Design in Gujarat is sardonically reminiscent of Jonathan Swift's imaginary Grand Academy of Lagado, as described in Gulliver's Travels. The Institute is engaged in developing "intermediate technology" for the poor, inventions that stunned him by their impracticality and ignorance of the real needs of the Indian peasant. This is for the most part, however, a sober book. Naipaul allows himself only a few outright jokes: such as the young foreign academic who swings "happily from branch to low branch in the grove of Academe" (IWC, 124) and the civil servant with "his plain wife and bespectacled adolescent son—old error, new hope" (IWC, 150).

As if to shore up some defenses against the protests he knows this book will arouse, from time to time he draws upon other opinions to support his views. He quotes an Indian psychotherapist's theory of the "underdeveloped" ego to help explain "India's intellectual second-rateness, which is generally taken for granted but may be the most startling and depressing fact about the world's second most populous country" (IWC, 109). But he manages to produce some optimism, albeit muted. Of the forays into "intermediate technology" he says, "It is something—perhaps a great deal—that India has felt the need to make the attempt" (IWC, 138); and at the end of the book he looks back at a pessimistic assessment he made in 1967 and comments, "That seemed to me a blacker time" (IWC, 191). However, the way ahead is dependent upon seeing the past as history rather than as a way of living: "The past has to be seen to be dead; or the past will kill" (IWC, 191).

One notable feature of India: A Wounded Civilization is its impersonal nature. The people he meets are not named. Even a man he spends some time with and whom he describes with respect as "a rare man in India, much more than the engineer he was by profession" (IWC, 62) is never mentioned by name. In his next travel book, Among the Believers: An Islamic Journey (1981), Naipaul seems to have decided that a more personal approach was needed.

In *Among the Believers,* Naipaul recounts his travels in four countries where Islam has been widely adopted: Iran, Pakistan, Malaysia, and Indonesia. His emphasis is on the conversion of non-Arab peoples and the Islamic attempt to extinguish all previous cultures and religions in these countries.

He visited Iran six months after the revolution in early 1979 that deposed the shah and brought to power the Islamic regime of Ayatollah Khomeini. He begins his narrative, before going back to describe his flight out from England, with his negotiations for an interpreter and guide to the holy city of Qom, firstly his encounter with Sadeq, "the kind of man who, without political doctrine, only with resentments, had made the Iranian revolution" (*AB,* 3). To Naipaul's considerable relief ("it would have been interesting to talk to him for an hour or two; it was going to be hard to be with him for some days" [*AB,* 3]) Sadeq's car refuses to start, and he is able to engage Behzad instead. When they meet, "I at once felt at ease with him. . . . There was nothing of the dandy about him, nothing of Sadeq's nervousness and raw pride" (*AB,* 5).

The importance of personal relationships like these is paramount in this book. In a way that harks back to his uncertain, touching friendship with Aziz in *An Area of Darkness,* Naipaul's narrative is immeasurably enriched by his acknowledgment of the importance of these personal contacts on his travels. It is easy to visit and look with a critical and pessimistic eye, recording dereliction, stupidity, and incompetence. When he allows himself to become close to people who have to make their lives in these societies where he is merely a passing observer, and introduces the reader to them as rounded personalities, effectively giving them a voice, his work takes on an extra dimension of humanity.

On the first day of their travels together, Naipaul and Behzad are walking through the busy streets of Tehran. Naipaul is deterred by the heavy traffic ("Iranians drove . . . like people to whom the motor-car was new. . . . This manner of driving didn't go with any special Tehran luck. . . . Two thousand people were killed or injured every month" [*AB,* 10]). Behzad goes ahead but soon looks back and sees that he has lost his companion.

> He understood my helplessness. He came back through the traffic to
> me and then—like a moorhen leading its chick across the swift current
> of a stream—he led me through dangers which at every moment seemed
> about to sweep me away. He led me by the hand; and, just as the moor-
> hen places herself a little downstream from the chick, breaking the force
> of the current which would otherwise sweep the little thing away forever,
> so Behzad kept me in his lee, walking a little ahead of me and a little to
> one side, so that he would have been hit first.

And when we were across the road he said, "You must always give your hand to me."

It was, in effect, what I had already begun to do. Without Behzad, without the access to the language that he gave me, I had been like a half-blind man in Tehran. (*AB*, 6)

With its uncharacteristic extended metaphor, this is an extraordinarily moving passage that binds the reader to Behzad and makes one care deeply about his future and his prospects. Something similar might well have happened to Naipaul on many of his previous foreign visits: he must often have had to rely on interpreters and guides. But never before has he expressed frankly, on such a personal level, the friendship he felt for one of these indispensable people.

Naipaul's affection for Behzad has nothing to do with political sympathy. Behzad is a revolutionary, but a Marxist, not a Muslim. Naipaul is clear-sighted about Behzad's beliefs: "His cause was as simple as his enemy's: and in the end really no more than a version of his enemy's. Both sides depended on revealed truth and a special reading of historical events; both required absolute faith. And both were fed by the same passion: justice, union, vengeance" (*AB*, 80).

With Behzad, Naipaul visits Ayatollah Shirazi, a teacher in Qom, and his usual difficulty in describing his origins takes on more serious implications. Nervous of acknowledging his Hindu background and lack of religious conviction, he allows Behzad to tell Shirazi that he was brought up a Christian: "And as soon as Behzad began to talk, I regretted what I had asked him to say. Shirazi hadn't been taken in by my equivocations; he knew that something was wrong. And I decided that I would never again on my Islamic journey, out of nervousness or a wish to simplify, complicate matters for myself like this, and consequently falsify people's response to me" (*AB*, 51). However, Behzad explains later that "if I had told him that you had no religion, he would have thought you were a communist. And that would have been bad for you" (*AB*, 53). So it may be that, despite Naipaul's resolve, Behzad had in this case saved him from a fate worse than being struck by a car in Tehran traffic.

After Iran, Naipaul moves on to Pakistan in his quest to understand the true meaning of the Islamic state, in search of "Islamic institutions and experiments" (*AB*, 112) in this country that was "meant to be . . . run on Islamic principles" (*AB*, 114). He searches in vain, finding no practical expressions of Islamic rule, only assertions that "if the state failed, it wasn't because the dream was flawed, or the faith flawed; it could only be because men had failed the faith. A purer and purer faith began to be called for" (*AB*, 90).

Once again, in Pakistan he makes friends: Ahmed, who "had known nothing about me before we met" and whose "response to me had been the pure response of man to man; and I had responded to that" (*AB*, 156), but who, in the end, distresses Naipaul by withdrawing his friendship without explanation; and Nusrat, the journalist with ambitions and "a great excited energy" (*AB*, 157), who asks Naipaul's advice about studying in the West and becoming a writer on third world journalism. Naipaul discourages him, then regrets what he has said: "Six months later, when I returned to Karachi and wondered who I should look up, I thought first of Nusrat. I found him changed. That bubbling, intelligent man had gone grey. The Islam he had wished to serve had pushed him deep into paranoia; and I regretted more than ever that momentary impulse of aggression towards him, who after all knew only Pakistan" (*AB*, 163–64). This acknowledgment goes even further than the friendship he admits for Behzad. It takes him beyond the role of observer and shows how the traveler can affect what he travels to see. Nusrat told Naipaul when he returned to Pakistan that "you've altered my life" (*AB*, 393). Although Naipaul feels that this is an exaggeration, it nevertheless shows another dimension to this kind of investigative writing.

Then there is Masood, whom Naipaul finds particularly appealing when he says, "In some countries you can believe in the life of struggle. . . . Here there is only luck." Naipaul goes on: "He didn't know how directly he was speaking to me. The idea of struggle and dedication and fulfilment, the idea of human quality, belongs only to certain societies. It didn't belong to the colonial Trinidad I had grown up in. . . . Masood's panic now, his vision of his world as a blind alley (with his knowledge that there was activity and growth elsewhere), took me back to my own panic of thirty to thirty-five years before" (*AB*, 194). With understanding and fellow-feeling, he sees Masood's simple origins in the way he eats, and "his distance from those origins . . . expressed in his fussiness and hypochondria" (*AB*, 196).

Naipaul does not condemn Islam: he can see its attractions. In Hyderabad, Pakistan, he visits a shrine and feels "that Islam had achieved community and a kind of beauty, had given people a feeling of completeness—if only the world outside could be shut out, and men could be made to forget what they knew" (*AB*, 145). However, a recurring theme in the whole book is that "parasitism is one of the unacknowledged fruits of fundamentalism" (*AB*, 158). The modern, Western world is to be spurned as corrupt and decadent, but at the same time it is to be depended upon. "All the rejection of the West is contained within the assumption that there will always exist out there a living, creative civilization, oddly neutral, open to all to appeal to" (*AB*, 168).

Muslim society is of course extremely protective of its women, and this accounts for the fact that everyone Naipaul gets to know well on this journey is male. He makes a point of meeting some "brave girls" in Malaysia after allowing himself to be vetted by their male friends, but once again, in Malaysia and Indonesia it is young men he befriends. Neither of these South-East Asian countries is an Islamic state, and he sometimes found it difficult to make contact with the Islamic organizations in these countries, where "people hide from the visitor for fear that they might be betrayed" (AB, 235). Nevertheless, in Kuala Lumpur, Naipaul is able eventually to meet Shafi, another person in whom the reader comes to feel a deep interest. Shafi, a Muslim worker for Anwar Ibrahim's youth movement, is a village boy, nagged, Naipaul suspects,

> by the inconsistency . . . between his longing for the purity of village life and his recognition of the backwardness of Malays. . . . I felt that for him the wish to re-establish the rules was also a wish to re-create the security of his childhood, the Malay village life he had lost. Some grief like that touches most of us. It is what, as individuals, responsible for ourselves, we constantly have to accommodate ourselves to. (AB, 242–43)

In Indonesia, Naipaul travels with the student Prasojo to a Muslim village school, a Pesantren, where he was astonished at the effort and organization that went into the attempt "to duplicate the village atmosphere, to teach villagers to be villagers!" (AB, 341). And then they travel to Bandung College near Jakarta to meet the famous Islamic instructor Imaduddin, who claims that he is "preparing the next generation of leaders of Indonesia . . . to replace all this"; but, Naipaul comments, "not by new institutions, but only by men as pure and cleansed as himself" (AB, 376–77).

Among the Believers is an engrossing book. It is full of judgments, many of them harsh, but, far from espousing "the cheapest and easiest of colonial mythologies about wogs and darkies," as Edward Said claims,[2] Naipaul's opinions are tempered by a feeling of personal connection with many of the people he meets, who are directly affected by and often even working for the advancement of the states that, politically and intellectually, Naipaul deplores. Its comments on Islamic fundamentalism, followed up by his later book Beyond Belief, have a lot to contribute to the understanding of more recent catastrophic events that have brought Islam dramatically to the attention of the Western world.

In his next book, Naipaul turns his analytical gaze back upon himself. Finding the Center is a short book consisting of two long essays. In his foreword he writes, "The two personal narrative pieces that make up Finding the Center were written one after the other and occupied the best part of two years. They are offered as a book principally for that reason; and also because, over and above their story content, both pieces are about the process of writing. Both pieces seek in different ways to admit the reader to that process" (FC, vii).

The first essay, "Prologue to an Autobiography," is Naipaul's first extended piece of autobiographical writing, but it is not autobiography in the sense of being a personal account of his life. When writing about Borges in "The Return of Eva Perón," he comments that "even the fifty-page 'Autobiographical Essay' doesn't violate his privacy. . . . The essay quickly becomes no more than a writer's account of his writing life" (REP, 124). Equally, "Prologue to an Autobiography" tells little about Naipaul's personal life. He writes of his family background in Trinidad, the knowledge on which he based his early books—and the facts of which he was unaware when he was writing them. Years after his father's death, Naipaul learned more from his mother about the mental disturbance his father had suffered, already described with uncanny accuracy in A House for Mr Biswas. One of the most significant things that emerges from this essay, as discussed in some detail in chapter 2, is the almost mythical status with which he endows the beginnings of Miguel Street. In many important ways, "Prologue to an Autobiography" anticipates the autobiographical tendencies of The Enigma of Arrival, a kind of impersonal but subjective writing in which there is "no family, no wife, no friends, no infidelities, nothing. . . . There's nothing about me apart from my writing."[3]

The second essay in Finding the Center, "The Crocodiles of Yamoussoukro," describes Naipaul's investigations in Ivory Coast. He explains the processes involved in his travel writing: "I travel to discover other states of mind. And if for this intellectual adventure I go to places where people live restricted lives, it is because my curiosity is still dictated in part by my colonial Trinidad background. I go to places which, however alien, connect in some way with what I already know" (FC, 90). While traveling he lives "in a novel of my own making, moving from not knowing to knowing. . . . The kind of understanding I am looking for comes best through people I get to like" (FC, 90); a fact that is clear from Among the Believers. He chose to go to Ivory Coast because "I wanted to be in an African country which, in the mess of black Africa, was generally held to be a political and economic success. African success, France in Africa—those were the glamorous ideas that took me out" (FC, 79).

Naturally, his idea of the glamour of this country becomes tempered by the reality. However, there are still many positive aspects to his assessment of this strangely mixed, modern and primitive society. He visits the presidential city of Yamoussoukro, a half-built monument to the president's benign power, and watches the emblematic crocodiles being fed their ritual meal of live chickens: "I saw the bird turned to a feathery debris in the seemingly grinning maw of one crocodile . . . round unseeing eyes apparently alight with pleasure, black feathers sticking out on either side of the jaw. A moment's ingestion, and all was gone, except for a mash in the hollow of the lower jaw. The ceremony was over. The feeder, skullcapped, prettily gowned, took his tin and walked back, unsmiling, to the Land-Rover" (*FC*, 146–47). In spite of his horrified distaste, he recognizes that this ritual "was proof both of (the President's) right to rule and the justness of his rule" (*FC*, 148). He recognizes that the Western ideal of democracy, imported to Ivory Coast, is not necessarily suited to the country:

> At the last election there had been an experiment. It was decreed that anyone in the party could contest any seat. . . . Eighty percent of the old deputies . . . had been voted out. . . . In the African tradition an elder remained an elder till he died. A man stripped of authority couldn't simply go back to being an ordinary villager; he had been personally degraded. So the democratic experiment had damaged the cohesiveness of village life. (*FC*, 85)

So, in spite of the claims of many of his critics that Naipaul idealizes Western civilization, it can be seen that he does not advocate indiscriminate Westernization in Africa. (In fact, in an interview in 1981 he had harsh words to say about his own adopted country: "England is the least-educated country in Europe. It isn't only Africans who are bow-and-arrow people, it's so many people here, living at a very high material level, who have allowed their minds to go slack."[4]) Nevertheless, considering his denunciation of expatriates in *In a Free State*, he makes a great concession here to people who work in Africa: "The doing of certain kinds of work in Africa, the practice of certain disciplines or skills from another civilization, can be like a disinterested exercise of virtue. Many expatriates—those who last in freed black Africa—become genuinely good people" (*FC*, 83). It is the expatriates, some of whom are of African descent but born, like Naipaul, in the West Indies, whom he gets to know best in Ivory Coast; and thus it is they, according to the logic of his travel writing, from whom he learns the most.

Naipaul said in 1977, after writing *India: A Wounded Civilization*, that "the book was very exhausting to write, this analysis, this shaping of chapters. I was unwilling always to describe simply; I always try to make description part of an argument." He wanted then, he said, to "go back to imagination," because "I regard the novel writing as engaging the truer part of me."[5] At that time he would have been writing *A Bend in the River*. However, he embarked on his Islamic journey only a couple of years later, presumably irresistibly drawn once more by the fascination of traveling and investigating, and came back to a kind of fictional writing only with the unique and masterly *Enigma of Arrival*.

CHAPTER NINE

A Definition of the Writing Self

The Enigma of Arrival

In an article published a year after finishing *The Enigma of Arrival*, a book concerned in a large part with the process of its own creation, Naipaul says:

> *Garden, house, plantation, gardener, estate:* these words mean one thing in England and mean something quite different to a man from Trinidad, an agricultural colony, a colony settled for the purpose of plantation agriculture. How, then, could I write honestly or fairly if the very words I used, with private meanings for me, were yet for the reader outside shot through with the associations of the older literature? I felt that truly to render what I saw, I had to define myself as writer or narrator; I had to reinterpret things . . . and after two years' work, I have just finished a book in which at last, as I think, I have managed to integrate this business of reinterpreting with my narrative.
>
> My aim was truth, truth to a particular experience, containing a definition of the writing self.[1]

Finding his own voice is only a part of Naipaul's almost obsessive interest in language in *The Enigma of Arrival* (1987), his autobiographical novel about ten years spent living in rural England. Some of this interest is explicit, some is not, but the writing constantly draws attention to itself in many different ways.

The narrative starts with literal obscurity: "For the first four days it rained. I could hardly see where I was" (*EA*, 5). As his years in the valley pass, he learns to see where he is, to understand and interpret, visually and verbally; and the two modes are closely linked: "I had slowly learned the names of shrubs and trees. That knowledge, helping me visually to disentangle one plant from another in a mass of vegetation, quickly becoming more than a knowledge of names, had added to my appreciation. It was like learning a language, after living among its sounds" (*EA*, 334).

When he first arrives at the cottage in Wiltshire, his attitude is still—at least in the hindsight of the rhetorical position of the novel—structured by his knowledge of English language and literature, his "half-English half-education" (*EA*, 245). He knows facts about the meanings of geographical names that the local people are unlikely to know—in this case, words are "shot through with associations of an older literature" that he knows and they do not. He knows, for example, "that both elements of Waldenshaw— the name of the village and the manor in whose grounds I was—I knew that both 'walden' and 'shaw' meant wood" (*EA*, 7). But even his theoretical knowledge is incomplete: it is some time before he is "able to think of the flat wet fields with ditches as 'water meadows' or 'wet meadows,' and the low smooth hills in the background, beyond the river, as 'downs'" (*EA*, 5). This passage from the second paragraph gives prominence to Naipaul's preoccupation with language and the part it plays in perception, which, together with change, decay, flux, death, and the passage of time, are deep themes in this novel.

His urge to explain and clarify differences in the meaning of words, and also social concepts, is pervasive. A discussion of the words "garden" and "gardener," for example, occupies several pages to explain why the Waldenshaw gardener, Pitton, "wasn't my idea of a gardener" (*EA*, 224). He gives a short history of gardening in Trinidad, emphasizing the low status of gardeners, an occupation for unskilled East Indians stranded in Trinidad after their periods of indentured labor had expired: "the gardener belonged to the plantation or estate past" (*EA*, 227). Even his ideas of English gardeners, picked up from P. G. Wodehouse and William Shakespeare, failed to prepare him for the reality of Pitton, "the carefully dressed, paunchy, staid figure" who "turned out to be only the gardener" (*EA*, 228).

The very fact that words have different associations in different societies, something of which he was no doubt aware when reading English books as a child, might have encouraged Naipaul's abiding interest in words —etymologies, catachreses, local usages. He loves language; he delights in words, and his delight takes him beyond the mere urge to clarify possible misunderstandings. When he was mentally ill at Oxford in the early fifties, he says, "The only thing that gave me solace, which didn't create pictures of human beings, was the intricacy of language. I lost myself in studies of the derivation of words, the design of the lettering."[2] Some of the terms he introduces in *The Enigma of Arrival* are no doubt in common usage, like "water meadows," but without any comment he calls the wide, flat way to Jack's cottage that "would have been used for carts in the old days" (*EA*, 8) the "droveway," a term that does not appear in the *Concise Oxford Dictionary*: persistent research in the *Oxford English Dictionary* reveals that its last quoted usage was in the Laws of Sewers, 1726. Whether in Wiltshire it is still in common use is not revealed in the novel; none of the other characters uses the word, but then there is not very much dialogue.

Another example is the word "accidia," in the form Naipaul uses it. In the *Concise Oxford* it occurs as "acedia" or "accidie," and only in the *OED* is it listed as a headword in the original medieval Latin form that Naipaul uses. His use of the word for his landlord's malaise, also, seems to be his own interpretation. He expresses his sorrow at Jack's illness and impending death in an oddly linguistic way, as well: "His face was waxen. I knew the word, from books. But never till now, seeing what it described on a white face, had I truly understood the word" (*EA*, 42). In this way Naipaul quietly reminds the reader of his racial difference, the color of his own face.

The interest he expresses when he learns a new usage might sometimes appear pedantic, although it is always tempered with delight. His novel is peopled with Dogberries and Mrs Malaprops, and sometimes he appears to be gently mocking them for their linguistic ineptitude. The language of these people—hard to think of them as fictional characters, although it seems that is what they are—is as crucial to his portrayal of them as their dress, habits, and behavior. Pitton, especially, is unwittingly a mine of fascinating linguistic information, to his occasional discomfiture. Naipaul remarks on the "new determinative use of the preposition 'in'" in the phrase "to pick the pears *in*—I liked that *in*. I played with it, repeated it" (*EA*, 61); and the "tying" of the saw in the wet wood they were cutting together: "I liked the word. I had never heard it before; but it was suggestive and felt right. Pitton became embarrassed" (*EA*, 264). Best of all, Naipaul loves the word "refuge," meaning "refuse" or "rubbish": "Refuse, refuge: two separate, unrelated words. But 'refuge,' which Pitton used for 'refuse,' did in the most remarkable way contain both words. Pitton's 'refuge' not only stood for 'refuse'; but had the additional idea or association, not at all inappropriate, of asylum, sanctuary, hiding, almost hide-and-seek, of things kept decently out of sight and mind" (*EA*, 201). He is further enchanted to find that the word is used in a similar way, to mean "rubbish collection," by several others in the valley. (It is, in fact, a usage listed in the *OED* as obsolete or dialectal.) Despite his idiosyncratic, or dialectal, usages and vocabulary, however, Pitton and his wife are "without the gift of words. They had trouble finding words for what they had to say, so it seemed that they had very little to say" (*EA*, 229). Bray, the car-hire man, on the other hand, is a confident talker with his own set of catachrestic usages: "'arrogant' was primarily Bray's version of 'ignorant,' but it also had the meaning of 'arrogant,' and this word, when used by Bray, with its two meanings and aggressive sound, was very strong" (*EA*, 240). And "'You know me,' he would say. 'I'm a down-and-out Tory.' Running together 'downright' and 'out-and-out'" (*EA*, 245). These people, in the heart of the

English countryside, use English just as idiosyncratically as the Trinidadians among whom Naipaul grew up, and cannot aspire to the correctness and depth of knowledge of this alien in their midst, despite his "half-education."

He is puzzled but sympathetic about people without "the gift of words." As much as he loves words himself, he is conscious of the dangers of a glib tongue, as demonstrated by Sandra in *The Mimic Men*; but to be entirely without this gift is unimaginable. A new dairyman and his wife arrive in the valley, from an unspecified "rough time in a town somewhere": "What terrors must there have been in the town for them! How could people like these, without words to put to their emotions and passions, manage? They could, at best, only suffer dumbly" (*EA*, 34). Often, though, those without the gift of words appear to greater advantage than those who use language confidently, like Bray or the central heating contractor, Michael Allen, who was "a great boaster . . . in the short time we spoke he boasted about many things, he asked me nothing about myself" (*EA*, 70). In contrast, when he finally meets Jack, the emblematic farmworker he has seen from afar working in his garden, they "looked at each other, examined each other, made noises rather than talked" (*EA*, 29). This is the way of the older generation of farmworkers—few words or none, expressing much. Jack's father-in-law, upon his only meeting with the narrator, manages only three words: "Dogs worry pheasants," but into that gnomic utterance he imparts "a little impulse of authority, even bullying, with someone who was a stranger. . . . But it was the briefest impulse in the old man; and perhaps it was also a social impulse, a wish to exchange words with someone new, a wish to add one more human being to the tally of human beings he had encountered" (*EA*, 22).

No such impulses are to be witnessed when the farm is modernized. The new farmworkers, driving to the new "milking parlour in brightly-coloured cars," are "tense young men, conscious of their style, their jeans and shirts, their moustaches and cars" (*EA*, 55), without the "dumb friendliness" (*EA*, 58) of the old farmworkers. When addressed, one of these young men "seemed bemused. . . . He mumbled something which I couldn't understand —all his style breaking down at this moment of speech" (*EA*, 56).

The way people dress and their vanities are as revealing as their speech. Naipaul dwells in some detail on Bray's chauffeur uniform: "A cardigan can be unbuttoned and buttoned in many ways; it can suggest formality, casualness, indifference . . . and the peaked cap—it could be set at many different angles: it could express regard or disregard. . . . It would have been harder for him without the cap; he would have had to find words, set his face in different ways. . . . The peaked cap, with its many angles, together with the various ways of wearing the cardigan, enabled Bray to make (and make clear) a whole range of subtle judgments" (*EA*, 247).

But styles of dress, like those of the young couple Brenda and Les, can show a more damaging self-obsession, and the narrator sees in their vanities the symptoms, if not the seeds, of their tragedy. After her brief affair with Michael Allen, Brenda returns to her husband and apparently taunts him into stabbing her to death. Once again the narrator is at odds with the society he inhabits: "It took some understanding that people who were so proud and flaunting in one way should be prepared in another corner of their hearts or souls or minds to go down several notches and be servants. . . . Within that condition (which should have neutered them) all their passions were played out." A startling observation: it is, however, immediately qualified: "But that might have been my own special prejudice, my own raw nerves. I came from a colony, once a plantation society, where servitude was a more desperate condition" (EA, 66). "Servant" is another word he might have added to his list of words that "mean something quite different to a man from Trinidad,"[3] and not only the word, but its application to the situation. Les and Brenda would not use the word to describe themselves, although Bray does share the narrator's prejudice: "His vocation was really to be a free man, not to be what his father had been, a man 'in service,' a servant" (EA, 243). For both men, the horror of servitude is a burden carried from childhood.

Sometimes the narrator's use of figurative language can be startling as well. He describes, for example, Jack's father-in-law's routine as "animal-like": "Like a rat, he seemed to have a 'run'" (EA, 23); but a few pages later he includes himself in his animal metaphor, describing "the [farm] manager's run, almost circular . . . ," which was "also Jack's; and it was partly mine" (EA, 28), turning his detached view of other characters onto his younger self.

Some of the people he describes are foreign to him in every way, and he observes them with a distant, if compassionate, interest. There are others, like Bray, for whom he has some fellow-feelings. The landlord also seems a kindred spirit: "coming to the manor at a time of disappointment and wounding, I felt an immense sympathy for my landlord, who, starting at the other end of the world, now wished to hide, like me. I felt a kinship with him. . . . I never thought his seclusion strange. It was what I wanted for myself at that time" (EA, 191–92). He compares stages of his own life with those of his landlord's, noting that "in 1949 or 1950–1950 being the year I had left my own home island . . . my landlord had withdrawn from the world" (EA, 217). The landlord, too, is or was an artist of sorts, claiming a kinship with the narrator by sending copies of his poems and drawings as gifts via the housekeeper Mrs Phillips, although they never actually meet.

More troubling for the narrator is Alan, the landlord's cousin, whom he gets to know well. Alan is, in himself, a cautionary tale—a warning of what can happen to an artist without the self-discipline or drive to produce work of any significance. He describes "Alan the writer, the man with the child-hood, the man with the sensibility. I understood this idea of the writer because it was so like my own when I had first come to England. . . . And that writer's personality of Alan's was partly genuine, and no more fraudulent than my own character, my idea of myself as a writer, had been in 1950" (*EA*, 287). But Alan, unlike Naipaul, could produce "no novel or autobiographical novel (setting the record straight, showing the truth behind the shiny bright clothes and the clowning manner); no critical study of contemporary literature (which he sometimes spoke about); no Isherwood-like book about post-war Germany, which he spoke about at other times" (*EA*, 287–88).

Alan's love of language and of idiosyncratic behavior is like the narrator's. The narrator is touched by his flattery: "It was hard, once Alan had told you he was making 'notes' about you, to ignore him, hard not to start acting up (even like my landlord) to an intelligent, friendly man who might indeed be making notes about all the things you were saying" (*EA*, 291). Alan's speech is as flamboyant as his dress. He refers to the landlord's style as that of "before the deluge" and sometimes refers to Mr Phillips (whom he usually calls Stan) as "Phillips" in the old style, as if he were a butler or a footman. But one day Alan rings the narrator, after an absence of a year, in a drunken state:

> hardly able to control his words, he was seeking only to send messages
> of love, to flatter, to speak to me about my work.
>
> And he was asking nothing in return. For there was, as it were, no
> means of getting back to the person from whom all this issued. The per-
> son that wished to buy peace from the world was beyond the reach of
> the world, was hardly known, it might be said, to Alan himself. It didn't
> matter how much one flattered back; it didn't matter how much love
> one sent back, one could never touch the true person. (*EA*, 292–93)

The portrait of Alan is the most poignant feature of a book full of poignancy. Not long after this phone call, he takes an overdose of pills and dies. "It was a theatrical kind of death. Theatre would not have been far from Alan's mind that evening" (*EA*, 294). Theatricality, or the feeling of being in a play or a film or a novel, forms a constant theme in Naipaul's description of his own youth—the feeling that the world of literature is "the real world" (*EA*, 129). Alan's tragedy is that he never manages, as Naipaul has managed, to discover himself and to enter the actual real world outside literature, despite his frankness on "approved topics" (*EA*, 288).

His friendship with Alan is one of the most intimate relationships the narrator describes with anyone in this novel. This is a measure of the novel's unusual nature, which reads like a prose poem, or an essay, or an autobiographical memoir. Critics have difficulty with the categorization of the book, some rejecting altogether its definition as a novel. Robert Royal, for example, writes, "The narrator's story is to all appearances a memoir of Naipaul's life";[4] and Selwyn R. Cudjoe mounts a political attack: "His studied act of refusal/defense in calling *The Enigma of Arrival* a novel can be described as nothing more than an attempt to deflect the painful consequences of his decision: his inability to face up to the implications of his colonial origins."[5] Cudjoe's reading is selective: the novel in several ways focuses directly on the very subject of his colonial origins. If he had described it as an autobiography, Naipaul himself says, "I think I would be run out of town, because there's no autobiography there—no family, no wife, no friends, no infidelities, nothing. That whole bit of life is torn out. There's nothing about me apart from my writing."[6]

In another interview he said, "I had to identify my narrator, my seeing eye, my feeling person. I didn't want to invent a character and give him a bogus adventure to set him there [in the English countryside]. I thought I should make the writer be myself—let that be true and within that set the fictional composite picture because you can't use real people to hang philosophical ideas about flux and change."[7]

The people of this novel, then, despite the ease with which critics "in the know" identify them with real-life equivalents, are to be regarded as fictional. The characters are viewed from a distance: their actions, their comings and goings, their deaths and loves —all occur offstage, as it were. The illusion of reality in this novel is, oddly, heightened by this scrupulous limitation of the narrator's point of view. The characters all seem to exist independently. Everything that he finds out about them comes to him either via his own observation and speculation or as hearsay through one of his informants—Bray, Mrs Phillips, Alan, Jack's wife. The uncertainty belongs equally to the narrator and the reader: any discussion of events outside his knowledge is clearly identified as speculation, such as his contemplation of Les's murder of Brenda: "And it was hard not to feel that she didn't have some idea of what she was provoking. And how, having started on the job of destruction—he had used a kitchen knife—having started on that, from which very quickly there was no turning back, however much in a corner of his mind he might have been wishing it all undone, healed again, how he must have struck, until the madness and the life was over! All in that little thatched cottage with the ruined garden" (*EA*, 74).

The expansive, digressive nature of the narrative is unusual for a novel. People who play hardly any part in the action are described in some detail, like Brenda's sister, coming to "collect Brenda's things" (*EA*, 75), who is treated in the way a real person would be treated in a memoir of someone linguistically perceptive. She describes her father's wartime dealings with

"Ministry of Defence," and the narrator comments, "I didn't think she was romancing. Her use of the words 'Ministry of Defence' without the definite article—the *the* that the average person would have wanted to add; was convincing" (*EA*, 77). In a more conventional fiction, there would be no need for the narrator—or the author—to comment on the verisimilitude of the character's vocabulary. The novel's peculiar brilliance lies in its convincingly incomplete portrayals of people who seem utterly real and its muted reportage of the events, major and minor, in their lives. It is ultimately unprofitable, however seductive it might be, to try to sift the fiction from the reality. It is certainly not the point of the novel.

Naipaul writes slowly and instructs his audience to read slowly: "You've got to rest after reading twenty good pages. You've got to stop and think. I read very slowly. It's very natural. My paragraphs are very rich—they have to be read. Many things are happening in the paragraph. If you miss a paragraph —if you miss a page—it's hard to get back into it."[8] He denounces conscious style, smoothness, and rhythm in prose, believing that these attributes lead to "the killing of sense."[9] It is undeniable that there is a Naipaul style, although it varies slightly from book to book; there is a dryness, a plainness, a hesitation to use adverbs, adjectives, or superlatives; there is sometimes a slightly unusual usage or an archaic word; there is frequent repetition and echoing of words and phrases; and sometimes a ruminative exclamation. In *The Enigma of Arrival* there is a particular emphasis on repetition.

Judith Levy has written perceptively on the language of this work (in a way that sometimes echoes Naipaul's discussion of the language of his characters). She draws attention to the "multiple effects" of the repetitions within a paragraph, and the use of repeated nouns where pronouns might be expected. To her, for one thing, "they indicate a tendency towards a more concrete, and hence, in developmental terms, a more primitive level of expression. For another, they create a process of defamiliarization, a drawing attention to the sound of the word that creates a split between the apprehension of the objects and the language used."[10] The repetitions give a rhetorical force—and, as Naipaul must surely realize, a rhythm—to the prose; but to break the trance this might produce in the reader, he will often digress in midsentence, referring to something distantly related to the theme in hand, which can result in long, complex sentences. The effect is to slow down the reading, to force the reader to go back, let the sense sink in.

Often these digressions will refer to something already mentioned; occasionally they foreshadow something to come. He describes, for example, the gardens of the row of cottages of which Jack's forms part: "Technically, the gardens were at the front of the cottages. In fact, by long use, the back of the cottages had become the front; and the front gardens had really become back gardens" (*EA*, 17). Thereafter, when he mentions Jack's garden he will say "the garden at the front (or back) of his cottage" (*EA*, 28), or "at the back of his cottage—the back being where the true front now was" (*EA*, 30). These echoes contribute to the timeless, or cyclical, nature of the novel, especially the parts that describe the narrator's time in Wiltshire: "Jack's Garden," "Ivy," and "Rooks." Part 2, "The Journey," and part 5, "The Ceremony of Farewell," are more chronologically linear; while the other parts, because of the echoing and foreshadowing, and the tendency to dwell on one theme or to tell one person's story complete and then come back and tell another, have a nebulous sense of time. This is in part a technique designed to emphasize the stages of human life: to see people as they change through time rather than to show them as actors in brief, dramatic episodes over which they have control. He meets the farm manager after his retirement and is moved to observe, "How quickly a man's time passed! So quickly, in fact, that it was possible within a normal span to witness, to comprehend, two or three active life-cycles in succession" (*EA*, 82). But although he describes them when he describes the encounter, he stresses that these thoughts came to him much later, when his time at the cottage and the manor was over and "middle age had come as abruptly to me as old age appeared to me to have come to the old manager" (*EA*, 83). The death of Jack is described early in the novel, and "the way he had asserted, at the very end, the primacy not of what was beyond life, but life itself" (*EA*, 93) becomes emblematic. His function as the inspiration for this novel is referred to, in self-referential, postmodern style, in the novel's final sentence.

The narrator's sense of history—where he is in his life, compared to other people and events, as well as the relation of his lifetime to the course of history—is constantly demonstrated by references to dates and inscriptions on buildings, and the rhetoric of architecture itself. He notices the "ordinary little houses, two or three of which carried—their only fanciful touch—the elaborate monogram of the owner or builder or designer, with the date, which was, surprisingly, a date from the war: 1944" (*EA*, 8). He discusses the churches of the district: the Gothic church with "a primitive painting of Doomsday" (*EA*, 300), the former Victorian Sunday school, the mission hut, the Wesleyan chapel, and the renovated church near the manor:

> This church was an age away from the religious anxiety of the Doomsday painting of St Thomas's in Salisbury: the sense of an arbitrary world, full of terrors, where men were naked and helpless and only God gave protection. The parish church had been renovated at the time the great Victorian houses and manors of the region were being built. And it was of that confident period: as much as a faith, it celebrated a culture, a national pride, a power, men very much in control of their destinies.

> ... The very scantiness of the parish-church congregation ... sup-
> ported the idea of an enclosed, excluding cultural celebration. (*EA*,
> 301–2)

This "celebration" has no room for "Jack, who celebrated life where he lived"
(*EA*, 302), or Bray (or, presumably, Naipaul himself). These people, whom
he sees as English "types" when he first comes to the manor, he can now see
do not belong to the smug security of English country life any more than he
does. He can feel himself included in their exclusion, breaking down the
alienation he feels as a colonial subject in the heart of the "mother country."

Along with his attention to dates and buildings, and their place in history,
he cultivates vagueness in quantifying his time at the manor cottage. It is
clear that he spent ten years there, and that he arrived there about twenty
years after his arrival in England in 1950. But within that stretch of years,
time seems elastic, and although it might be possible to construct a chronology for the novel's events during those ten years, the narrative deliberately
discourages such attempts, in parallel with the narrator's difficulty in dating
events after the memorable first year: "Time altered for me. At first, as in
childhood, it had stretched. The first spring had contained so much that was
clear and sharp—the moss rose, the single blue iris, the peonies under
my window. I had waited for the year to repeat. Then memories began to be
jumbled; time began to race; the years began to stack together; it began to
be hard for me to date things" (*EA*, 299). Distances, also, are rarely given
exactly, or even quantities or dimensions: "two or three" houses (*EA*, 8), the
"very big silage pit" (*EA*, 57), the "very wide" droveway (*EA*, 23).

In part 5 this reluctance to specify dates disappears, and the reader is encouraged to put a time scale against events, starting with "a journalistic assign-
ment ... in August 1984" (*EA*, 344). Itineraries of the travels of Naipaul and
his brother Shiva, taking them to and from Trinidad on the occasion of their
sister's death, are given in some detail. With part 5, the healing of the time
in Wiltshire is completed and it is time to reenter the real world; not the
"real world" of literature, but the real world where relatives die, where planes
must be caught and arrangements made. The time in Wiltshire, which is the
true subject of the novel, is to be considered whole, not broken down into
quantities or time spans: just a magical decade of healing, for the narrator,
and a procession of people to be observed, to exemplify "philosophical ideas
about flux and change."[11]

His place in this world, which at the time he arrives seems "perfection,"
he recognizes, is a by-product of the empire and cannot last, but he does not
regard this as a disadvantage, compared to the "privilege" of his landlord:
"Whatever my spiritual state at the moment of arrival, I knew I would have
to save myself and look for health; I knew I would have to act at some time.

His privilege—his house, his staff, his income, the acres he could look down at every day and know to be his—this privilege could press him down into himself, into non-doing and nullity" (*EA*, 192). His image of his landlord, constructed from hearsay, is valuable to him, and he is "nervous of undoing the magic of the place. If I had seen my landlord . . . he would have been endowed with a 'character,' with vanities, irritations, absurdities; and this would have led me to make judgments—the judgments that, undoing acceptance, can also undo a relationship" (*EA*, 192–93). The distance between them is somehow contained in Naipaul's failure ever to use his landlord's name, although the term he always uses, "my landlord," has an oddly intimate, proprietary ring. Perhaps "my landlord" in the novel is just that—the concept the narrator has of the man that belongs to him alone.

Naming is, as always, important. The narrator himself never reveals his own name. A letter from Angela, his 1950 boardinghouse friend, is addressed to "Victor," because this was the English name she had given him when they first met, his "Hindi or Sanskrit name [being] too hard for her" (*EA*, 175). Since the narrator is so little an actor in the Wiltshire sections of the narrative, no other character ever speaks his name in dialogue. The assumption is there to be made that the narrator can be identified with Naipaul himself, even without the external evidence. His presence in the novel is pervasive and provides an overall context for his judgments. He views his characters without condemning them, but judgments, discriminations, and even criticism are certainly not absent. Yet, seeing so clearly the frame within which the narrative is set and the angle from which the narrator is seeing, it is not possible for the reader to interpret his judgments as anything but provisional. For example, when Bray, the car-hire man, begins to talk of religion, "I barely took it in, heard it simply as part of his chattering everyday irony. . . . As soon as I understood that he was speaking in earnest, my vision of him changed. In the same features, the same way of speaking, I saw not the glibness of his cynicism but personal feeling and, soon, passion" (*EA*, 302–3). The narrator, also, makes these judgments only in the sense that he measures people's behavior against his own explicitly personal and idiosyncratic value system, then attempts to understand, with a deep acceptance, how those values differ.

In describing his relations with other characters in the novel, the narrator is detached, an observer rather than an actor, even when he is personally involved. One friendship ends when Pitton, having lost his job as gardener at the manor, manages after a difficult period to begin a new life in Salisbury: "Pitton, in this last decade of active life, grew out of what he had been. He got to know more people, at work, and on the council estate where he lived. . . . Gradually he stopped acknowledging me from the laundry van.

One day in Salisbury, in that pedestrian shopping street where he had tried to fill me with his own panic, one day he saw me. And then—the new man—he didn't 'see' me" (*EA*, 283–84). There is no reference to the pain this snub might have caused the narrator; the context is wholly that of Pitton's recovery after a difficult period, his becoming a "new man."

The Enigma of Arrival is about flux and decay, change, life cycles, and death; but it is also a meditation, an essay, even a treatise, on language. Everything about it is artful, and attention is constantly drawn to the fact. Naipaul traces the development of his novel in part 5:

> I had thought for years about a book like *The Enigma of Arrival*. . . .
>
> My theme, the narrative to carry it, my characters—for some years I felt they were sitting on my shoulder, waiting to declare themselves and to possess me. But it was only out of this new awareness of death that I began at last to write. Death was the motif; it had perhaps been the motif all along. (*EA*, 243–44)

Death is not an oppressive motif, but one that shows "life and man as the mystery" (*EA*, 354). It is typified by the narrator's inference that Jack asserted "at the very end, the primacy not of what was beyond life, but life itself" (*EA*, 93).

Perhaps for someone like Jack—with his "intellectual backwardness, his purely physical nature" (*EA*, 233)—wordless happiness is possible, but for Naipaul the joy of words is fundamental. Talking of his father, he said, "He was unhappy much of the time. But he had a tremendous gift for joy which I share. Happiness is a kind of passive animal state, isn't it? Whereas joy is a positive sensation of delight in a particular thing—a joke, another person, a meal—and you can have it in the middle of deep gloom."[12] In his best writing, whatever its subject, delight in words and language is one of Naipaul's most attractive characteristics. He describes how, when writing *A House for Mr Biswas*, "the right words seemed to dance above my head; I plucked them down at will,"[13] and a similar assurance and ease characterizes *The Enigma of Arrival*. Memento mori this book might be, but its gloom is suffused with the unquenchable joy in words that Naipaul evinces on every page; "that reawakened delight in language" (*EA*, 344) that came with the acknowledgment of the experience that prompted the writing of the book.

But the narrator of *The Enigma of Arrival*, who seems so transparently the author, is, of course, a creature made only of language. English critic John Bayley, in his review of the novel, perceives this duality: "To such a writer as Naipaul, for the purpose of understanding himself and others, and for the purposes of fiction, it is clearly necessary to have a deep and imaginative sense of the dual nature of individuals, their existence in two worlds, both in different ways precarious. Naipaul thoroughly understands the romance of himself . . . the inner saga of himself and his destiny which each person secretly carries alongside the physical circumstances of his existence. His own sense of himself comes out in this book with a gentle, meticulous candor, wholly absorbing and illuminating."[14] And putting this self in the foreground, focusing the narrative almost pedantically through it, is designed to provide the moral context for his own vision. As Peggy Nightingale says, "The goal of all Naipaul's writing, which arises from his personal need to explain his own dislocation and to triumph over its debilitating effects, is to order experience in such a way that readers discern the elements of fantasy which distort perception and understanding."[15] It is in *The Enigma of Arrival* that he has most perfectly achieved this goal. Bayley says, "No other writer today could produce anything like it,"[16] and this is not an empty truism but a recognition of the very essence of this novel.

CHAPTER TEN

Capturing the Reality Later Travel Books

Naipaul has always been tempted by the idea of endings: of finishing his career, writing his last book. Even death has its attractions for him. His desire for completion seems especially strong in respect to his travel writing. Speaking in 1977 of *India: A Wounded Civilization*, he said: "I take it very seriously, this part of my work. But this is the end. The book was very exhausting to write. . . . I've spent all this year trying to wash myself clean of this. I want to go back to imagination. I want to stay here. It doesn't mark the beginning, it marks the end."[1]

India: A Wounded Civilization has, nonetheless, been followed by four significant books of travel; *Among the Believers*, which was discussed in chapter 8, and three books that will be looked at in this chapter: *A Turn in the South, India: A Million Mutinies Now,* and *Beyond Belief.*

This inclination for renunciation may be related to the need he sees to "write every book as though it is the final work, the summing up,"[2] although something new always appears after all to occupy his attention. In 1995 he said: "I can't do things again once I've done them as well as I can do them. . . . So it's time to do something else. There are always more things to do. I have a restless mind. It is my age, my health and my vitality that are now getting in the way and making me slow up a little. The world is full of excitement for me. Reality is always changing. It changes constantly and the writer has to find new ways of capturing the reality."[3]

In regard to *A Turn in the South*, he gave a very practical reason for resuming travel writing. A technological innovation came to his aid: "I was physically tired of the act of writing, my wrists ached and my handwriting became illegible. I became very agitated about the way I would keep my journal, keep my notes. . . . [A small electronic typewriter] was like an answer to my prayers. It has altered my life; I was able to make my notes by hand and then work almost immediately on this wonderful instrument."[4]

Also, he says that in the southern states of the United States, he learned "how to travel in a new way."[5] He allowed himself to be guided to a greater extent by the people he met on his journey. He let them speak for themselves and he stayed in the background, moving on in this way from his subjective travel books, which were as much about himself as the places he visited, to a more transparent representation of the points of view of the people he met. This new technique was hardly a sudden revolution, however. In *Among the Believers* he had already started to let his interpreters and guides play an important part in his narrative. In *A Turn in the South,* of course, there was no need for interpreters (although he sometimes had trouble with the southern accents), and therefore in many ways it describes a different kind of experience.

Stephen Schiff remarks that this book "is virtually gaga about the redneck culture and country-music lyrics and black church choirs. There is little about racism in it."[6] But on the contrary, the book deals directly with racial issues, and the word "redneck" is not even used in the first two-thirds of the book. Perhaps Schiff was expecting a more political book denouncing white racism without attempting to understand its history, a kind of book Naipaul is not equipped to write.

In the first half of *A Turn in the South* Naipaul visits Atlanta, Charleston, Tallahassee, and Tuskegee. Explaining the genesis of this project, which he first contemplated when attending the 1984 Republican National Convention in Dallas, he once again explicitly states that this book is the end, rounding off a career of travel writing begun more than twenty years before:

> My first travel book . . . had been about some of the former slave colonies of the Caribbean and South America. . . . It seemed to me fitting that my last travel book—travel on a theme—should be about the old slave states of the American Southeast.
>
> My thoughts . . . were about the race issue. I didn't know then that that issue would quickly work itself out during the journey, and that my subject would become that other South—of order and faith, and music and melancholy—which I didn't know about. (*TS,* 25)

For Naipaul, the South is full of small surprises. Indeed, there would hardly be any point in traveling and writing such books if this element of the unexpected were not present. The first surprise came to him at the Easter service in Bowen, North Carolina:

> I began to feel the pleasures of the religious meeting: the pleasures of brotherhood, union, formality, ritual, clothes, music, all combining to create a possibility of ecstasy.

> It was the formality—derived by these black people from so many
> sources—that was the surprise; and the idea of community. (*TS*, 15)

This church service, which he attended on a preliminary foray into the
South from New York before the main journey started later in the year, was
just the beginning of his discovery of "the other South." He can hardly be
said to ignore the issue of race: for the first half of the book he concentrates
on meeting black people and other minorities. And he always relates what
he sees to his own background: "Perhaps in a society of many groups or races
everyone, unless he is absolutely secure, lives with a special kind of stress.
Growing up in multiracial Trinidad as a member of the Indian community
. . . I always knew how important it was not to fall into nonentity" (*TS*, 33).

With this consciousness, and the history of the South—slavery and the
Civil War—always in mind, Naipaul explores the present. He speaks with
sympathetic perplexity about the Confederate Memorial in Columbia, South
Carolina: "On one side: birth, faith, duty, suffering, and death. On the other
side: the nameless, undefined cause, ennobled by these virtues. . . . The pain
of defeat is something that can be shared by everyone, since everyone at
some stage in his life knows defeat of some sort and hopes in his heart to
undo it, or at least to have his cause correctly seen" (*TS*, 100). But, he continues, "how could such a cause"—that is, slavery—"be defended?" (*TS*, 101).
He never finds an adequate intellectual solution to this question. As he sees
it, the cause is suppressed, never mentioned, and what remains on the surface is the melancholy of defeat, suffusing the culture. However, in spite
of this disturbing undercurrent, he found that "the great discovery of my
travels . . . in the South" had been that "in no other part of the world had I
found people so driven by the idea of good behavior and the good religious
life. And that was true for black and white" (*TS*, 164).

The career of Booker T. Washington, and the college he founded at
Tuskegee, is of special interest. Naipaul visits Tuskegee and finds himself
impressed by its grandeur: "There was nothing slavelike or Trinidad-like about
Tuskegee: nothing to be excused. . . . It was an achievement on the American
scale: scores and scores of dark-red Georgian brick buildings" (*TS*, 139). He
soon notices, however, that dilapidation is setting in, although he cannot
mention it to his hosts: "A kind of silence was imposed on the visitor, as in a
private house; certain things were not to be seen" (*TS*, 149). He reads and
rereads the works of Washington and W. E. B. DuBois with a growing sensi-
tivity to the circumstances in which they were written: "I began to see [Wash-
ington's *Up From Slavery*] as a painful coded work, making separate signals
even in a single paragraph to Northerners, Southerners, and blacks," all the
time "making it clear that as a black man he knew his place" (*TS*, 153). He

goes on: "So many snares: so many people to please; so many contradictions to resolve; so many possibilities of destruction. The achievement was great. But at what cost. He died at the age of fifty-nine" (*TS*, 154).

In the second half of the book, Naipaul decided "to consider things from the white point of view, as far as that was possible for me" (*TS*, 158), a muted reminder of his own racial difference not only from southern Blacks but from white people as well. His discovery of redneck culture was the kind of accident upon which his work thrives. Meeting Campbell, who he had been told was "the new kind of young conservative," Naipaul spoke with him "of family and values and authority . . . all quite predictably, until it occurred to me to ask, 'Campbell, what do you understand by the word "redneck"?'" (*TS*, 204). What resulted was "a full and beautiful and lyrical account, an account that ran it all together, by a man who half looked down on and half loved the redneck" (*TS*, 203–4). Moved by this account, Naipaul began to look more closely and sympathetically at redneck culture. But never far from his mind is "the old sentimentality of the South, the divided mind, the beauty and sorrow of the past containing the unmentionable, ragged, black thing of slavery" (*TS*, 218–19).

Naipaul does not make himself disappear completely in this book. He often contrasts what he finds, in the history of the South and the legacy of that history, with his Caribbean past. He comments from time to time on the pains and difficulties of his journey, such as the severity of his asthma in the humidity of Tallahassee and Tuskegee, and the relief of an air-conditioned hotel room in Jackson. But there are positive pleasures as well:

> Driving back one stormy afternoon in Mississippi from the Delta to Jackson . . . I began to be aware of the great pleasure I had taken in traveling in the South. . . .
>
> And I thought that afternoon that it would have completed my pleasure if I didn't have to write anything. . . . But if I wasn't writing, if I didn't have a purpose and at times a feeling of urgency . . . would I have even come to Mississippi? (*TS*, 221)

As so often, he expresses that tension between the urge to exercise the vocation and the wish to be rid of it.

Naipaul's experience in the South was of a different order to that related in *Among the Believers*. In the Muslim countries he usually needed an interpreter, and this gave a special quality to his travels. In the South, although he met and perhaps befriended many people, there is rarely such an immediate sense of close personal connection as he had with Behzad and his other guides in the earlier book. One of the exceptions is a conversation with a waitress in the Research Triangle in North Carolina. Paula abruptly abandons her professional spiel and confides that she is about to leave her job and move to Wilmington. Naipaul responds immediately on a personal level, asking if she had finished packing, and she reassures him:

> "I'll just throw it all in the Chevy.". . .
> "You really think it will all go in the Chevy?" It had become one of my own little anxieties about traveling and the hotel life. (*TS*, 280)

After the rather detached, contemplative character of the book, Naipaul's conversation with Paula is a delightful glimpse not only of this young woman and her beliefs, the practicalities and ideals of her individual existence, but also of Naipaul's gift of empathy, his willingness to listen to her story. For this reason, although he also describes a sympathetic connection with other people he meets, such as the poet James Applewhite, this short passage is one of the most appealing parts of the book, giving the impression of a genuine two-way communication with someone unexpected.

Naipaul often found in the South that people he spoke to were defensive at first about their beliefs and way of life, which were "easy to ridicule," and that they found his "degree of understanding" surprising and pleasing (*TS*, 295). Nowhere does Naipaul allow himself to ridicule beliefs that he does not share. There is no satire in this book, any more than there is in *Among the Believers,* although white, rightwing southerners of the United States might seem to many liberals an easy and natural target for satire. Perhaps it is for this reason that Schiff made the comment that "there is little about racism" in *A Turn in the South.*[7]

The great achievement of Naipaul's next book, *India: A Million Mutinies Now,* is to see through the difficult, painful, and often threatening present to a vision of hope for the future. *India: A Wounded Civilization* ended on a note of muted optimism. Twelve years later Naipaul allows this optimism to blossom into a prediction that India will grow in stature, find its feet in the world, and become a mature, thinking society conscious of its own history. Such a transition will not be easy, however. He believes the country will have to go through a period of troubled adolescence to reach maturity: "Independence had come to India like a kind of revolution: now there were many revolutions within that revolution. . . . All over India scores of particularities that had been frozen by foreign rule, or by poverty or lack of opportunity or abjectness had begun to flow again" (*IMMN*, 6). Pf course this new freedom has a dangerous aspect: "Independence was worked for by people more or less at the top; the freedom it brought has worked its way down. People everywhere have ideas now of who they are and what they owe themselves. . . . The liberation of spirit that has come to India could not come as release alone. In India, with its layer below layer of distress and cruelty, it had to come as disturbance. It had to come as rage and revolt. India was now a country of a million little mutinies" (*IMMN*, 517).

On this journey though India, Naipaul talks to people involved in many conflicting campaigns and battles, some of them violent. In the south he talks to Brahmins and anti-Brahmins; in the north he gets to know Sikh terrorists and their victims. He meets communists and descendents of Rajas, politicians and journalists. Commenting upon the passion of magazine editor Vishwa Nath, he admits with something like regret what has elsewhere been a matter of pride: "he had what I had never had: a clear idea of the enemy" (*IMMN*, 400). The idea of the enemy, relatively benign in this journalist committed to producing simple instruction and reassurance for underprivileged women in his magazine *Women's Era*, becomes lethal in the case of the terrorists. The psychology of their reactions upon witnessing the outcome of their attacks is expounded with disturbing clarity: "The resulting shock and grief would have confirmed the terrorists in their idea of power, would have confirmed them in their fantasy that it was open only to them to act, and that—as in some fairytale—an enchantment lay over everyone else, rendering them passive" (*IMMN*, 424). And further, "in that atmosphere some of the good and poetic concepts of Sikhism were twisted. One such idea was the idea of *seva* or service. When terror became an expression of the faith, the idea of seva altered" (*IMMN*, 446). Naipaul is hardly condoning terrorism, but he is attempting to explain its origins and motives, which is indisputably an urgent task in the contemporary world.

He is equally interested in finding out about the genesis of people's commitment to causes, whether they are Sikh, Hindu, Muslim, or communist, because the promptings are remarkably similar. He notes that for Mr Palani, an anti-Brahmin in Mylapore, "his cause made his world complete, left no room for doubt, supplied explanations for everything" (*IMMN*, 235). In the same manner, he was struck by the way that the Naxalite communist activist Dipanjan in Calcutta "spoke of the distress of India: as though it was a personal idea, a personal observation, as though his group observed it better than others and with more understanding, as though this distress was something they were entitled to refer to, to explain their actions" (*IMMN*, 316). It takes a very cool head to refrain from condemnation of actions that include murder, especially when the terrorists' cause is not felt to be just. But, as Naipaul has said, he is "not interested in attributing *fault*,"[8] he is interested in understanding. He has also made the point that this book "is not oral history: it's an account of a civilization at a hinge moment. It's done through human experience. . . . The idea came to me that the truth about India wasn't what I thought about India, it's what they are living through."[9]

The nearest he seems to come to criticizing anyone in this book is, strangely, when describing the sheltered life of a *pujari,* a performer of Hindu religious rites, in Bombay: "He looked inwards and was serene: he shut out the rest of the world. Or, as might be said, he allowed other people to keep the world going. It wasn't a way of looking which his fellows in the community had. . . . But it made him a good pujari" (*IMMN,* 84). One might remark that this man was doing little harm compared with the terrorists and others given to violent actions on behalf of their causes, who attract less of his criticism, although certainly not his active approval. However, in this book Naipaul seems determined to revise his own well-documented distrust of causes, perhaps bending over a little too far backward to acknowledge the importance of commitment and the "million mutinies" in contributing to India's progress. On the other hand, several of his Brahmin friends who seem as inward-looking as the *pujari,* their way of life threatened, are treated with more sympathy. It is hard for him, he says, "not to feel sad at the undoing of a culture. But the brahmin cause—if such a cause existed—could not be isolated from all the other Indian causes. It was better to see the undoing of a culture . . . as part of a more general movement forward" (*IMMN,* 274).

He does not, of course, claim that India's situation has improved uniformly throughout the country. He notices, on the road south from Goa, that "there was nothing like the destitution I had seen 26 years before. . . . The land was almost beautiful, almost without pain for the beholder" (*IMMN,* 149). But Indian cities are still not good places to live: "Bad architecture in a poor tropical city is more than an aesthetic matter. It spoils people's day-to-day lives; it wears down their nerves; it generates rages that can flow into many different channels" (*IMMN,* 281). Calcutta, especially, is a dying city: "Everybody was suffering, . . . transport was so hard that working people gave up jobs they needed because they feared the suffering of the travel; . . . no one had clean water or air; and no one could go walking" (*IMMN,* 347). Indian traffic was hellish; in Bangalore overloaded trucks "were driven fast and close to one another, as though metal was unbreakable and made man a god" (*IMMN,* 150).

He feels empathy with a young woman he meets in Bangalore who had had a similar clannish Indian childhood to his own, "an early introduction to the ways of the world, and to the nature of cruelty," which, he suspected, gave them both "a taste for the other kind of life, the solitary or less crowded life" (*IMMN,* 178). But he makes sure that other preferences are also represented in his account. There is a remarkable description of a family of five who choose to live in a *chawl,* a single room, ten feet square, rather than the larger apartment their improved circumstances have made possible. It was not an ideological decision. Mrs Ghate "had suffered in the comparative seclusion and spaciousness of the self-contained apartment"—three hundred square feet—and it became necessary for her emotional stability and the family's happiness to return to the crowded family life they had been used to, the same environment that drove Naipaul himself, when visiting, "near to stomach-heave, by the smell" (*IMMN,* 60).

Characteristically, Naipaul makes the process of his research part of his narrative. "On this kind of journey knowledge can sometimes come slowly; the traveler can sometimes listen selectively; and certain things—because they appear to fit the country or the culture—can be taken too much for granted" (*IMMN,* 243). On this journey, as well, there were some problems with language: not all the people he spoke to were English-speakers. Interviewing some Maoist anti-Brahmin rebels in Madras via an interpreter, he was puzzled: "I didn't know what to make of what I had heard. There were so few word-pictures in what they had said, so few details. That might have been because of the translation, or because of the formality of our meeting, or because they had spoken their stories too often" (*IMMN,* 277).

For similar reasons, he was careful about choosing whom to interview in the Bombay mafia: "I thought it would be better for me to meet someone lower down, not of don status, someone not so interviewed, someone who had not formalized his experience to such a degree, and might still have something to say" (*IMMN,* 70). Always wishing to provide concrete details for his readers, he tries to get people to help him see things as they do. Talking to Dipanjan, the Naxalite activist, he said, "I hadn't got many pictures from his narrative. He had gone to the villages—how had he done that? Had he just taken a bus or a train to a particular village? Could he go beyond certain abstractions—'workers,' 'villages,' 'peasants,' 'repression'?" (*IMMN,* 320).

He is also intent upon letting the reader share his own experiences: the journey (often difficult) in a hire car or taxi to the interview, the room in which the interview takes place, and the physical appearance of the people he meets, their mannerisms and dress, are often described vividly. A lengthy and affectionate description of the sitting room of a Shiv Sena activist in Bombay concludes: "The little pink-walled room was really quite full of things to look at: much thought here, much pride. . . . The glass cabinet and the things in it . . . were like things I had known in my childhood. . . . My heart went out to them" (*IMMN,* 20).

Naipaul's personal reaction broadens out occasionally to support a political point, although he is never dogmatic. A book he read while on this journey, *My Diary in India* by William Howard Russell, a nineteenth-century journalist, crystallized some of his feelings. He had trouble appreciating the book, "like the trouble I used to have, when I was a reviewer, with good books with which I was nonetheless out of sympathy. . . . The trouble I had with the book was a trouble with history" (*IMMN*, 394). He will not simply condemn the British Raj. He admits that, despite all its painful aspects, there were some positive results: "It is hard for an Indian not to feel humiliated by Russell's book. Part of the humiliation the Indian feels comes from the ambiguity of his response, his recognition that the Indian system that is being overthrown has come to the end of its possibilities . . . that out of the encompassing humiliation of British rule, there will come to India the ideas of country and pride and historical self-analysis" (*IMMN*, 395).

Remembering from his Trinidad childhood the "shoddiness of the Indian books we bought . . . this other idea of the Indian reality, of poor goods, of poor machines poorly used" (*IMMN*, 157–58), he compares notes with Pravas, a Bangalore engineer, about "the psychological effects on him, as he was growing up, of the shoddiness of Indian manufactured goods." Pravas's response puts the issue into context: "Compared with contemporary goods elsewhere, they are bad. Compared with the nothing we had 50 years ago, it is something. It only means we have started late" (*IMMN*, 171). This "new world" had, after all, begun only "for some people with their grandfathers, and for most with their fathers" (*IMMN*, 171). In *India: A Million Mutinies Now*, Naipaul perceives a marked improvement in living conditions since his previous visits and acknowledges that "hundreds of thousands of people all over India, perhaps millions of people, had worked for this for four decades, in the best way: very few of them with an idea of drama or sacrifice or mission, nearly all of them simply doing jobs" (*IMMN*, 149).

No such optimism is evident in his description of Iran and Pakistan in *Beyond Belief: Islamic Excursions among the Converted Peoples*. He compares both countries unfavorably with India: "India, almost as soon as it became a British colony, began to be regenerated. . . . Iran was to enter the twentieth century only with an idea of eastern kingship and the antiquated theological learning of places like Qom. Iran was to enter the twentieth century only with a capacity for pain and nihilism" (*BB*, 234). The revolution that deposed the shah and the war with Iraq had "eviscerated" the country, and "all that could be said was that the country had been given an almost universal knowledge of pain" (*BB*, 240). It could not be said that life had improved since the shah's time.

Naipaul's main friend and interpreter in Iran this time is Mehrdad, a university student. Mehrdad's pain, about the war and about his country, is virtually inexpressible: "When . . . I had asked Mehrdad what he felt about the war, he had said, 'I feel nothing about it.' He hadn't meant that. What he had meant was. . . . : 'Sometimes I feel I can't bear any more'" (*BB*, 230–31). Mehrdad is sardonic about the "meaningless rules" imposed on the country: Ayatollah Khomeini had written many books of rules, and they were enforced by Revolutionary Guards, "their beards and guerrilla gear now the sign of authority, and not young rebellion" (*BB*, 137). It was easy enough for an outsider to wonder at and ridicule the rules, but "it took time to understand how far the restrictions reached, though it was easy enough to state what they were; and it took time to understand how they were deforming people's lives" (*BB*, 225). Even the word "revolution" had been spoiled: it had been "taken over by the religious state. No one ever spoke of the possibility of political action. There were no means, and no leaders in sight. No new ideas could be floated. The apparatus of control was complete" (*BB*, 226).

In Pakistan, on the other hand, the stranglehold on power is not so complete. The law courts, "with all their apparatus, . . . didn't deliver, the lawyers said. There was too much political interference, too much litigation; there were too many false witnesses" (*BB*, 256). The basis of the claims of Mohammed Iqbal, the poet who made the case for Pakistan in 1930, was in essence a "rejection of Hindu India" (*BB*, 251). But "what didn't exist, and what Iqbal's proposal didn't even attempt to define, was the new Muslim polity that was to come with the new state. . . . This polity is an abstraction; it is poetic" (*BB*, 251–52).

The contrast between India and Pakistan, according to Naipaul, arises out of the subcontinent's history of conquests:

> The Hindus . . . welcomed the New Learning of Europe and the institutions the British brought. The Muslims, wounded by their loss of power, and out of old religious scruples, stood aside. It was the beginning of the intellectual distance between the two communities. This distance has grown with independence; and it is this—more even than religion now—that at the end of the twentieth century has made India and Pakistan quite distinct countries. India, with an intelligentsia that grows by leaps and bounds, expands in all directions. Pakistan, proclaiming only the faith and then proclaiming the faith again, ever shrinks. (*BB*, 247)

Naipaul is uncharacteristically damning and almost brutal about Iqbal and his vision of a pure Islamic state: "Poets should not lead their people to hell" (*BB*, 356). The Pakistani state had "shown itself dedicated only to the idea of the cultural desert here, with glory—of every kind—elsewhere" (*BB*, 357). In the fundamentalist Islamic ideology, the conquered become converts and must set about dismantling and denying their cultural heritage: "The cruelty of Islamic fundamentalism is that it allows only to one people—the Arabs, the original people of the prophet—a past, and sacred places, pilgrimages and earth reverences. . . . It is the most uncompromising kind of imperialism" (*BB*, 64).

In Pakistan, nevertheless, certain ineradicable elements of the past persist. The idea of caste remains intact in many respects; and among the Pathans there is a strict code of honor of which they are very proud, and with which Naipaul has some sympathy: "Language, home territory, hospitality, sanctuary, revenge: honor extended to all of these things. . . . Without that idea men who have no voice or representation in the world can become nothing" (BB, 321–22). The fact that the region that became Pakistan had an ancient heritage came as a surprise to the Muslim migrants who came from India at partition: "They had agitated more than anyone else for the separate Muslim state, and they came to Pakistan and to Sindh as to their own land. They found that it belonged to someone else; and the people to whom it belonged were not willing to let go" (BB, 341). This is just one more example of the intellectual failure of those who fought for the idea of the Muslim homeland: a failure of foresight and imagination, the practical consequences ignored for the sake of the abstract, "almost unbearable beauty" of the Islamic state (BB, 153).

In *Beyond Belief* Naipaul naturally meets few women, but their plight, especially in Iran and Pakistan, is treated with considerable sympathy. Mehrdad's sister in Tehran "had little chance of getting married, since too many men of suitable age had been killed in the eight-year war. She simply stayed at home . . . silent, full of inward rage, her unhappiness a shadow over the house. . . . In this she was like the fifteen-year-old daughter of a teacher I had got to know. This girl had already learned that she could be stopped by the Guards and questioned if she was alone on the street. She hated the humiliation, and now she didn't like to go out. The world narrowed for her just when it should have opened out" (BB, 225).

This "old-fashioned tormenting of women" (BB, 225) was, he believes, unlikely to be what the young people of the revolution had dreamed of in 1979. In Pakistan he is severe on one woman he encounters, who had chosen, dramatically, to go into purdah but who, Naipaul suspects, like H. G. Wells's Invisible Man, "had wrapped herself up to conceal a vacancy" (BB, 301). But Islam had failed to help the serf women of Pakistan, "chattels of their landlords and their husbands, unprotected by law or custom or religion," who "lived with cruelty" (BB, 338). Under Islamic law, with all its rhetoric of protection and respect for women, bigamy is allowed, and Naipaul often heard stories of families fractured by the desertion of the father for a second marriage: "The adventure had religious sanction, but the consequences never ended for the two families. It made for a society of half-orphans, in a chain of deprivation and rage" (BB, 95). In Pakistan, men are allowed four wives under Islamic law, and once again Naipaul is brutal about "the veiling and effective imprisoning of women, and giving men tomcatting rights over four women at a time, to use and discard at will" (*BB*, 251).

Beyond Belief begins in Indonesia, where the "crossover between faiths" was still in progress (*BB*, 129). At the time of this visit, Jakarta was booming and wealthy, "the new wealth . . . changing landscape and lives too fast, or so it seemed" (*BB*, 133). He once again visits the Islamic intellectual and teacher Imaduddin, whom he had met during his 1979 journey. In 1979 Imaduddin was regarded as subversive and had recently spent time in jail, but now, fifteen years later, he is the "Man of the Moment," close to the powerful who are now leaning toward Islam. Despite his personal liking for Imaduddin, Naipaul is struck anew by the propensity of people like him to ignore "the implications of the asylum and law and learning he had traveled to find" in the United States and other Western countries: "In his world-view . . . nothing seemed owed to the world outside Islam" (*BB*, 46).

There is a brief postscript—less than fifty pages—to *Beyond Belief* describing Naipaul's visit to Malaysia. He seeks out Shafi, his guide and interpreter from his previous visit, but is unable to find him, suspecting that his former associates did not want him to be found. It is interesting when he does manage to revisit old acquaintances, but, he says in his prologue, in a sense it does not matter whom he encounters: "It may be asked if different people and different stories in any section of the book would have created or suggested a different kind of country. I think not: the train has many coaches, and different classes, but it passes through the same landscape. People are responding to the same political or religious and cultural pressures" (*BB*, xii).

Beyond Belief is, to date, Naipaul's final book of travel writing. His next major book is the first "conventional" novel in many years, *Half a Life,* but before that, in 2000, a slim volume appeared containing two essays previously published in the *New York Review of Books. Reading and Writing: A Personal Account* is a literary memoir in two parts, "Reading and Writing" and "The Writer and India." Satisfying in themselves, they nevertheless add little to the material already covered in *Finding the Center, The Enigma of Arrival, A Way in the World,* and earlier essays. One has the impression with these pieces that Naipaul's fascination with his own career is beginning to border on an obsession.

CHAPTER ELEVEN

Three Novels *A Way in the World, Half a Life,* and *Magic Seeds*

The Enigma of Arrival is very unlike a novel, and many critics have rejected the definition. In 1994, with *A Way in the World,* Naipaul stretched the definition even further. Indeed, he preferred not to call it a novel, and the English edition was subtitled "A Sequence." For the American edition, however, he agreed to the publisher's wish to use the word "Novel" instead.[1] As he told Mel Gussow, "These are arbitrary divisions," and this is especially true in relation to Naipaul's mature work.[2]

It is perhaps best to view *A Way in the World* as a sequence of linked narratives rather than a novel. There are nine sections, combining history, autobiography, and historical fiction. In the section on Sir Walter Raleigh, the remark is made that Raleigh's book on El Dorado was "a book no one could ever disentangle," a conflation of fantasy and reality (*WW,* 177). One immediately thinks of the relevance of this to *A Way in the World,* in which it is also difficult to sift the fiction from the literal fact. There is, however, a difference. Naipaul is openly using fictional events and characters to illuminate reality, while Raleigh was attempting to pass off his fantasy of fabulous riches as truth. It was a fantasy by which he seemed to have duped himself more than anyone, since he forfeited his life trying—though not very convincingly —to prove it was true.

A Way in the World retells some of the material Naipaul uncovered in his research for *The Loss of El Dorado.* In fact, in an interview with Gussow, he refers to the book as a "corrective" of both that book and *Mr Stone and the Knights Companion.* It addresses *The Loss of El Dorado* far more directly than *Mr Stone,* however. In another 1994 interview,[3] he was still concerned —"tormented" was the word he used—about his misuse of the material for *Mr Stone,* which he seems to have revisited when writing his 2001 novel *Half a Life.* But in relation to *The Loss of El Dorado,* he told

Gussow that "I wasn't writing my own kind of book. . . . I borrowed the form of the history and *damaged* the work."[4]

A Way in the World is undeniably his "own kind of book." It spreads its narrative, without concern for the conventional novelistic unities of time, place, and character, over several centuries and continents. Each section deals mainly with one "character," sometimes a historical figure, sometimes fictional. Sometimes it is impossible to distinguish the real from the imaginary. There is, of course, thematic unity. Questions of perception and self-deception are continually raised, as well as the Naipaulian themes of exile and displacement. There is also unity in the more literal sense that each of the people dealt with has had some connection with Trinidad or South America.

The first part, "Prelude: An Inheritance," is a short sketch of a Trinidad esthete. After a page of preparation to introduce the idea of the "shifting about of reality"—of light and dark, of cool and warm—a "pleasant sensation" that Naipaul found he could call up on his return visits to Trinidad after time spent overseas, he tells the story, at one remove, of Leonard Side. Side is a creature of hybridity, a Muslim who keeps a Christian image in his overdecorated bedroom; a florist equally comfortable decorating cakes for the Women's Institute and corpses for the Funeral Parlor. The narrator does not meet Side; he is described by a female schoolteacher the narrator knows. It is too literal to assume that Naipaul tells the story this way because that is how he actually heard it. The schoolteacher, whether real or fictional, is given few personal characteristics apart from her sex. Her prose, quoted directly for six pages, is indistinguishable from Naipaul's. It does not matter whether she exists, but it is significant that he chooses to relate this passage in her voice. This use of reported speech in narrative has been an increasingly common device in Naipaul's work since *A Bend in the River* and usually allows Naipaul to write directly about characters and situations it would be implausible for him, or his narrator, to know at first hand. When her narrative finishes, Naipaul comments on it, speculating on Side's possible future, which "the teacher couldn't tell me. . . ; she had never thought to ask"; and also on his "nature," the "mystery of [his] inheritance." He concludes this short prelude with the comment that "we cannot understand all the traits we have inherited. Sometimes we can be strangers to ourselves" (*WW*, 8–9).

Part 2, "A Smell of Fish Glue," brings readers to an autobiographical reminiscence of Naipaul's brief time working in the civil service in Trinidad before leaving for Oxford in 1950. The Trinidad of this period is contrasted with what he found on later visits. Then, senior positions were reserved for the English, and everyone else—the vast majority—lived with the knowledge that their expectations of advancement were limited. Returning after six years, with independence in the wind, Naipaul finds "something new" (*WW*,

28). "Black Power" is beginning to emerge as a force in the colony, and with it "the idea of an impossible racial righteousness" (*WW*, 36) that has little to do with real grievances and is directed more against the equally underprivileged Indian community than the tiny white population. The chaos and violence that ensues reduces some parts of Port of Spain to ruins and makes Naipaul ponder the earlier occupants of this land, the indigenous population wiped out by the Spanish and the English colonists: the layers of history that can now be seen, or remembered, or imagined, on this small island.

The next part is the first of three "Unwritten Stories." It is one of the few instances of explicit fiction in the book. His story, set in the South American jungle, "shaped itself in my mind, over some years. But it never clothed itself in detail, in the 'business' necessary to a narrative" (*WW*, 45). What makes this an unwritten story is not that it has not been artfully arranged into a narrative, but that Naipaul, as he writes, explains the creative processes involved in establishing characters and setting: "To make the narrator a writer or traveller would be true to the actual experience; but then the fictional additions would be quite transparent. Can the narrator be a man in disguise, a man on the run?. . . A man on the run would be true to the place. But narrative has its own strictness. It requires pertinence at all times, and to have given that character to the narrator would have introduced something not needed, a distraction" (*WW*, 45–46). He decides to make his narrator "a carrier of mischief. A revolutionary of the 1970s" (*WW*, 46). This narrator, never named and referred to throughout simply as "the narrator," falters in his resolve to incite the people he meets to rebellion when he conceives an affection for them and begins to wish to bring them no harm. He then discovers that there is a memory, apparently recent, among these people of a previous European visitor. But this turns out to have been Raleigh, more than 350 years before. The "unwritten" story ends here with his realization that these people have already been long ago betrayed by false promises that they are expecting him to fulfill. The theme of unreasonable expectations encouraged, probably thoughtlessly, for ulterior motives is thus linked with Raleigh, preparing the reader for the later exploration of his final fatal journey to Trinidad.

The next part of the book, "Passenger: A Figure from the Thirties," is partly autobiographical but introduces a fictional character called Foster Morris, who wrote a book on Trinidad in the 1930s. Like *The Enigma of Arrival*, this section uses Naipaul's "feeling person" as the narrator but renames and perhaps remolds this minor literary figure, who gives Naipaul advice that is alternately bracing, encouraging, and dismissive when he is starting out as a writer in London. Whether Morris has a real-life equivalent, the fictional character plays a crucial role in Naipaul's narrative of his career. The recent publication of Naipaul's family correspondence dating from his first years in England throws a little more light on his experiences of this time—but only a little. "Last year," he writes to his sister Kamla in early 1956, "I wrote not one, but three books. The first I sent to a critic who criticised it so severely that I gave it up altogether and didn't even send it out to a publisher. I think it was the best thing. Because after that I decided to change my style of writing completely."[5] The result was *Miguel Street*, his first publishable book. The critic is not named in the letters, but they show at least that there was a real person who played the role he assigned, nearly forty years later, to the fictional Morris.

Lebrun, another fictional character, is the subject of the next section, "On the Run." He was based, according to the critics, on C. L. R. James,[6] a Trinidadian writer and politician whose famous book on the game of cricket in the West Indies, *Beyond a Boundary,* Naipaul reviewed in his essay "Cricket."[7] Lebrun, like James, "belonged to the first generation of educated black men in the region" (*WW,* 119). In *A Way in the World* they meet after the narrator writes to Lebrun in response to a "marvellous article" he had written about the narrator's books. Whether one can conflate the narrator and Naipaul here is a tricky point. However, since Lebrun is fictional, even if he is based on fact, it is no doubt worth making the same distinction in the case of the narrator. Literal truth it may not be, but Naipaul is making a statement about various larger truths in a passage like this: "The revelation of Lebrun's article became a lasting part of my way of looking. I suppose I was affected as I was, not only because it was the first article about my work, but also because I had never read that kind of political literary criticism before. I was glad that I hadn't. Because if I had, I mightn't have been able to write what I had written. Like Foster Morris and others, I would have known too much before I had begun to write, and there would have been less to discover with the actual writing" (*WW,* 110).

Lebrun, however, becomes a threat to the young writer, and at a dinner in New York given by Lebrun's American friends in honor of the narrator, whom they clearly see as his revolutionary protégé, Naipaul begins to worry: "No other group would ever again make me an invitation so wholehearted or so seductive. But to yield was to cease to be myself, to trust to the unknown. And . . . I became very frightened" (*WW,* 124). This fright manifests itself— typically—in something concrete: he is revolted by the gefilte fish that the hostess has prepared especially for him, and, to his embarrassment, he cannot eat it.

One of the notable features of this section is that it reuses in a different way some of the material Naipaul had used in *Finding the Center.* In "The Crocodiles of Yamoussoukro," he had described getting to know an expatriate French-speaking West Indian African woman, Arlette, in Ivory Coast. In

A Way in the World, Arlette reappears, fictionalized, as Phyllis. Comparing the two accounts of the same person, it is possible to see how fiction allows Naipaul more scope to speculate and to include more detail about personal lives and circumstances than he would allow himself to in a nonfiction account. From their style, though, if taken out of context either account could be nonfiction, and the significant difference is in the purpose for which Naipaul is using the material. In *Finding the Center* Arlette is a person through whom he can find out about Ivory Coast, one of those "people I get to like" (*FC,* 90). She is interesting in herself, but her principal role in this book is as an interpreter and guide to her adopted country. In *A Way in the World* Phyllis becomes part of Lebrun's story, the means for the narrator to find out about Lebrun's activities in western Africa, and provides an illustration of the mischief he brought about with his revolutionary talk, "never having to live with the consequences of his action, always being free to move on" (*WW,* 155). Phyllis, the fictional character, is viewed more objectively and coolly than Arlette, the real person: moving her across to fiction, as it were, allows a good deal more freedom in characterization and imaginative expansion.

Part 6 of *A Way in the World* is another "Unwritten Story," a new version of the futile last months of Sir Walter Raleigh. Much of this section takes the form of a dialogue between Raleigh and his surgeon onboard the *Destiny* in 1618, near the mouth of the Orinoco River. The section begins, "Perhaps a play or screen play, or a mixture of both—that is how it came to me, an unrealizable impulse, a long time ago" (*WW,* 157); unrealizable, perhaps, because Naipaul feels that writing drama is not his strength. There is drama in this dialogue, but it is muted. As with the schoolteacher in the first section, there is no attempt to color the words of these characters. It is as if the surgeon is speaking for Naipaul, putting to Raleigh the history of his activities in Trinidad and Venezuela, occasionally asking him for clarification on points that have puzzled him, but in the main, setting out the facts as in an indictment. There is a quasijudicial air about it, like a police officer reading his evidence in court.

The second half of this part of the sequence gives the testimony, as told to a priest in New Granada, of Don José, an Indian claiming to be the natural son of the former Spanish governor of Trinidad, Fernando Berrio. Don José was captured by Raleigh's lieutenant, Keymis. He was befriended and employed by Raleigh, and he was therefore able to relate Raleigh's last months in the Tower.

Here Naipaul is, as he promised, revisiting some of the material he felt he had spoiled in *The Loss of El Dorado.* In the genre of fiction there is more scope for the concrete detail that gives Naipaul's best work its capacity to draw the reader imaginatively into the world he is describing. The title of this section, "A Parcel of Papers, A Roll of Tobacco, A Tortoise," describes the gifts sent to Raleigh, along with Don José, and the news of the death of his son. The irrelevance of these gifts—the insensitivity of Keymis in sending these things at such a time, as if they were some compensation for Raleigh's loss: these add novelistic point and poignancy to a scene that had not been so imaginatively re-created in *The Loss of El Dorado*. Telling this part of the story in the earlier book, Naipaul had confined himself scrupulously to narrative and direct quotation from the archival sources.[8]

Part 7, "A New Man," brings readers once again to the recent past and is another piece of seductive narrative, the literal truth of which is impossible to determine. Flying from Trinidad to Venezuela, the narrator meets Manuel Sorzano, a Trinidad East Indian, like Naipaul, who has moved to Venezuela and taken on a new name and identity. Manuel gradually opens up to the narrator, and their conversation comes round to a discussion of his son's troubles with his girlfriend. The son, Antonio, starts living with a Venezuelan girl, but in his inexperience he does not know what to do when he finds out she has been unfaithful. Manuel explains his difficulties: "The boys have to go out and get. They have to be men in a new way, and they don't really know what to do. They don't have the example from me. They just copying people outside without really understanding. And is extra hard for them, because all the time they still have the old-fashioned bashfulness which they get from me" (*WW*, 232).

These are themes that become central in Naipaul's next novel, *Half a Life*. But this is a vignette of the challenges faced by people transplanted from one culture to another. Manuel, and by association Naipaul, does not entirely deplore the new world. Manuel tells his son, "I never had the kind of excitement in my life that you and your generation looking for in yours. Yours is the modern way, and I must tell you I jealous you a little bit for it, for the freedom it give. But if you want this kind of excitement, you have to pay the price. Other people must have their excitement and freedom too. You can't tie them down. You can't start thinking of fair and unfair. Once you start looking for this excitement, you have to put away this idea of fair and unfair" (*WW*, 233).

The "New Man" is Manuel, remade in Venezuela after escaping his first family in Trinidad, but also Antonio, having to remake himself as a Venezuelan, competing with other men, "going out to look for boy friend and girl friend among strangers," as Manuel puts it (*WW*, 233). They are both hybrid, displaced creatures of the modern world, caught between their half-remembered traditional cultures and the emotional demands made on them by exposure to unfamiliar ways. At the end of this section, Manuel once again shows his ambivalence toward his adopted country—"a great country" where "they treat you according to what you show yourself to be," but where, also, "you have to know how to handle yourself" to deal with the guerrillas and kidnappers. It is a dangerous world that is nevertheless full of possibilities.

Venezuela, two hundred years before, had seemed full of possibilities for Francisco Miranda, the subject of the next section of the book. Miranda, like Raleigh, appeared in *The Loss of El Dorado,* and Naipaul comes back to his story here. This section, "In the Gulf of Desolation," is the third of the "Unwritten Stories," imagined as a screenplay or a play. In *The Loss of El Dorado* Naipaul talked of Miranda as a colonial. He revises this opinion in *A Way in the World:*

> I thought of him as a precursor. I saw him as a very early colonial, someone with a feeling of incompleteness, with very little at home to fall back on, with an idea of the great world out there, someone who, when he was out in this world, had to reinvent himself. . . .
>
> I feel now that I was carried away by a private idea of an ancestry, and overlooked too much of what was obvious. There is something in the idea of colonial incompleteness, and his political cause cannot be denied. But Miranda was also, right through, from the time he left home, something of a confidence man. (*WW,* 243–44)

However, Miranda's fraud, like Raleigh's, is as dangerous to himself as to his followers. His fantasy of the capacity and desire of the Venezuelan people to rebel against Spain brings him back again and again despite what seems, surely not only in hindsight but at the time, proof to the contrary. In the end, as Naipaul observes, Miranda traveled out from England again to help the revolution that had finally taken place under Simón Bolívar, and "found a country split into all its racial and caste groups, a civil war beyond any one man's managing, and far beyond his military skill." So his long-dreamt-of revolution was defeated, "and Miranda—like a man who had run to meet a fate from which he had more than once escaped—was a prisoner himself" (*WW,* 326).

The bulk of this section of the book—the longest of the nine parts—concerns Miranda's stay in Trinidad in 1806. Aged fifty-six, "he has been out of Venezuela for thirty-five years. For more than twenty of those years . . . he has been touting around an idea of Spanish-American liberation," which is "his only asset" (*WW,* 238). He has come to South America to attempt, finally, to bring his revolution about. His first attempt is a disaster, and he retreats to Trinidad to gather forces for a second try. When this fails he returns to Trinidad and stays there "like a man marooned" for a whole year (*WW,* 239).

Naipaul tells the outline of this story first, then comes back to offer a kind of cinematic version of it. He imagines Miranda arriving in Trinidad after his failed first invasion, to be greeted by General Hislop, the governor. The governor "is a man of jangled nerves" (*WW*, 249) who cherishes pathetic hopes of military glory with Miranda's revolutionary government. In *The Loss of El Dorado* Naipaul did not invent conversations that were not in the archival sources, but in *A Way in the World* he allows his novelistic imagination to re-create these situations. During this first period, Miranda is welcomed at Government House, and his conversations with Hislop, as between two men with unrealistic ambitions nurturing each other's fantasies, are touching. Naipaul has them addressing each other, tenderly and respectfully, as "General" in their conversations. When Miranda returns after his second failure, Hislop makes a point of addressing him as "Mr Miranda."

Much of the "action" in this section is also related in Miranda's partly real, partly imagined correspondence with his long-term companion in London, the mother of his two sons, Sarah. Sarah's letters had been used also in *The Loss of El Dorado*, but here Naipaul composes frank, confessional letters from Miranda to Sarah as a way of imagining his feelings and his continuing self-deception, at the same time showing his dawning realization of his doomed prospects.

At the end of this section, Miranda, imprisoned in Venezuela, is visited by Andrés Level de Goda, politically speaking an enemy of Miranda. Level de Goda wrote about Miranda in his memoirs, years later, and once again Naipaul uses their conversations as a dramatic device. As with Raleigh and the surgeon in the earlier section of the book, the questions Naipaul puts into Level de Goda's mouth might have been those Naipaul himself would like to have asked Miranda. "In all your years of writing about Venezuela and South America, you simplified, General," Level de Goda remarks (*WW*, 331). Naipaul allows Miranda to explain himself, making few authorial comments. He concludes this section with a description of Miranda's papers, some of which were published in Havana in 1950: "These Havana volumes, in which the papers appear just as Miranda preserved them, the ephemeral mixed up with more formal things, without editorial gloss or interference, seem still warm with the life of the man" (*WW*, 341). Naipaul's account, also, allows the reader to see not only the folly and self-deceit, which are self-evident and need little elaboration, but also the life and personality of this extraordinary man.

The final, ninth section of *A Way in the World* is titled "Home Again." In it Naipaul brings to the fore a character he described in passing in the second section, someone he met when working in the civil service before leaving for England in 1950. This time, Naipaul meets him in East Africa, where he is living for a short time as a visiting lecturer. Blair, a black Trinidadian, comes to the country as the president's adviser. He seems to be riding on the wave of a new respect for black intellectuals and politicians, but before long he is murdered by the president's opponents and his body is shipped back to Trinidad to the very funeral parlor where Leonard Side, in the first section of the book, was exercising his esthetic sense. The book is thus neatly brought full circle. But this short final section also shows two different types of expatriates. One, known as Richard, is a blistering portrait of a type for whom Naipaul has nothing but contempt.

> Richard kept an eye on the expatriates. . . . He invited people to dinner in his apartment when he felt they were straying. . . . He wrote of socialism as of an austere faith that was its own reward. . . .
>
> Richard had an easy, self-mocking manner which made you feel that he was half on your side and that you could joke with him about what he had written. You couldn't. He was humourless: he simply couldn't take in a point of view that was different from his own. (*WW*, 346–47)

The other expatriate, De Groot, was in Africa because he enjoyed living there. "In Africa he had no special cause; people looking for a man with a cause found him incomplete" (*WW*, 360). The narrator likes and respects De Groot and seeks him out when planning a return trip to Africa years later. However, whereas Richard has left Africa and fallen on his feet, without revising any of his opinions, in eastern Europe, "still concerned only with the rightness of his principles, and somehow still safe" (*WW*, 369), De Groot is dying in an African hospital, deluded and living out a "settler parody at the end" (*WW*, 362). The comparison is not explicitly drawn: it is left to the reader to ponder the effects of the postimperial world on these two very different men.

A Way in the World, moving as it does through various periods and places, showing lives both real and imaginary, gives Naipaul boundless scope to illustrate his insights into the history of the modern world, "the interplay of various peoples" that has "gone on forever."[9] Every character is restless, rootless, or exiled; unsettled in some way by the immense shifts of peoples that have convulsed the world since the beginning of the age of exploration. These upheavals have only grown more commonplace as the centuries have passed, until world conflicts in the twentieth century, following mass migrations of forced labor in the eighteenth and nineteenth, have made displacement an almost universal human condition.

Naipaul's next novel was published in 2001. It represents a return to the conventional novel for the first time since *A Bend in the River*. Although it is still very much an idiosyncratic work that could have been written by nobody else, *Half a Life* centers on one fictional character, giving his family background and relating his childhood, youth, and first marriage. The third-person narrator is detached, omniscient, and impersonal, although within the framework of the third-person narrative, large sections of the book are narrated by the characters, first Willie's father to Willie, and later Willie himself to his sister.

At the beginning of *Half a Life,* Willie Chandran asks his father why his middle name is Somerset. His father replies, "without joy, 'You were named after a great English writer'" (*HL,* 1). The phrase "without joy" could equally be applied to the whole novel. It begins with an account of the dreary, futile life of Willie's father, a high-caste Indian sadhu who, in a moment of perverse political protest, spoils his life by marrying a low-caste woman he despises. The narrative continues with Willie's own years as a foreign student in London and afterward as the husband of a "half-and-half" Portuguese African on her East African estate.

The London section of the novel can be partly seen as Naipaul's revision of his "errors" in writing his earlier London novel, *Mr Stone and the Knight's Companion.* The seedy Earls Court life that is briefly glimpsed in the earlier novel is like the life of Willie and his acquaintances, socially and sexually insecure in the racially mixed London of the 1960s.

The title of *Half a Life* can be interpreted in several ways. Literally, the book takes Willie's life to a notional midpoint of forty-one years, and its main characters are racially or socially mixed—half-and-half. On a deeper level, it is implied that Willie and his father only live half lives, having been stunted sexually by their upbringing in a ritualized society where marriages are arranged and boys are not taught how to seduce. This theme also occurred in *A Way in the World* and was mentioned in a 1994 interview. Recalling his earlier years in London, Naipaul said: "I was a very passionate man. I wasn't spurned; it was incompetence. I didn't know how to seduce the girl. . . . I didn't know about the physical act of seduction, you see. I didn't know, because I had never been told. I was too shy."[10] More than anything, Willie and his father both lack the joy of satisfying sexual relationships. In London, Willie finds that making love to his friends' girlfriends "is quite an easy thing to do. But I know it to be wrong, and it would get me into trouble one day" (*HL,* 117). Eventually, after many years of marriage to the first unattached woman who shows a serious interest in him, he finds satisfaction for a time in an affair with a married neighbor:

> I thought how terrible it would have been if, as could so easily have happened, I had died without knowing this depth of satisfaction, this other person that I had just discovered within myself. It was worth any price, any consequence. . . .
>
> I thought with sorrow . . . of my poor father and mother who had known nothing like this moment. (*HL,* 205)

He soon finds, however, that "some half-feeling of the inanity of my life grew within me, and with it there came the beginning of respect for the religious outlawing of sexual extremes" (*HL*, 211). He subsequently discovers that his lover is deranged, and doubts the reality of what they had together, so that even this brief experience of sexual satisfaction is compromised.

But the half life is not just sexual. It also includes the placelessness that is Willie's lot. His mother's family, low-caste and "backward," knew so little that they sent her to a Hindu caste school where she was persecuted: "They didn't know about the religion of the people of caste or the Muslims or the Christians. They didn't know what was happening in the country or the world. They had lived in ignorance, cut off from the world, for centuries" (*HL*, 39). His love for his mother changes to distant rejection as he grows up and learns more about the world. His father despises him, partly for his similarity to his mother.

Alienated from his family in India, he has no wish to return there after leaving for London to study, and after taking his degree he finds, as Naipaul did, that there was no job for him in England. Unlike Naipaul, however, his writing career, promising at first, peters out. Willie is thus a kind of cautionary tale for what Naipaul's life might have been without the impulse or discipline to keep writing in spite of early discouragement. This frightening sense of the blankness of the life he feels he narrowly missed feeds into the desolation and despair of this novel.

His sister, Sarojini, ineligible in the Indian marriage market because of her mixed-caste background, makes an international marriage and moves from place to place as her husband's work requires. There is nowhere either she or Willie feels is home. In the same way, Willie is never certain of his feelings. Especially in London, he lives "in a daze. . . . He was unanchored, with no idea of what lay ahead" (*HL*, 58). He converts this for a time into an opportunity: "Towards the end of his second term, he saw with great clarity that the old rules no longer bound him. . . . The possibilities were dizzying. He could, within reason, re-make himself and his past and his ancestry" (*HL*, 60). But he finds that this is not a basis for a life of fulfillment. It fails to provide a sense of belonging. At the end of the novel, Willie leaves Ana, his wife of eighteen years, telling her "I'm tired of living your life" (*HL*, 227). He joins Sarojini, her husband apparently no longer present in her life, at her flat in Germany. No future is projected for them: the first half of their lives has passed in futility, the other half is unknown.

Racial tensions play their part in the novel, but Willie has no allegiance to any group, and his only solution to such situations is avoidance and flight. Asked by a radio producer for whom he had done some work to investigate the Notting Hill riots in 1958, he refuses to pose as "a man from India who has come to have a look at Notting Hill, . . . a man looking for trouble, a man looking to be beat up" (*HL*, 110), and by his caution, or cowardice, foregoes any future radio commissions. And, leaving Ana in her East African country at the end of the novel, he reports, "I didn't think I could live through another war. I could see that it would have a point for Ana. I didn't see that it had a point for me" (*HL*, 227).

The lives this novel describes are mostly joyless, but the novel is not without its moments of rather grim humor. Sarojini visits a reluctant Willie at his college in London and insists on cooking for him in his room:

> She came every day to Willie's college room and prepared a rough little meal. She asked for his help in nothing. . . . She lay the heater on its back and she set the pots on the metal guards above the glowing electric coils. . . . Sarojini had never been a good cook, and the food she cooked in the college room was awful. The smell stayed in the room. Willie was worried about breaking the college rules, and he was just as worried about people seeing the dark little cook—clumsily dressed: with a cardigan over her sari and socks on her feet—who was his sister. In her new assertive way, but still not knowing too much about anything, in five minutes she would have babbled away all Willie's careful little stories about their family and background. (*HL*, 116)

In this novel Naipaul has come back to pure fiction for the first time in more than twenty years. In the two books he has called novels during that period, his own presence as narrator is central. In this desolate tale of unfulfilled lives, however, he has used only fictional characters, perhaps to distance himself from its frank (although not explicit) treatment of sexual matters. It is beautifully written and well crafted, but the joyfulness of the best of his earlier works is missing, and overall it is rather a depressing book.

In *Magic Seeds* (2004), Naipaul takes up Willie's story where he left off in *Half a Life*. Despite the many thematic links between his previous books, this is the first sequel he has produced. Willie is no more resolute than before. By the end of *Magic Seeds* he has learned but not developed: all the wisdom he has gained during the decade or so of the action is negative.

A short, untitled prologue begins the novel. In characteristic fashion Naipaul sketches the plot—the "numbing guerrilla years," Willie's time in jail "with its blessed order"—as usual refusing the temptations of suspense. In the prologue he talks of the perspective Willie has gained during these years: "Later it was possible to work out the stages by which he had moved from what he would have considered the real world to all the subsequent areas of unreality: moving as it were from one sealed chamber of the spirit to another" (*MSeeds*, 3). The implication is that the stages of his career as a guerrilla with the Tamils in India seem inevitable and logical, and it is only with hindsight that Willie can see how he might have prevented the mistakes he has made.

Taking refuge with Sarojini in Berlin after his separation from his wife, Ana, he allows her to shame him into believing that he did have a place in the world, and it was with the oppressed, the freedom fighters. With Naipaul's deep suspicion of "the corruption of causes," it is no surprise that Willie soon finds that the struggle in which he enlists is futile, corrupt, and destructive. He writes to Sarojini: "That war was not yours or mine and it had nothing to do with the village people we said we were fighting for. We talked about their oppression, but we were exploiting them all the time. Our ideas and words were more important than their lives and their ambitions for them-selves" (*MSeeds*, 161). He nevertheless is committed to—or trapped in—the movement and stays for many years. Luckier than some, he manages at last to leave by surrendering to the police rather than by meeting a violent death at the hands of his fellows.

Sarojini's role in this novel is full of ironies. She is prosperous, living in Berlin with a part-time husband—"There's his other family. That's a great help. I don't have to be with him all the time" (*MSeeds*, 20)—but acts as a self-appointed recruiter for the guerrillas, while living "on a subsidy from some West German government agency" (*MSeeds*, 12). She and her husband make documentaries: she has been to guerrilla camps. However, once her brother has been dispatched to his fate, she begins to have second thoughts and admits, "I am not too happy with what I have done, though everything was done with the best of intentions. It is awful to say, but I believe I have sent many people to their doom in many countries" (*MSeeds*, 153). When Willie is in an Indian jail, she retreats to their father's ashram and extricates him from his prison by contacting his publisher in London and arranging for a letter to be written on his behalf. Willie finds, to his surprise, that he is "a pioneer of modern Indian writing" (*MSeeds*, 168).

He returns to London and his former aimless life, sleeping with his friends' wives now rather than their girlfriends, attending futile training courses and empty social events. The only real difference is that he is older, less driven sexually, and moving in more prosperous circles. He finds it difficult to find anything to write to his sister about. On the night after a particularly con-fronting wedding, with loud African music, he thinks he has "found some-thing good to write to Sarojini about. The thing eluded him. He looked for it, through all the slave music, and in the morning all he was left with was: 'It is wrong to have an ideal view of the world. That's where the mischief starts. That's where everything starts unravelling. But I can't write to Saro-jini about that'" (*MSeeds*, 280).

This is the end of the novel: frustration, passivity, and a negative wisdom, affirming Naipaul's long-standing distrust of causes. Ironically, Willie believes that this message, on which Naipaul has based much of his work, is not even suitable for a letter to his sister. It is unlikely that Naipaul is now repudiating the lesson he has spent so many years advocating, so perhaps this is another example of Willie's shortsightedness. In the same way that Willie was unable to use his writing to find his way out of the wilderness of his early years, and was led instead to an unfulfilling life in Africa with Ana, he is now unable to see that this discovery is a worthwhile and important one that could be made the basis of not just a letter to his sister, but a whole writing career.

Magic Seeds is in many ways a more engaging book than *Half a Life*. The language of both novels is simple and fablelike, the dialogue emblematic rather than natural, with long, well-formed sentences. Descriptions are also simple: a setting or a character is drawn with a few strokes; a kind of roof, a paint color, certain types of shoes or hairstyle can all be made to signify much. But the life of action, albeit futile, that Willie lives through gives the first half of *Magic Seeds* a dynamism that *Half a Life* never quite achieves. The political adventure of *Magic Seeds,* though no more fulfilling for Willie than the sexual adventure of *Half a Life,* gives it more shape and substance, and although Willie does not realize its importance, he has learned a valuable lesson from his experiences. Sarojini too has redeemed herself somewhat and apologized. Although the future is as uncertain at the end of this novel as it was at the end of *Half a Life,* there is nevertheless a suggestion that some progress has been made.

Magic Seeds—the title a reference, of course, to the story of "Jack and the Beanstalk," with its theme of a simple, magical route from poverty to riches—is partly based on material Naipaul gathered for *India: A Million Mutinies Now.* Despite the personal bravery of some of the novel's characters, the admiration Naipaul seems to have felt for Indian freedom fighters, never wholehearted, is tempered in this book by his more habitual caution. As Sarojini acknowledges, Willie has been "sent to the wrong people, and as it turned out the other lot were not going to be much better" (*MSeeds,* 153). There is no sense in the novel that Willie could have discovered a just struggle elsewhere. The India of the "million little mutinies" arises from that fact that "people everywhere have ideas now of who they are and what they owe themselves" (*IMMN,* 517). These people are not like Willie, who understands "with the deepest kind of ache that there was no true place in the world for him" (*MSeeds,* 228), but who nevertheless seeks a place and a purpose by enlisting himself in the causes of others. Naipaul has always understood the criminal folly of such revolutionary tourists.

CHAPTER TWELVE

Conclusion

Speaking at his Nobel Prize acceptance lecture in 2001, Naipaul said, "I am the sum of my books. Each work . . . stands on what has gone before, and grows out of it. I feel that at any stage of my literary career it could have been said that the last book contained all the others."[1]

Good writing, according to Naipaul, should be unexpected, unstable, and not entirely respectable. It must have a moral sense, while avoiding political and social simplifications, but should be fun to read. Above all, it should show the writer's "whole response to the world"[2] honestly and with clarity, not hiding behind a false persona, clever postmodern rhetoric, or consciously beautiful prose; and the content should be matched by the form that expresses it most clearly, without any regard for formal categories such as "novel" or "essay." The extent to which he has succeeded can be seen in a comment like that of Nan Doerksen: "Perhaps where Naipaul's genius lies is in his ability to take an existing literary genre, or idea, and bend it to his own peculiar vision, finally creating something that is definitively his own as Shakespeare did."[3]

Naipaul has retold the narrative of his own career many times: the early difficulties, the breakthroughs, the disappointments, the times of healing, the journeys and arrivals, the fear and the panic that have compelled him to keep going. His life as a writer became his subject, and the writing self became foregrounded to the extent that there was for many years no doubt that one was reading a subjective view of the world, sometimes tactless, never free from prejudice, but always candid and unblinking: the view of "an extraordinarily sensitive and extraordinarily self-conscious man who has chosen to travel through the chaotic, cruel, and yet elusive territory of darkness with the hope that he might, at some future time, triumph over it";[4] abraded by the world into creating patterns in his writing to explain it. Peter Hughes notes that "the reversion to overgrown and savage life of what was once trained and tamed has a special horror for Naipaul":[5] in *The Enigma of*

Arrival he says he overcomes this horror by "meeting distress half-way" and holding "on to the idea of a world in flux" (*EA,* 54).

Because he has felt the need to make his own career and find the forms that best express "the material that possesses" him,[6] his work, despite a lack of overt "structural deformations,"[7] has always been idiosyncratic and has become more so throughout his career. The form of the early works is basically that of the novel or short story, but even so, *Miguel Street,* the first work he was able to sell for publication, was not published straightaway because "the publisher required something less unconventional in form first, something more recognizable by the trade as a novel" (*WW,* 88). Its narrator is a prototype for a long line of Naipaul-like narrators that he resumed, first with his travel writing and later with parts of *In a Free State,* and that came to full novelistic fruition in *The Enigma of Arrival.* In the early books it is not so much the form as the vision that is unique; the vision that never romanticizes its subjects and finds in them a source of spontaneous comedy.

His writing is certainly unexpected, and in unexpected ways. In *A House for Mr Biswas* he deliberately resists surprise and suspense in the narrative line, sketching the broad lines of Mr Biswas's life in the first few pages of the novel and beginning part 2 with the statement: "To the city of Port of Spain, where with one short break he was to spend the rest of his life, and where at Sikkim Street he was to die fifteen years later, Mr Biswas came by accident" (*HMB,* 277). The unexpectedness resides not in narrative surprises but in observations of relations between characters, such as the unsentimental but eventually respectful partnership of Mr Biswas and his wife, Shama, or the changed dynamics of the marriage of Chinta and Govind when the wife-beating began: "Her beatings gave Chinta a matriarchal dignity and, curiously, gained her a respect she had never had before" (*HMB,* 416); or in Mr Biswas's own idiosyncratic characterizations. He has the impression, for example, whenever he sees his cousin Jagdat that he "had just come from a funeral." Sober, or tearful, or weighed down with grief, the reader might presume, but he continues: "Not only was his manner breezy; there was also his dress, which had never varied for many years: black shoes, black socks, dark blue serge trousers with a black leather belt, white shirt cuffs turned up above the wrist, and a gaudy tie: so that it seemed he had come back from a funeral, taken off his coat, undone his cuffs, replaced his black tie, and was generally making up for an afternoon of solemnity" (*HMB,* 224). This passage perfectly exemplifies Christopher Hope's observation (quoted by Mel Gussow) that "his writing is always unexpected, and it's never entirely respectable."[8] It is not events that are unexpected, it is the reactions to them, the impulse to look below the surface to something that lies beneath, refusing to be content with political or social analyses that encourage simple answers.

As his career progressed, Naipaul started to incorporate some of this unexpectedness into the form of his books. *In a Free State,* the first of his fictions to make clear formal innovations while still being called a novel, is in five sections, the central three not linked to the prologue and epilogue or each other by any continuities of character or setting; and the beginning of each part gives the reader a slight, unexpected jolt. *The Enigma of Arrival* once again has unexpectedness embedded in the narrative, in the characterizations and observations, but also in its form and its denial of the reader's expectations of something resembling a plot. Naipaul does his best to dispense with the mechanics of plot in *The Enigma of Arrival,* by blurring time and thus causing uncertainty in the logic of cause and effect that is basic to plotting, but he cannot avoid the emergence of plots from his narrative: the story of Brenda and Les, for example, becomes a small plot in the reader's mind; how they come to live in the valley, become friendly with the Phillipses at the manor, and enjoy a brief happy period that ends when Brenda runs away to Italy with the central heating man, who "kicked her out," and how upon her return she taunts Les into killing her with a kitchen knife. Details are filled in later, of a phone message for Les from Brenda in Italy that was not passed on, the kind of petty accident that has large and unexpected effects and that normal plots thrive on. The difference is that it is filtered through Naipaul's mind—the reader finds out about each fact only when he learns it. But as in all narrative, the reader is invited to reconstruct the train of events from the material provided by the narrator. The point of view makes *The Enigma of Arrival* an unusual book, rather than the lack of plot.

The need Naipaul has felt throughout his career "to make a pattern of one's observations"[9] has led him to become an increasingly autobiographical writer. This can make him appear to be obsessed with various aspects of his life, particularly his writing career. He explains this impression when describing the origins of *The Enigma of Arrival* in the period after his manuscript for *The Loss of El Dorado* was rejected, when he had to return to England and start again:

> It was out of this grief, too deep for tears or rage . . . that I began to write my African story, which had come to me as a wisp of an idea in Africa three or four years before.
>
> The African fear with which as a writer I was living day after day; the unknown Wiltshire; the cruelty of this return to England, the dread of a second failure; the mental fatigue. All of this, rolled into one, was what lay on the spirit of the man who went on the walks down to Jack's cottage and past it. Not an observer merely, a man removed; but a man played on, worked on, by many things.

> And it was out of that burden of emotions that there had come to the writer, as release, as an idyll, the ship story, the antique-quayside story, suggested by "The Enigma of Arrival";[10] an idea that came innocently, without the writer suspecting how much of his life, how many aspects of his life, that remote story . . . carried. But that is why certain stories or incidents suggest themselves to writers, or make an impression on them; that is why writers can appear to have obsessions. (*EA*, 102–3)

He believes, as a writer, that he cannot avoid revealing himself and his preoccupations: this being so, the pretense of disinterest and objectivity is of no value and must be abandoned. As Bibhu Padhi says, "It is only by easing himself into his problem—in Naipaul's case, it is basically one of a deep-seated feeling of homelessness, an ominous sense of incompletion at every level of human life and every point of human history—that the novelist can responsibly pursue his vocation and, at the same time, allow his sensibility to shine through his words."[11] This has led him to what might seem the extreme of making his narrative persona, in all his books between *Among the Believers* and *Beyond Belief,* indistinguishable from himself.

However, in works in which he has used a third-person narrator, or a fictional first person, there is no impression of fraudulence. *A House for Mr Biswas* works superbly as a third-person narrative, with the control of distance perfectly adjusted to keep the reader sympathetic but not uncritical of the main characters. *In a Free State* contains a mixture of narrative styles; and the two stories that are written in the fictional first person have an impact that could not be achieved in any other form. It is obvious that this is not the undisguised voice of Naipaul, but that does not prevent the reader from being convinced that the sensibilities dramatized in these stories are authentic. In reviewing the story "In a Free State," Angus Calder complains that, having "lived for three years in East Africa," he "can see how Naipaul . . . has squeezed more intensity out of this arena than can actually be found there"[12] —precisely the point, surely, of writing imaginative fiction. However, when he uses an autobiographical narrator it precludes this type of fiction, since he remains reticent about areas of his life he would regard as private, such as his marriages and close friendships; and in his narrative persona, he cannot plausibly allow himself to indulge too much in the imaginative reconstruction of even fictional events. What this technique achieves is to make the framework of his judgments explicit and to show clearly that these judgments, whether expressed or implied, are his alone, not the decrees of a superhuman being.

"Compassion," he claims, "is a political word" that "I take care not to use."[13] However, with its slight connotation of distance, it seems a more suitable term for his relation to many of the characters in his mature work than its Greek cognate, "sympathy," while "pity" is too condescending. In *A House for Mr Biswas* there is certainly sympathy, and sometimes empathy, for Biswas and his children—and here is an example, too, of a subjective view that is prejudiced in order to see more clearly. Biswas's wife, Shama, might have been portrayed as more of a person in her own right: perhaps this was the intention of Naipaul's brother Shiva in his novel *Fireflies,* which tells the life story of a woman in some ways similar to their mother, in the same way that his brother's novel celebrates their father's life. But each novel makes its choice of where its sympathies will lie, and having done so, to retain clarity, must keep faith with its own vision. Mr Biswas is never presented as a moral paragon, and the negative attitudes toward Shama in the book are clearly his subjective views, even though they are narrated in the third person.

In a Free State takes another step toward empathy, in the two shorter stories written in the first person. Moral judgment is held in abeyance in these stories: clearly no reader is expected to agree with Santosh in his views on black Americans, or with the attitude of Dayo's brother toward "the schoolgirls sitting young and indecent on the concrete kerb in their short blue skirts, laughing and talking loud to get people to look at them" (*IFS,* 100); but neither are the narrators judged for their beliefs and actions. These stories make it possible for the reader, temporarily, genuinely to feel with their narrators, to see English and American society from an unfamiliar point of view.

With *The Enigma of Arrival,* the empathy ceases. Naipaul's persona does not demand empathy for itself, and the most appropriate term for his attitude toward the characters in the novel is "compassion," in which is encompassed tolerance, understanding, and a detached fascination with their affairs and way of life. In *Enigma* everyone is of interest: this is something Naipaul discovers in the course of the novel. He comes to understand the valuable "material" he failed to notice during his early years in London— displaced people from Europe, elderly people with memories of the previous century. He does not withhold judgment on his characters in the later work, but he makes it clear that his judgments are provisional, and they are always tempered by his tendency to see through the eyes of others. "I could meet dreadful people and end up seeing the world through their eyes, seeing their frailties, their needs," he said to Gussow in 1987.[14] There is a more important truth about people than a political or economic view: as he said to Ian Hamilton, "even when people make the most fantastic assumptions about their place in the world, they still have these enormous personal problems."[15] As Bruce King says, "his views often have the effect of paradox and surprise forcing a re-examination of received opinions."[16]

It is a feature of the unexpectedness of his books that they constantly dramatize this kind of paradox: the rich landlord driven into himself by his wealth in *The Enigma of Arrival,* the English expatriates caught in the aftermath of independence in "In a Free State," and Santosh, prosperous but bereft in "One out of Many." Insight into these apparently atypical situations, and exploration of personal relations that do not conform to narrative stereotypes— the refusal to romanticize or sentimentalize—gives his writing its power to surprise, sometimes to shock, at other times to delight. Hughes notes that at times his "poise and concision seem to contradict the disorder that is their argument":[17] the contradictions pervade style and form as well as content.

Naipaul's style is unique without being outlandish or showy. He says, "Style in itself has no value. I just try to write as clearly as I can to let those thoughts appear on the page. I don't want the style to stand out, I don't want the words to get in the way. I wish to create something the reader does not notice and which he reads very quickly. It took a lot of work to do it."[18] His prose can be read with ease, but there is an odd quality that gradually makes itself felt. His sentences can be long, with parenthetical interjections, but he usually repeats the subject of the sentence after an interjection. This serves to keep the reader oriented, but also often produces the effect of an incantation. His language is never flamboyant. He uses figurative language rarely, and although he often uses similes, they are not fanciful or highly inventive. He will say, for example, that "religion was like something in the air" (*TS,* 69), or the latrine in an Indian village house was "like an extravagance" (*IWC,* 82). The image is hardly even an image: using the convention of the simile is just a way of drawing back from making too absolute a statement.

Starting in the right way is, as Naipaul realizes, essential. The first sentence of *Miguel Street* has an almost legendary value to him as the magical way his writing career finally began, as he describes it in *Finding the Center.* Later he found he had to work hard for his apparently simple beginnings, and he has had to make them his own. "I will not let anyone tell me that I must have people coming in through the door and describe the room . . . so people know what's happening. No, my writing is something else now. It is carefully done, like a watch."[19]

Naipaul's vocabulary is part of his uniqueness. It is not that he uses recondite or unusual words, but there are certain words he has taken up and used in his own special way. There might be fifty or a hundred of these "Naipaulian" words: "glamour," "desolation," "panic," "corruption"; "group," used to mean the nation or race or community to which one owes loyalty; "taint," "drama," and "style." Sometimes he will use an abstract noun in the plural, such as "excitements," which can give it a faint blush of irony. He will use "bush" or "simple" to describe societies that might more tactfully be called "developing" societies. "Nerves" or "raw nerves" is often used to describe his feelings of anxiety as a young man. The continual use of these words becomes part of Naipaul's implied worldview, in which things are seen directly and with a kind of fastidious detachment. He uses adverbs and adjectives sparingly, drawing back from extravagant descriptions. He will, however, quite frequently—especially when writing in his own voice—use sentences of one or two words with an exclamation mark as a comment on a fact he has just related; "Peonies, China!" for example, toward the end of the epilogue of *In a Free State*, or "Energy!" to describe Les's after-hours work in *The Enigma of Arrival*. There is often a certain muted humor in these exclamations.

Most critics feel that after *A House for Mr Biswas,* Naipaul abandoned comedy. Phillip Langran declares that "the comic mode has no place" in the "new vision" of *In a Free State*,[20] and William H. Pritchard believes that "even admirers of" the novels of the 1970s "might admit that they're not much fun to read."[21] However, Naipaul says, "I think there is a good deal of comedy right through the work, a good deal of humour. It is contained in the actual tone of the writing, which probably comes over best during one's reading of it. I write for the voice. . . . The early comedy was really hysteria, the hysteria of someone who was worried about his place as a writer and his place in the world. When one is stressed one makes a lot of jokes. . . . That's not healthy. The profounder comedy comes from greater security."[22]

In *A Way in the World*, he says in criticism of an early unpublished story that the humor depended "more on words than on observation or true feeling" (*WW*, 27). Cleverness with words, facile wit, "the gift of the phrase" that Sandra has in *The Mimic Men* (*MMen*, 65) all needed to be unlearned, in favor of "plain concrete statements, adding meaning to meaning in simple stages" (*WW*, 87), before he could begin to make his way as a writer. It would, of course, be fascinating to read some of his early unpublished fiction to see whether it was as unpromising and pretentious as he would have us believe: but certainly the style that he has developed by the avowed means of resisting style, rhythm, and poetry has proved a very flexible and powerful instrument for him. As for humor, it appears to have receded in the period between *A House for Mr Biswas* and *The Enigma of Arrival*, but the title story of *In a Free State,* when read aloud, often raises unexpected laughter. The humor is embedded in the ironies of the situations characters have found themselves in, in their vanities and hypocrisies, and these are sketched economically in a few words that are easy to miss in silent reading. The dialogue, too, when spoken, betrays the characters' comical attempts at self-promotion and self-justification.

Political ideologies have always repelled Naipaul. His distrust of "the corruption of causes" and the mind-numbing propensities of political commitment is well-known, but he feels, too, that political beliefs would have seriously hampered him at the start of his career, as he said in *A Way in the World*. He prefers not to analyze his writing in an abstract way at all, whether political or otherwise. In his Nobel speech, talking about *The Mimic Men*, he said it occurred to him thirty years after writing it that it was "about colonial schizophrenia." He continued, "But I had never used abstract words to describe any writing purpose of mine. If I had, I would never have been able to do the book. The book was done intuitively, and only out of close observation."[23]

He believes a sense of inconstancy and change is important in good writing, and there is rarely a feeling at the end of a Naipaul novel of closure or stability: struggles as difficult as his, or worse, may be in store for Mr Biswas's widow and her children after his death; Bobby's troubles are only beginning at the end of "In a Free State"; and even in the less dramatic *Enigma of Arrival*, the narrator seems to be bracing himself at the end for a future away from the serenity of his "house in the woods." Ideas of flux, decay, renewal, and exchange are constant themes in both his fiction and his nonfiction.

The texture of his prose has become denser with the years, but it is not the density of difficulty. By the time of *A Bend in the River*, his chapters, or parts, are long, but within each chapter there are many breaks where the reader is invited to stop and think and rest. This is what makes the novel, which is less than three hundred pages, seem longer than it is. It was the last of his books until *Half a Life* that could be unambiguously called a novel; in between there were several travel books and two works of fiction mingled with autobiography and history. In his work Naipaul intentionally avoids creating the compulsion that characterizes the reading experience for novels of a more conventional kind. He writes, as he says, to try to slow the reader down, and the new style of fiction that he developed was designed with this purpose. The machinery of plot is suppressed in favor of an implicit demand to ponder the significance of what he had written. Factual uncertainty plays its part: in *A Way in the World*, for example, the fictional character Foster Morris, an aging author, is the subject of a discussion between Naipaul and Graham Greene. Did the discussion take place, but about someone different; did Naipaul ever talk to Greene; is the whole situation utterly imaginary, or is there a grain of truth? In this way the reader is led to consider larger philosophical questions of the relationship between fiction and history. According to Hughes, "Naipaul's vision of the world . . . depends upon its power to translate one history or story into others, to show that the relation between fiction and history is not the difference between falsehood and truth, but rather a distinction between converging narratives with different origins."[24]

When his work is measured against his own stipulations for good writing, he has largely succeeded. He is a very self-aware writer, very conscious of his purpose, which is to be as true to his vision of the world as he can be. The form he has developed with *The Enigma of Arrival* and *A Way in the World* is an adaptation peculiarly his own, meeting his own needs as an author, but not what he would recommend to any other writer: his advice is that every writer must "find the correct form" for the "material that possesses you . . . the one that feels true to you."[25] In his novels of the 1970s, what Naipaul calls "the element of pleasure" that "is almost inevitably paramount"[26] in the reading of fiction has been played down, but it is revived, at least temporarily, with *The Enigma of Arrival,* where a subdued joy, in words, in characters, in the natural world and human history, mingles easily with an unsentimental poignancy and a philosophical melancholy. The moral sense that he believes literature must have is never lacking, although the vision has become broader and more tolerant as he has matured. He claims never to have been a satirist and that "laughing at people . . . would be bad manners and pointless writing."[27] The most obvious candidates to be labeled satire are his two first published novels, *The Mystic Masseur* and *The Suffrage of Elvira,* of which the first perhaps might be excused because of its genial and ironic attitude toward its protagonist. Whether the early novels are categorized in that way, however, the satirical impulse has long been replaced by a broader view, where "the most dreadful people" can be understood even while they are, provisionally, judged.

Fellow West Indian writers will perhaps never be happy with Naipaul: Derek Walcott, in his review of *The Enigma of Arrival,* despite his admiration of "our finest writer of the English sentence," abhors his "author's lie," objecting to many things—"the genteel abhorrence of Negroes, the hatred of Trinidad, the idealization of History and Order"—and the fact that he prefers the heat and light of New York to that of Trinidad.[28] King points out that Naipaul's critics "desire a literature of cultural affirmation which is part of the struggle for decolonization. Naipaul does not ignore the effects of colonialism or fail to see injustice, but his writing treats such themes in a complex way."[29] Stella Swain, in *The Dictionary of Literary Biography,* notes that "his postcolonialism should be understood in the widest sense"; he is "not so much the voice of any particular newly independent or decolonized nation as . . . the chronicler of diverse global experiences of alienation and loss,"[30] and, as P. S. Chauhan observes,

> His critics, confining themselves to a biographical perspective or to occasional ideological forays, get into high dudgeon because Naipaul would not engage in either formulaic denunciations of the colonial

masters or the self-righteous praise of the land of his ancestors, the two favorite tacks of colonial writers. An open reading of Naipaul's work would suggest that if his critics, instead of imposing their expectations upon it, related his individual statements to the unifying philosophic outlook that underlies his writing, they might recognize that his work carries a more devastating judgment upon the dreams and deeds of the colonizer than would any wholesale ritualistic denunciation.[31]

Naipaul makes no apology for his views; they are his principal subject, and they are formed through the process of writing, which means that everything he writes is part of a progression toward understanding rather than an exposition of views already held. His resistance to plots and the apparatus of fiction is important in this respect: plot, as he sees it, "assumes that the world has been explored and now this thing, plot, has to be added on. Whereas I am still exploring the world. And there is narrative there, in every exploration."[32] The narrative of this exploration, since *Finding the Center* at least, has been a major subject: his determination to face unpleasant truths unflinchingly, despite his fastidiousness and his horror of mess and noise, causes the "creative abrasion" (*EA*, 282) that keeps him writing and prevents him from succumbing to the temptation of idleness, which, however tempting, represents "death of the soul" (*EA*, 282).

NOTES

CHAPTER 1

1. V. S. Naipaul, "Two Worlds: The Nobel Lecture," in *Literary Occasions: Essays* (New York: Knopf, 2003), 181–82.

2. Seepersad Naipaul, *The Adventures of Gurudeva and Other Stories,* with a foreword by V. S. Naipaul (London: Deutsch, 1976).

3. A chronology of Naipaul's life and work is available on the Web site of the V. S. Naipaul Archive at the University of Tulsa Library (www.lib.utulsa.edu/speccoll/naipavs0.htm).

4. Lillian Feder, *Naipaul's Truth: The Making of a Writer* (Lanham, Md.: Rowman & Littlefield, 2001), 5.

5. Edward Said, "Intellectuals in the Post-Colonial World," *Salmagundi* (Spring/Summer 1986): 53.

6. Quoted in Scott Winokur, "The Unsparing Vision of V. S. Naipaul," in *Conversations with V. S. Naipaul,* ed. Feroza Jussawalla, 121 (Jackson: University Press of Mississippi, 1997).

7. Amit Chaudhuri, "On V. S. Naipaul," in *V. S. Naipaul: An Anthology of Recent Criticism,* ed. Purabi Panwar (Delhi: Pencraft International, 2003), 188.

8. Michiko Kakutani, "Naipaul Reviews His Past from Afar, "*New York Times,* December 1, 1980, late city final edition, C15.

9. Ibid.

10. Stephen Schiff, "The Ultimate Exile," in *Conversations with V. S. Naipaul,* ed. Jussawalla, 141.

11. Adrian Rowe-Evans, "V. S. Naipaul: A *Transition* Interview," in *Conversations with V. S. Naipaul,* ed. Jussawalla, 30.

12. Israel Shenker, "V. S. Naipaul," in *Critical Perspectives on V. S. Naipaul,* ed. Robert D. Hamner, 51 (Washington, D.C.: Three Continents Press, 1977).

13. Schiff, "The Ultimate Exile," 153.

14. Ibid.

15. Rowe-Evans, "Naipaul: A *Transition* Interview," 33.

16. Linda Blandford, "Man in a Glass Box," in *Conversations with V. S. Naipaul,* ed. Jussawalla, 56.

17. Bernard Levin, "V. S. Naipaul: A Perpetual Voyager," in *Conversations with V. S. Naipaul,* ed. Jussawalla, 94.

18. Charles Michener, "The Dark Visions of V. S. Naipaul," in *Conversations with V. S. Naipaul,* ed. Jussawalla, 65.

19. Shenker, "V. S. Naipaul," 53.

20. Schiff, "The Ultimate Exile," 141.

21. Mel Gussow, "V. S. Naipaul in Search of Himself, "*New York Times Book Review,* April 24, 1994, 30.

22. Aamer Hussein, "Delivering the Truth: An Interview with V. S. Naipaul," in *Conversations with V. S. Naipaul,* ed. Jussawalla, 155.

23. Rowe-Evans, "Naipaul: A *Transition* Interview," 30.

24. Bharati Mukherjee and Robert Boyers, "A Conversation with V. S. Naipaul," in *Conversations with V. S. Naipaul,* ed. Jussawalla, 90.

25. Rowe-Evans, "Naipaul: A *Transition* Interview," 35.

26. Charles Wheeler, "It's Every Man for Himself—V. S. Naipaul on India," in *Conversations with V. S. Naipaul,* ed. Jussawalla, 44.

27. Mukherjee and Boyers, "A Conversation," 85.

28. Schiff, "The Ultimate Exile," 137–38.

29. Kakutani, "Naipaul Reviews His Past."

30. Hussein, "Delivering the Truth," 155.

31. Robert Siegel, "Author V. S. Naipaul Interviewed," *All Things Considered,* NPR, May 23, 1994, http://proquest.umi.com (last accessed August 14, 2005).

32. Shenker, "V. S. Naipaul," 50.

33. Mukherjee and Boyers, "A Conversation," 75–76.

34. Ibid., 77.

35. Rowe-Evans, "Naipaul: A *Transition* Interview," 34.

36. Hussein, "Delivering the Truth," 160.

37. Schiff, "The Ultimate Exile," 149.

38. Gussow, "Naipaul in Search of Himself," 29.

39. Ibid.

40. Wheeler, "Naipaul on India," 43.

41. Ahmed Rashid, "The Last Lion," in *Conversations with V. S. Naipaul,* ed. Jussawalla, 167.

42. Hussein, "Delivering the Truth," 161.

43. Rashid, "The Last Lion," 166.

44. Michener, "Dark Visions," 69.

45. Mukherjee and Boyers, "A Conversation," 92.

46. Ibid., 81–82.

47. Schiff, "The Ultimate Exile," 148.

48. Rowe-Evans, "Naipaul: A *Transition* Interview," 27, 29.

49. Michener, "Dark Visions," 71.

50. Edward Behr, "People Are Proud of Being Stupid," *Newsweek,* August 18, 1980, 38.

51. Mukherjee and Boyers, "A Conversation," 91.

52. Derek Walcott, "Interview with V. S. Naipaul," in *Conversations with V. S. Naipaul,* ed. Jussawalla, 8.

53. Rowe-Evans, "Naipaul: A *Transition* Interview," 34.

54. Ibid., 24.

55. Mukherjee and Boyers, "A Conversation," 79.

56. Walcott, "Interview," 8.

57. Cathleen Medwick, "Life, Literature, and Politics: An Interview with V. S. Naipaul," in *Conversations with V. S. Naipaul,* ed. Jussawalla, 61.

58. Winokur, "The Unsparing Vision," 117–18.

59. Elizabeth Hardwick, "Meeting V. S. Naipaul," in *Conversations with V. S. Naipaul,* ed. Jussawalla, 46.

60. Mukherjee and Boyers, "A Conversation," 86.

61. Hussein, "Delivering the Truth," 160.

62. Siegel, "Naipaul Interviewed."

63. Alistair Niven, "V. S. Naipaul Talks to Alistair Niven," in *Conversations with V. S. Naipaul,* ed. Jussawalla, 163.

64. Ian Hamilton, "Without a Place: V. S. Naipaul in Conversation with Ian Hamilton," in *Conversations with V. S. Naipaul,* ed. Jussawalla, 17.

65. Naipaul, "The Little More," in *Critical Perspectives,* ed. Hamner, 15.

66. Hamilton, "Without a Place," 19.

67. Ronald Bryden, "The Novelist V. S. Naipaul Talks about His Work to Ronald Bryden," *Listener* 89 (March 22, 1973): 368.

68. Shenker, "V. S. Naipaul," 53.

69. Michener, "Dark Visions," 64.

70. Siegel, "Naipaul Interviewed."

71. Rowe-Evans, "Naipaul: A *Transition* Interview," 31.

72. Gussow, "Naipaul in Search of Himself," 30.

73. Schiff, "The Ultimate Exile," 149.

74. Michener, "Dark Visions," 73.

75. Andrew Robinson, "Going Back for a Turn in the East," in *Conversations with V. S. Naipaul,* ed. Jussawalla, 112.

CHAPTER 2

1. "Speaking of Writing VI: V. S. Naipaul," *Times* (London), January 2, 1964, 11.

2. Naipaul to Kamla Naipaul, London, February 10, 1956, *Letters between a Father and Son,* ed. Gillon Aitken (London: Little, Brown, 1999), 321.

3. Naipaul to Naipaul family, Oxford, April 11, 1951, in *Letters between a Father and Son,* ed. Aitken, 87.

4. Naipaul to Naipaul family, Oxford, August 25, 1953, in *Letters between a Father and Son,* ed. Aitken, 291.

5. Seepersad Naipaul, *Adventures,* 18–19.

6. Naipaul to Naipaul family, Oxford, May 10, 1952, in *Letters between a Father and Son,* ed. Aitken, 193.

7. Seepersad Naipaul, *Adventures,* 17.

8. Naipaul to Droapatie Naipaul, Oxford, October 28, 1953, in *Letters between a Father and Son,* ed. Aitken, 305.

9. Seepersad Naipaul, *Adventures,* 21.

10. Mukherjee and Boyers, "A Conversation," 85.

11. For a discussion of women in Naipaul's novels, see Gillian Dooley, "Naipaul's Women," *South Asian Review* 26, no. 1, special issue on V. S. Naipaul (2005): 88–103.

12. Naipaul to Kamla Naipaul, Trinidad, September 21, 1949, in *Letters between a Father and Son,* ed. Aitken, 3.

13. "Speaking of Writing," 11.

14. Seepersad Naipaul, *Adventures,* 24.

15. Suman Gupta, *V. S. Naipaul* (Plymouth: Northcote House, 1999), 17.

16. Ibid., 9.

17. George Lamming, *The Pleasures of Exile* (Ann Arbor: University of Michigan Press, 1992 [1962]), 225.

18. Rowe-Evans, "Naipaul: A *Transition* Interview," 31.

CHAPTER 3

1. Rashid, "The Last Lion," 166.

2. Rashid, "Death of the Novel," *Observer* (London), February 25, 1996.

3. D. S., "N. B.," *Times Literary Supplement* (London), March 8, 1996, 18.

4. Naipaul, "On Being a Writer," *New York Review of Books,* April 24, 1987, 7.

5. Naipaul, "Writing *A House for Mr Biswas,*" *New York Review of Books,* November 24, 1983, 22.

6. Jim Douglas Henry, "Unfurnished Entrails: The Novelist V. S. Naipaul in Conversation with Jim Douglas Henry," in *Conversations with V. S. Naipaul,* ed. Jussawalla, 23.

7. Gordon Rohlehr, "Character and Rebellion in *A House for Mr Biswas,*" in *Critical Perspectives,* ed. Hamner, 87–88.

8. Naipaul, "Images: *Commonwealth Literature,*" in *Critical Perspectives,* ed. Hamner, 29.

9. Kakutani, "Naipaul Reviews His Past."

10. Gussow, "Travel Plus Writing Plus Reflection Equals V. S. Naipaul," *New York Times,* January 30, 1991, late edition , C9.

11. Shenker, "V. S. Naipaul," in *Conversations with V. S. Naipaul,* ed. Jussawalla, 51.

12. Gordon Burn, "The Gospel According to Naipaul," *Weekend Review,* July 9–10, 1994, 4.

13. Gussow, "Enigma of V. S. Naipaul's Search for Himself in Writing," *New York Times,* April 25, 1987, late city final edition , I16.

14. Seepersad Naipaul to V. S. Naipaul, Trinidad, March 12, 1952, in *Letters between a Father and Son,* ed. Aitken, 177.

15. Seepersad Naipaul, *Adventures ,* 8.

16. Seepersad Naipaul, "They Named Him Mohun," in *Adventures,* 125.

17. Ibid.

18. Seepersad Naipaul, *Adventures,* 16.

19. Ibid.

20. Naipaul, "Writing *A House,*" 22.

21. Mukherjee and Boyers, "A Conversation," 78.

22. Rohlehr, "Character and Rebellion," 92.

23. Naipaul, "Images," 26.

24. Naipaul, "Jasmine," in *The Overcrowded Barracoon* (London: Deutsch, 1972), 25.

25. Ibid., 28–29.

26. Hamilton, "Without a Place," 17.

27. Gussow, "Enigma."

28. Ibid.

29. Naipaul, "Writing *A House*," 23.

30. Ibid.

31. Melvyn Bragg, "V. S. Naipaul," *Southbank*, ABC, London Weekend Television, London, 1987.

32. Winokur, "The Unsparing Vision," 116.

33. Ibid., 128.

34. James Wood, "Tell Me What You Talked," *London Review of Books*, November 11, 1999, 25.

35. For a detailed discussion of the relationship between Naipaul's family life as revealed in the letters and *A House for Mr Biswas*, see Dooley, "Those Difficult Years," *CRNLE Journal* (2000): 147–54.

Chapter 4

1. Walcott, "Interview," 5.

2. Mukherjee and Boyers, "A Conversation," 82.

3. Ibid., 83.

4. Naipaul, "The Shipwrecked Six Thousand," in *The Writer and the World: Essays* (New York: Knopf, 2002), 88.

5. Rowe-Evans, "Naipaul: A *Transition* Interview," 26.

6. See, for example, Gupta's discussion of *The Mystic Masseur* and *The Suffrage of Elvira* in relation to the political history of Trinidad (*V. S. Naipaul*, 7–13).

7. Naipaul, *The Middle Passage*, 2nd ed. (London: Macmillan, 1995), vi.

8. Walcott, "Interview," 5.

9. Ibid., 5–6.

10. Ibid., 6.

11. James Atlas, "V. S. vs the Rest: The Fierce and Enigmatic V. S. Naipaul Grants a Rare Interview in London," in *Conversations with V. S. Naipaul*, ed. Jussawalla, 104.

12. Naipaul, *The Loss of El Dorado*, rev. ed. (Harmondsworth: Penguin, 1973), 316.

Chapter 5

1. Search performed online, January 2005.

2. Paul Theroux, *V. S. Naipaul: An Introduction to His Work* (London: Deutsch, 1972), 7.

3. Oscar Wilde, "The Importance of Being Earnest," in *Plays* (Harmondsworth: Penguin, 1954), 261.

4. For example, he used Waugh as an example to draw attention to the absurdity of some of his own critics: "Imagine a critic in Trinidad writing of *Vile Bodies*: 'Mr Evelyn Waugh's whole purpose is to show how funny English people are. He looks down his nose at the land of his birth. We hope that in future he writes of his native land with warm affection.'" (Naipaul, "London," *Times Literary Supplement* (London), August 15, 1958, reprinted in *The Overcrowded Barracoon* [London: Deutsch, 1972], 11.)

5. Evelyn Waugh, *The Loved One* (Harmondsworth: Penguin, 1948), 117.

6. Mukherjee and Boyers, "A Conversation," 78.

7. Naipaul, "London," 14.

8. Hussein, "Delivering the Truth," 156.

9. Ibid.

10. Naipaul, "London," 14.

11. Theroux, *Sir Vidia's Shadow* (Boston and New York: Houghton Mifflin, 1998), 286.

12. Mukherjee and Boyers, "A Conversation," 91.

13. James Anthony Froud, *The English in the West Indies, or The Bow of Ulysses* (London: Longmans, 1888).

14. Hussein, "Delivering the Truth," 154.

15. See Bruce King, *Derek Walcott: A Caribbean Life* (Oxford: Oxford University Press, 2000), 214–15.

CHAPTER 6

1. Burn, "The Gospel," 4.

2. See William Walsh, *V. S. Naipaul* (Edinburgh: Oliver & Boyd, 1973), 64; Shashi Kamra, *The Novels of V. S. Naipaul* (New Delhi: Prestige, 1990), 149; King, *V. S. Naipaul,* 2nd ed. (Basingstoke: Palgrave Macmillan, 2003), 86ff.; Peter Hughes, *V. S. Naipaul* (London: Routledge, 1988), 50.

3. John Rothfork, "V. S. Naipaul and the Third World," *Research Studies* 49, no. 3 (1981): 185.

4. Bragg, "V. S. Naipaul," 1987.

5. Rowe-Evans, "Naipaul: A *Transition* Interview," 36.

6. Levin, "A Perpetual Voyager," 98.

7. Rowe-Evans, "Naipaul: A *Transition* Interview," 27.

8. Hughes, *V. S. Naipaul,* 33.

9. Rowe-Evans, "Naipaul: A *Transition* Interview," 31.

10. Landeg White, *V. S. Naipaul: A Critical Introduction* (London: Macmillan, 1975), 205.

11. Andrew Gurr, "The Freedom of Exile in Naipaul and Doris Lessing," *Ariel* 13, no. 4 (1982): 12.

12. Rothfork, "Third World," 187.

13. King, *V. S. Naipaul,* 88.

14. For example, Selwyn R. Cudjoe, *V. S. Naipaul* (Amherst: University of Massachusetts Press, 1988).

15. Fawzia Mustafa, *V. S. Naipaul* (Cambridge: Cambridge University Press, 1995), 119.

16. Robert K. Morris, *Paradoxes of Order: Some Perspectives on the Fiction of V. S. Naipaul* (Columbia: University of Missouri Press, 1975), 104.

17. Rob Nixon, *London Calling: V. S. Naipaul, Postcolonial Mandarin* (New York: Oxford University Press, 1992), 54.

18. P. S. Chauhan, "V. S. Naipaul: History as Cosmic Irony," in *Reworlding: The Literature of the Indian Diaspora* (New York: Greenwood Press, 1992), 22–23.

19. Rowe-Evans, "Naipaul: A *Transition* Interview," 26.

20. Rothfork, "Third World," 187.

21. Gupta, *V. S. Naipaul*, 53.

22. Michener, "Dark Visions," 64.

23. Schiff, "The Ultimate Exile," 150.

24. Richard C. Morais, "Tribal Tribulations," *Forbes* 161, no. 4, February 23, 1998, 149–50. *Expanded Academic ASAP*, Online, May 13, 1998.

25. Hardwick, "Meeting Naipaul," 47.

26. Hamilton, "Without a Place," 20.

CHAPTER 7

1. Naipaul, "London," 13.

2. Gussow, "V. S. Naipaul: 'It Is Out of This Violence I've Always Written,'" *New York Times Book Review*, September 16, 1984, 38.

3. This article, published in *The Return of Eva Perón with the Killings in Trinidad* in 1980, will be discussed in chapter 8.

4. Bragg, "V. S. Naipaul," 1987.

5. Mukherjee and Boyers, "A Conversation," 86.

6. Ibid.

7. Ibid.

8. Ibid.

9. Ibid.

10. Wayne C. Booth, *The Rhetoric of Fiction*, 2nd ed. (Chicago: University of Chicago Press, 1983).

11. Mukherjee and Boyers, "A Conversation," 86.

12. Michener, "Dark Visions," 76.

CHAPTER 8

1. Wheeler, "Naipaul on India," 39.

2. Said, "Intellectuals," 53.

3. Gussow, "Enigma."

4. Michener, "Dark Visions," 64.

5. Wheeler, "Naipaul on India," 43.

CHAPTER 9

A different version of this chapter was published in *V. S. Naipaul: An Anthology of Recent Criticism*.

1. Naipaul, "On Being a Writer," 7.

2. Michener, "Dark Visions," 66–67.

3. Naipaul, "On Being a Writer," 7.

4. Robert Royal, "This Little World," *National Review* (August 28, 1987): 50.

5. Cudjoe, *V. S. Naipaul*, 215.

6. Gussow, "Enigma."

7. Niven, "V. S. Naipaul Talks," 163.

8. Schiff, "The Ultimate Exile," 149.

9. Ibid.

10. Judith Levy, *V. S. Naipaul: Displacement and Autobiography* (New York: Garland, 1995), 111.

11. Niven, "V. S. Naipaul Talks," 163.

12. Michener, "Dark Visions," 66.

13. Naipaul, "Writing *A House,*" 23.

14. John Bayley, "Country Life: *The Enigma of Arrival,*" *New York Review of Books,* April 9, 1987, 3.

15. Peggy Nightingale, *Journey through Darkness* (St. Lucia: University of Queensland Press, 1987), 237.

16. Bayley, "Country Life," 3.

CHAPTER 10

1. Wheeler, "Naipaul on India," 43.

2. Niven, "V. S. Naipaul Talks," 165.

3. Ibid.

4. Robinson, "Going Back," 110.

5. Ibid.

6. Schiff, "The Ultimate Exile," 150.

7. Ibid.

8. Michener, "Dark Visions," 64.

9. Hussein, "Delivering the Truth," 157.

CHAPTER 11

1. See Gussow, "Naipaul in Search of Himself," 29.

2. Ibid., 3.

3. Hussein, "Delivering the Truth," 156.

4. Gussow, "Naipaul in Search of Himself," 3.

5. Naipaul to Kamla Naipaul, London, February 10, 1956, in *Letters between a Father and Son,* ed. Aitken, 321.

6. See, for example, William H. Pritchard, "Naipaul's Written World," *Hudson Review* 47, no. 4 (1995): 595.

7. Naipaul, "Cricket," in *The Overcrowded Barracoon.*

8. "Dialogue occurs as dialogue in the sources." Postscript to *The Loss of El Dorado,* 323.

9. Hussein, "Delivering the Truth," 161.

10. Schiff, "The Ultimate Exile," 145.

CHAPTER 12

1. Naipaul, "Two Worlds," 182–83.

2. Rowe-Evans, "Naipaul: a *Transition* Interview," 29.

3. Nan Doerksen, "*In a Free State* and *Nausea,*" *World Literature Written in English* 20 (1981): 113.

4. Bibhu Padhi, "Naipaul on Naipaul and the Novel," *Modern Fiction Studies* 30, no. 3 (1984): 465.

5. Hughes, *V. S. Naipaul*, 22.

6. Burn, "The Gospel," 4.

7. Hardwick, "Meeting Naipaul," 46.

8. Gussow, "Naipaul in Search of Himself," 29.

9. Rowe-Evans, "Naipaul: A *Transition* Interview," 31.

10. A painting by Giorgio de Chirico.

11. Padhi, "Naipaul on Naipaul," 464.

12. Angus Calder, "Darkest Naipaulia," *New Statesman*, October 8, 1971, 483.

13. Robinson, "Going Back," 111.

14. Gussow, "Enigma."

15. Hamilton, "Without a Place," 20.

16. King, *V. S. Naipaul*, 4.

17. Hughes, *V. S. Naipaul*, 19.

18. Rashid, "The Last Lion," 168.

19. Schiff, "The Ultimate Exile," 149.

20. Phillip Langran, "V. S. Naipaul: A Question of Detachment," *Journal of Commonwealth Literature* 25, no. 1 (1990): 135.

21. Pritchard, "Naipaul's Written World," 594.

22. Niven, "V. S. Naipaul Talks," 164.

23. Naipaul, "Two Worlds."

24. Hughes, *V. S. Naipaul*, 24.

25. Burn, "The Gospel," 4.

26. Mukherjee and Boyers, "A Conversation," 92.

27. Walcott, "Interview," 8.

28. Walcott, "The Garden Path," *New Republic*, April 13, 1987, 29.

29. King, *V. S. Naipaul*, 195.

30. Stella Swain, "V. S. Naipaul," *Dictionary of Literary Biography*, vol. 207. *Detroit*: Gale, 1999, 203.

31. Chauhan, "Cosmic Irony," 13–14.

32. Schiff, "The Ultimate Exile," 148.

BIBLIOGRAPHY

WORKS BY V. S. NAIPAUL

Unpublished Material
V. S. Naipaul Archive, University of Tulsa Library.

Published Fiction
A Bend in the River. London: Deutsch, 1979; New York: Knopf, 1979.
The Enigma of Arrival. London: Viking, 1987; New York: Knopf, 1987.
A Flag on the Island. London: Deutsch, 1967; New York: Macmillan, 1967.
Guerrillas. London: Deutsch, 1975; New York: Knopf, 1975.
Half a Life. London: Picador, 2001; New York: Knopf, 2001.
A House for Mr Biswas. London: Deutsch, 1961; New York: McGraw-Hill, 1961.
In a Free State. London: Deutsch, 1971; New York: Knopf, 1971.
Magic Seeds. London: Picador, 2004; New York: Knopf, 2004.
Miguel Street. London: Deutsch, 1959; New York: Vanguard, 1960.
The Mimic Men. London: Deutsch, 1967; New York: Macmillan, 1967.
Mr Stone and the Knights Companion. London: Deutsch, 1963; New York: Macmillan, 1964.
The Mystic Masseur. London: Deutsch, 1957; New York: Vanguard, 1959.
The Suffrage of Elvira. London: Deutsch, 1958; New York: Knopf, 1982 (in *Three Novels*, omnibus edn. with *Miguel Street* and *Mystic Masseur*).
A Way in the World. London: Heinemann, 1994; New York: Knopf, 1994.

Published Nonfiction
Among the Believers: An Islamic Journey. London: Deutsch, 1981; New York: Knopf, 1981.
An Area of Darkness. London: Deutsch, 1964; New York: Macmillan, 1965.
Beyond Belief: Islamic Excursions among the Converted Peoples. London: Little, Brown, 1998; New York: Random House, 1998.
A Congo Diary. Los Angeles: Sylvester & Orphanos, 1980.
Finding the Centre. London: Deutsch, 1984; *Finding the Center*. New York: Knopf, 1984.
India: A Million Mutinies Now. London: Heinemann, 1990; New York: Viking, 1991.
India: A Wounded Civilization. London: Deutsch, 1977; New York: Knopf, 1977.
Letters between a Father and Son. London: Little, Brown, 1999; New York: Knopf, 1999.

Literary Occasions: Essays. Introduced and edited by Pankaj Mishra. New York: Knopf, 2003.

The Loss of El Dorado. London: Deutsch, 1967; New York: Knopf, 1970.

The Middle Passage. London: Deutsch, 1962; New York: Macmillan, 1963.

The Overcrowded Barracoon. London: Deutsch, 1972; New York: Knopf, 1973.

Reading and Writing: A Personal Account. New York: New York Review of Books, 2000.

The Return of Eva Perón with the Killings in Trinidad. London: Deutsch, 1980; New York: Knopf, 1980.

A Turn in the South. London: Viking, 1989; New York: Knopf, 1989.

The Writer and the World. London: Picador, 2002; New York: Alfred A. Knopf, 2002.

Articles and Parts of Books

Foreword to *The Adventures of Gurudeva and Other Stories,* by Seepersad Naipaul. London: Deutsch, 1976.

"The Anxious Gardener." *Harper's Magazine* (May 1986): 28–29.

"The Documentary Heresy." *Twentieth Century* 173 (Winter 1964/5): 107–8.

"Images: *Commonwealth Literature.*" In *Critical Perspectives on V. S. Naipaul,* edited by Robert D. Hamner, 26–29. Washington, D.C.: Three Continents Press, 1977.

Introduction to *East Indians in the Caribbean: Colonialism and the Struggle for Identity: Papers Presented to a Symposium on East Indians in the Caribbean, The University of the West Indies, June 1975.* Millwood, N.Y.: Kraus International Publications, 1982. 1–9.

"The Little More." [1961] In *Critical Perspectives,* ed. Hamner, 13–15.

"On Being a Writer." *New York Review of Books,* April 24, 1987, 7.

"Writing *A House for Mr Biswas.*" *New York Review of Books,* November 24, 1983, 22–23.

SELECTED WORKS ABOUT NAIPAUL

Books

Cudjoe, Selwyn R. *V. S. Naipaul.* Amherst: University of Massachusetts Press, 1988. Cudjoe's book is at the extreme of postcolonial criticism of Naipaul.

Feder, Lillian. *Naipaul's Truth: The Making of a Writer.* Lanham, Md.: Rowman and Littlefield, 2001. Feder describes Naipaul's methods for discovering the truth about himself and the world he explores.

Gupta, Suman. *V. S. Naipaul.* Plymouth: Northcote House, 1999. Gupta is critical of Naipaul's "black and white" attitudes, while conceding the objective truth of much of his writing.

Hamner, Robert D., ed. *Critical Perspectives on V. S. Naipaul.* Washington, D.C.: Three Continents Press, 1977. A useful early collection of essays by and about Naipaul.

Hayward, Helen. *The Enigma of V. S. Naipaul.* New York: Palgrave Macmillan, 2002. A thematic examination of Naipaul's work.

Hughes, Peter. *V. S. Naipaul.* London: Routledge, 1988. A short introduction to the earlier works.

King, Bruce. *V. S. Naipaul.* 2nd ed. Basingstoke: Palgrave Macmillan, 2003. A comprehensive survey of Naipaul's work, including a chapter on "Naipaul's Critics and Postcolonialism."

Nixon, Rob. *London Calling: V. S. Naipaul, Postcolonial Mandarin.* New York: Oxford University Press, 1992. A critique of Naipaul's "rejection" of his colonial roots.

Panwar, Purabi, ed. *V. S. Naipaul: An Anthology of Recent Criticism.* Delhi: Pencraft International, 2003. A collection of essays by Indian and international scholars.

Theroux, Paul. *Sir Vidia's Shadow: A Friendship.* Boston: Houghton Mifflin, 1998. A memoir of the author's long friendship with Naipaul, which ceased unexpectedly upon Naipaul's second marriage in 1996.

————. *V. S. Naipaul: An Introduction to His Work.* London: Deutsch, 1972. The first book-length critical work on Naipaul.

Walsh, William. *V. S. Naipaul.* Edinburgh: Oliver & Boyd, 1973. An important early study of Naipaul's work to date.

Articles and Parts of Books

Applewhite, James. "A Trip with V. S. Naipaul." *Raritan* 9, no. 4 (1990): 48–54.

Bayley, John. "Country Life: *The Enigma of Arrival.*" *New York Review of Books,* April 9, 1987, 3–4.

Calder, Angus. "Darkest Naipaulia." *New Statesman,* October 8, 1971, 482–83.

Chaudhuri, Amit. "On V. S. Naipaul." In *V. S. Naipaul: An Anthology of Recent Criticism,* edited by Purabi Panwar, 187–90. Delhi: Pencraft International, 2003.

Chauhan, P. S. "V. S. Naipaul: History as Cosmic Irony." In *Reworlding: The Literature of the Indian Diaspora,* 13–23. New York: Greenwood Press, 1992.

Dooley, Gillian. "Alien and Adrift: The Diasporic Sensibility in V. S. Naipaul's *Half a Life* and J. M. Coetzee's *Youth.*" *New Literatures Review,* no. 40 (Winter 2003): 73–82.

————. "The Horizon Conquerors: Post-War London through Colonial Eyes." *New Literatures Review,* no. 39 (Summer 2003): 75–88.

————. "Looking Back in Anger: The Transformation of Childhood Memories in Naipaul's *House for Mr Biswas* and Jamaica Kincaid's *Annie John.*" In *The West Indian Fiction,* edited by R. K. Dhawan, 164–72. New Delhi: Prestige, 2000.

————. "Naipaul's Women." *South Asian Quarterly* 26, no. 1 (2005): 88–103.

————. "Those Difficult Years." Review of *Letters between a Father and Son. CRNLE Journal* (2000): 147–54.

Gurr, Andrew. "The Freedom of Exile in Naipaul and Doris Lessing." *Ariel* 13, no. 4 (1982): 7–18.

Huggan, Graham. "V. S. Naipaul and the Political Correctness Debate." *College Literature* 21 (October 1994): 200.

Kermode, Frank. "In the Garden of the Oppressor." *New York Times Book Review,* March 23, 1987, 11–12.

Naipaul, Shiva. "A Trinidad Childhood: Beyond the Dragon's Mouth." *New Yorker,* September 17, 1984, 57–113.

Padhi, Bibhu. "Naipaul on Naipaul and the Novel." *Modern Fiction Studies* 30, no. 3 (1984): 455–65.

Pritchard, William H. "Naipaul's Written World." *Hudson Review* 47, no. 4 (1995): 587–96.

Ramchand, Kenneth. "The World of *A House for Mr Biswas.*" In *The West Indian Novel and Its Background,* 189–204. 2nd ed. London: Heinemann, 1983.

Rohlehr, Gordon. "Character and Rebellion in *A House for Mr Biswas.*" In *Critical Perspectives,* ed. Hamner, 84–93.

———. "The Ironic Approach: the Novels of V. S. Naipaul." In *The Islands In Between,* edited by Louis James, 121–39. London: Oxford University Press, 1968.

Rothfork, John. "V. S. Naipaul and the Third World." *Research Studies* 49, no. 3 (1981): 183–92.

Said, Edward. "Intellectuals in the Post-Colonial World." *Salmagundi* (Spring/Summer 1986): 44–64.

Suleri, Sara. "Naipaul's Arrival." *Yale Journal of Criticism* 2, no. 1 (1989): 25–50.

Walcott, Derek. "The Garden Path." *New Republic,* April 13, 1987, 27–31.

Wyndham, Francis. "V. S. Naipaul." *Listener,* October 7, 1971, 461–62.

Interviews

Bingham, Nigel. "The Novelist V. S. Naipaul Talks to Nigel Bingham about His Childhood in Trinidad." *Listener* 88 (September 7, 1972): 306–7.

Bragg, Melvyn. "V. S. Naipaul." *Southbank.* ABC. London Weekend Television, London. 1987.

Bryden, Ronald. "The Novelist V. S. Naipaul Talks about His Work to Ronald Bryden." *Listener* 89 (March 22, 1973): 367–70.

Burn, Gordon. "The Gospel According to Naipaul." *Weekend Review,* July 9–10, 1994, 4.

Gussow, Mel. "Enigma of V. S. Naipaul's Search for Himself in Writing." *New York Times,* April 25, 1987, late city final edition: I16.

———. "Travel Plus Writing Plus Reflection Equals V. S. Naipaul." *New York Times,* January 30, 1991, late edition, C9.

———. "V. S. Naipaul in Search of Himself." *New York Times Book Review,* April 24, 1994, 3, 29–30.

———. "V. S. Naipaul: 'It Is Out of This Violence I've Always Written.'" *New York Times Book Review,* September 16, 1984, 37–38.

———. "Writer without Roots." *New York Times Magazine,* December 26, 1976, 9, 12, 22.

Jussawalla, Feroza, ed. *Conversations with V. S. Naipaul.* Jackson: University Press of Mississippi, 1997. A valuable collection of interviews covering Naipaul's career from the early 1960s to the mid-1990s.

Kakutani, Michiko. "Naipaul Reviews His Past from Afar." *New York Times,* December 1, 1980, late city final edition: C15. *New York Times Online.* Nexis.

Rashid, Ahmed. "Death of the Novel." *Observer,* February 25, 1996.

"Speaking of Writing VI: V. S. Naipaul." *Times,* January 2, 1964, 11.

Tejpal, Tarun, and Jonathan Rosen. "V. S. Naipaul: The Art of Fiction CLIV." *Paris Review* 148 (1998): 39–66.

Wyndham, Francis. "Writing Is Magic." *Sunday Times,* November 10, 1968, 57.

Videos and Web Sites

Nobel Prize in Literature 2001 http://www.nobel.se/literature/laureates/2001/.

V. S. Naipaul Archive, University of Tulsa Library http://www.lib.utulsa.edu/speccoll/naipavs0.htm.

V. S. Naipaul. Great Writers of the Twentieth Century. Videocassette. Script edited by Tom McCarthy. Produced by Bob Portway. BBC Education, 1996.

INDEX

ABOUT THE AUTHOR

GILLIAN DOOLEY is a literary critic and librarian living in Adelaide, South Australia. A specialist in the study of Iris Murdoch, V. S. Naipaul, and Doris Lessing, she is the editor of *From a Tiny Corner in the House of Fiction: Conversations with Iris Murdoch* and writes regularly for Australian literary magazines.